Trade Wars

Phillip Oppenheim

TRADE WARS
Japan versus the West

Weidenfeld and Nicolson · London

To Birdie and Skip

© 1992 Phillip Oppenheim

All rights reserved. No part of this publication may be reproduced, stored in a retrieval system, or transmitted, in any form or by any means, electronic, mechanical, photocopying, recording or otherwise, without the prior permission of the copyright owner.

Weidenfeld and Nicolson Ltd
Orion House, 5 Upper St Martin's Lane
London WC2H 9EA

ISBN 0 297 82144 X

Filmset by Selwood Systems, Midsomer Norton, Avon
Printed in Great Britain by Butler & Tanner Ltd,
Frome and London

Contents

	Prologue	1
1	The Grey Zone	5
2	Managing Trade	23
3	Getting Tough	30
4	Scotch and Snow	40
5	Survival of the Fattest	54
6	The Protection Racket	66
7	An Overanxious Mother	78
8	Industrial Policy	94
9	Trade Barriers	108
10	Honourable Rice	121
11	The Roots of Competitive Advantage	130
12	The Bicycle Economy	149
13	No New Fish	168
14	More of the Same?	186
15	Stumbling Blocs	205
16	Trade War	225
	Index	236

Introduction

If democratic Western states began preventing their citizens from freely moving around their countries or travelling abroad, there would be an outcry. Yet our governments habitually prevent us from buying goods from overseas, or limit the amount we can buy, or place restrictions on such goods in such a way as to force up prices – and few people notice.

Such restrictions are generally referred to as protectionism and our governments usually impose these limits on us in the name of the overall well-being of our economies, or in retaliation at alleged unfair trade by other nations. Yet the truth is that protectionism is almost invariably a convenient short-term response to special pleading by uncompetitive industries and rarely, if ever, assists the protected industry. It usually, moreover, severely penalizes the economy as a whole. For by furnishing protection to one industry, others are inevitably disadvantaged.

If, for example, the steel industry is protected – as it is in Europe and North America – that has the effect of limiting competition from imports, so prices rise, steel-consuming industries have to pay more and as a result are less competitive. If the car industry is protected, as it has been in most Western countries in recent years, consumers pay more for their cars and have less to spend or invest in other industries.

Even if economic benefits from trade barriers can be proved, is the state really justified in telling its citizens what they should or should not buy? In a free society, should not people be allowed to make their own choices?

Unfair trade by competitor nations is an increasingly common justification for protectionism. Yet, as I attempt to show, the trade laws in most European countries, the United States and other industrialized nations are so slanted as to find that other countries have been trading unfairly even when they haven't. It is simply too easy for industrialists from companies which have lost their edge to cry foul rather than to

Introduction

admit their own shortcomings. It is more convenient for politicians to join in the chorus when it helps to cover up policy failures which have led to weak economies. And it is comforting for the public to believe that economic defects can be attributed to devious, unprincipled foreigners rather than reasons nearer to home.

So the impetus for protectionism has been powerful and the easy course for governments has been to accede to the special pleading of industrialists and impose trade barriers, usually citing the benefits of job preservation, despite the manifest long-term disadvantages and resultant job losses elsewhere in the economy.

These protectionist pressures have intensified over the past couple of decades for a number of reasons. First, the recent international downturn has made trading conditions very difficult, while high unemployment in the developed world has led politicians to give priority to the maintenance of threatened industries and jobs, however unviable in the long term. Second, the world is undergoing a fundamental economic shift away from Europe and America to Japan and East Asia. Western industrialists, unable to compete with the efficient economies of the Eastern Pacific seaboard, have trooped to their governments cap in hand for subsidies and protection. Moreover, the common perception that Japan itself has prospered to a significant degree through deliberate government policies of protection and intervention, especially through the agency of the feared trade and industry ministry, MITI, has provided ammunition for those arguing for such policies in the West.

I seek to demonstrate that trade barriers in Japan have been and are exaggerated, often for self-serving reasons, by Western industrialists, politicians and commentators; that the impact of MITI's policies have similarly been overstated; that these policies have, anyway, been tried and failed in the West; and that the real sources of Japan's competitive advantage lie elsewhere – in sound education, the fundamental attitudes of the Japanese people and the economic policies of Japan's government. These have given priority to economic growth over domestic consumption by maintaining relatively low state spending and taxation, tight monetary policies and incentives for people to save rather than to spend – the mirror image of the policies pursued in many Western countries. Moreover, if protectionism and so-called 'industrial strategies' were the key to economic success, countries like India and Brazil – which have practised such policies more than most – would be economic superpowers rather than the failed and distorted economic entities that they are.

The problem is that it has been too easy for Western politicians to pay lip-service to the need for free trade while in practice imposing more and more trade barriers on their economies. It has also been easier for American and European businessmen to whinge about unfair trade and whisper warnings about devious orientals, rather than address their fundamental competitive shortcomings. Yet the hypocrisy of many such industrialists is illustrated by the enormous quantities of Japanese goods which they themselves buy-in to sell under their own brandnames. Who would believe that Chrysler's Jap-bashing hero, Lee Iaccoca, has himself presided over his company importing millions of Japanese-made cars to sell in his dealerships under all-American brandnames?

Import restraints are increasingly moving away from overt barriers such as tariffs towards ever more sly forms of protection such as shadowy and little reported import quotas, spurious anti-dumping duties and, increasingly, managed trade agreements which are imposing the failed central-planning policies of the former Eastern-bloc countries on Western economies.

Not only do such policies damage the West by raising prices, preventing resources from being allocated to where they can best be utilized and delaying necessary structural reforms, but they also threaten to divide the global economy into hostile trading blocs based on Europe, North America and Japan in an ominous echo of the 1930s. It is too easy for trade disputes to degenerate into political tensions and henceforth into military conflict, as happened once before.

Trade restraints against Third World countries and the former-communist nations which are struggling to transform their economies in the direction of the free market also severely penalize their relatively unsophisticated goods such as textiles, bulk chemicals, agricultural products and steel. Unless these countries can freely export such products, they are unlikely to be able successfully to reform and develop their economies and in turn buy more sophisticated goods from richer countries. By imposing trade barriers these richer nations may well turn out to be tragically short-sighted.

Many people believe that the defeat of communism heralds an era of unfettered free markets and the triumph of economic liberalism. But when a senior economist at the OECD, the premier economic think-tank of the industrialized world, warns that the global economy is now less integrated and more divided than it was in 1914 and that most developed countries now maintain more trade barriers than they did a decade ago, we should all be concerned. For the world is, in fact, slipping into a mess of protectionism and interventionism that at the very least will impoverish poorer countries and prevent the West from

Introduction

making the reforms necessary truly to take up the Japanese challenge; and at worst could contribute to the type of conflicts which were heralded by the trade disputes of the 1930s.

Phillip Oppenheim
House of Commons
London

July 1992

Acknowledgements

I am particularly grateful to the journalist, Claudia Cragg, for her great knowledge of Japan and editorial help. Likewise, Cynthia Mack, who has lived in Japan with her grandmother, provided valuable insights into the Japanese way of life. Other people with great experience of Japan whose assistance was much appreciated include Richard Greer of Baring Securities' Tokyo office, David Mathew and Anthony Garner. Needless to say, any opinions expressed or errors in this book are my own and should in no way reflect on them.

Chris Norall of Forrester and Norall was immensely generous in providing me with help and information on the European Community's trade policy, as was Neville Williams, formerly of the Department of Trade and Industry. Michael Perry of Unilever also contributed greatly to the section on selling in Japan. I would like particularly to thank Professor Richard Boyd of the School of Oriental and African Studies of the University of London for providing me with invaluable information on MITI and Japanese industrial policy.

I would like to sincerely thank David Menhennet, Head of the House of Commons Library, together with his staff for the speed and efficiency with which they invariably responded to requests for books, journals and information.

The teams at the New York and London offices of *What to Buy for Business*, the consumer report for businesses, also provided enormous assistance with research and background material.

I also owe a great debt to Sarah Harding, for her suggestions, invaluable editing and stylistic assistance.

The author is indebted to a large number of books, magazines and newspapers from which he has quoted. He has always endeavoured to acknowledge the sources of quotations or information and is particularly

Acknowledgements

grateful to those publications and publishers who gave permission to quote where permission was necessary.

Particularly valuable was *The Financial Times*, whose coverage of trade and industry issues was of enormous help. Also of great assistance were: *The Wall Street Journal, The Economist, Business Week, Fortune, US News and World Report, Time, Newsweek, The Daily Telegraph, The Independent, The Times, The Observer* and *Car* magazine.

Prologue

Late in September 1986, the slightly seedy Uruguayan seaside resort of Punta del Este, deserted in the dead winter season, was the unlikely scene of a gathering of 4,000 trade ministers, delegates and officials from most of the world's nations. They were meeting to inaugurate the so-called Uruguay round of the General Agreement on Tariffs and Trade, the organization which acts as a referee for world trade. Their ambition was to build on the post-war advances in freeing up world trade in manufactured goods by extending trading agreements to the hitherto largely untouched areas of agriculture and textiles, as well as services such as insurance and banking, so opening up a brave new era of unfettered free trade.

Five years later, with deadline after deadline for the completion of the Uruguay round being missed, the French prime minister, Edith Cresson, describing the Japanese as 'little yellow dwarves who sit up all night thinking of ways to screw the Americans and Europeans'; a leaked CIA report portraying the Japanese as committed to 'the economic domination of the world'; more than thirty anti-Japan bills being tabled by American senators; and the US government claiming that Canadian-built Honda cars should be subject to import duties, the high hopes of Punta del Este seemed a very distant memory. Rather, to many people the world's trading system appeared on the verge of collapse.

When the great and the good met at the Bretton Woods conference in 1944, their intention was to establish a new world order. The aim of the delegates, economists and finance ministers from Allied countries, was to expunge the disorders and rivalries of the pre-war international financial and trading system, problems which had led to the Great Depression and slump of the early 1930s, contributing significantly to

Prologue

the global tensions which resulted in the fiercest and most destructive war the world had ever seen.

To that end, Bretton Woods established the charters of the International Monetary Fund, designed to ease the ebbs and flows of the global monetary systems, and the World Bank, which was to finance development projects in poorer countries. There was also a recognition of the need for an international trade body to adjudicate and ensure fair play in the world's trading system, but nothing of significance was done until 1946 when the newly formed United Nations proposed to establish an international trade organization.

At first, progress was rapid. Many countries were more amenable to exposing their economies to foreign competition as they were underpinned by the assurance that the IMF provided a mechanism for the co-operative management of balance of payments deficits, so limiting the threat of damaging runs on currencies caused by trade deficits.

The positive attitude of the US president further reinforced the moves towards an international trade body, and it was the United States which published a draft charter for the new organization. Meetings were also held to draft a treaty covering general obligations to reduce tariffs, which were then the main impediments to trade. These obligations were called the General Agreement on Tariffs and Trade, or GATT. The plan was that GATT would be a general charter, enforced by the trade body called the International Trade Organization (ITO).

Although the ITO constitution was completed, it never came into being. The stumbling block was the United States Congress, which made it clear on several occasions between 1948 and 1951 that it would not approve the ITO code. So the body originally envisaged by a far-sighted American president to act as the umpire of world trade was, ironically, rejected by a US Congress more mindful of the fears of their voters about overseas competition to their industries. Ever since, GATT has limped along as little more than an international treaty to which countries contract.

Subsequent attempts to make GATT into a more formal trade body with real powers – most notably in 1955 when an Organization for Trade Co-operation was proposed – all fell to the veto of the US Congress. And therein lies the problem, for although most politicians pay lip service to the benefits of free trade, almost invariably more pressing short-term political considerations predominate.

For the question posed in the minds of the world's leaders is rarely: 'How much would the economy benefit overall by having greater access to lower-cost, better-quality goods from overseas, and how many extra jobs will be created as a result of having a more efficient economy which concentrates on what it can best make, buying in what it cannot?' Rather it is: 'How many jobs will be lost in the short term if we expose a particular industry to the rigours of full-blown competition from more efficient producers?' Of course, such considerations are made all the more urgent when the potentially threatened industry is located in an area of high unemployment – or when an election is near.

Despite these constraints, GATT has evolved into an organization of sorts with its own secretariat. But it really relies on an elaborate group of committees, working parties, panels and other bodies staffed by representatives of GATT's member nations. Inevitably such a setup has resulted in more trade-offs between contracting nations than would have been the case with a fully fledged trade body, independent of individual countries.

Nonetheless, GATT has made great progress in liberalizing the international trade between developed countries in most types of manufactured and industrial goods. This has been achieved in a series of negotiating 'rounds', some of which lasted several years. The first round at Geneva in 1947 saw twenty-three countries agree to relatively free trade covering $10 billion worth of goods. By the end of the Tokyo round in 1979, no fewer than ninety-nine nations were contracted to GATT and had agreed to liberalize $155 billion worth of trade. Between 1948 and the conclusion of the Tokyo round, world trade, excluding the Eastern bloc, grew almost fivefold in real terms, and average tariff levels in the major industrialized countries had fallen by 1979 to a mere 2–3 per cent compared with the 50–60 per cent common in the 1940s. That GATT achieved so much was in no small measure due to the devotion and ingenuity of its leaders over the years.

Indeed, so successful had GATT become in reducing import tariffs on manufactured products that by the end of the 1970s it began to turn its attention to other fields. Principal among these was services, such as finance and insurance. These were almost invariably subject to barriers against foreign competition because of their regulated nature – and the regulations are apt to be used to exclude foreign competition. Then there was agriculture, probably the most subsidized and protected industry in the developed world and excluded from GATT in 1955 as a result of American pressure. Textiles, too, were considered ripe for GATT's attention as exports from developing to industrialized countries had, since 1974, been covered by a series of successive four-year agreements, the so-called Multi-Fibre Arrangement, whereby developed countries limited imports of low-cost textiles by quotas. Together, these industries accounted for more than a third of world trade.

But there was a cruel irony in store. For at the very moment that the GATT pioneers felt confident enough to attempt to push forward the frontiers of world trade into these hitherto virgin territories, it was becoming alarmingly apparent that many of the existing post-war gains in trade in manufactured goods were coming under threat.

The fact that officials from the EC, the United States and Australia spent ten hours wrangling over ten words in the text of the negotiating parameters on agriculture at the very beginning of the Uruguay talks in 1986 was an ominous portent. For by then the global trading system was already backsliding into protectionism at an accelerating rate. What is more, it was not merely relapsing into open and above-board means of restricting trade, such as tariffs on imported products. Rather, the system was slipping into a grey zone of covert trade barriers which bypassed GATT, a hazy world of 'unofficial' import quotas, agreed between industries in the importing and exporting countries.

So bad was the situation becoming that, with more than a touch of irony, the buzz word at the GATT negotiations soon became 'tariffication' – meaning the conversion of covert grey area protectionist measures to tariffs, which at least had the virtue of being clear and conspicuous.

As these so-called 'voluntary restraint agreements' mushroomed, the Uruguay round itself became increasingly bogged down with wrangles over farm trade and missed its 1990 deadline for completion. So as the new decade dawned it was becoming abundantly clear that, far from entering a brave new world of unconstrained global trade, the international economy was in reality steadily regressing into competing trading blocs and the type of bitter trade dispute which played such a conspicuous role in raising tensions in the 1930s.

1 The Grey Zone

Anti-dumping policy in the EC seems now to be used covertly as industrial policy for the purpose of promoting particular industries.
Michael Davenport, former European Community economist[1]

According to *Newsweek* magazine, the latest New York scam is for conmen to bump into Japanese tourists, drop bottles of cheap wine at their feet and then claim the wine was a vintage. Eager to avoid a scene, Japanese visitors will sometimes hand over as much as $100.[2] The newly wealthy, camera-toting Japanese tourist has, to a large extent, replaced the innocent American holidaymaker as the butt of jokes and rip-offs.

More damaging to Americans' self-esteem than their displacement by the Japanese as the archetypal tourist is the speed with which Japanese interests have been purchasing large chunks of corporate America, especially as among Japanese industry's acquisitions are some of America's best-known names, including CBS Records, Firestone, Intercontinental Hotels and Columbia Pictures – this last being described by *Newsweek* as 'buying America's soul'.

Nor is the body escaping, for the Japanese are also buying up America itself, particularly prime real estate in downtown Los Angeles, where nearly half the commercial property is now owned by foreigners – predominantly Japanese. But perhaps the most potent token of the relative change in the positions of Japan and America was the sale to Mitsubishi Estates in 1989 of the epitome of American capitalism, a group of mid-Manhattan skyscrapers including the Rockefeller Center.

Behind this reversal of roles lies Japan's seemingly inexorable economic rise. Bombed into near oblivion in 1945, Japan's per capita GNP had overtaken that of the United States by 1986; and by that time the 500 kilometre-long belt between Tokyo and Kobe represented the greatest concentration of industrial power the world had ever seen. At the end of the 1980s, moreover, Japan not only supplied the world with manufactured goods, but also lent it the money to pay for Japanese products. For the Japanese had also become the world's creditors, with net external assets of close to $600 billion and dollar reserves of more than $1,000 billion. Nine out of the world's ten largest banks were, by then, also Japanese.

The amazingly rapid turn-round in the position of the United States provided the other half of the equation. In 1980 the USA had a trade surplus of $17 billion, an accumulated federal debt of only $650 billion and a budget deficit which was barely 2 per cent of GNP, and America was still the world's largest creditor nation. American electronics, semiconductor and computer industries at that time dominated the commanding heights of the global economy.

By 1986, however, the US trade surplus had turned into a deficit of $136 billion, the debt had tripled to around $2,000 billion and the budget deficit had risen to nearly 5 per cent of GNP. Moreover, the United States had, in six years, switched from being the largest creditor in history to being the biggest borrower, with its debts dwarfing those of the Third World. Perhaps most galling of all, Japanese electronics and semiconductor companies had ousted their American rivals from the top positions, while Japan's computer industry was catching up with startling rapidity.

Then there are the four tigers – the Asian newly industrialized countries of South Korea, Taiwan, Singapore and Hong Kong. In the last three decades, the NICs have more than doubled their share of the free world's GNP to 6 per cent. Together with Japan and the other fast-expanding east Asian economies, they make up the most rapidly growing region in the world. Symbolizing this shift in the gravity of world economic power is the fact that more wide-bodied jets now fly across the Pacific each day than cross the Atlantic, while Japanese Air Lines (JAL) has become the largest jumbo operator with a fleet of nearly seventy planes.

It is the emergence of Japan as the world's premier economic superpower, dominating the rapidly growing east Asian region, which underlies worsening trade tensions. For as the West faces sharpened competition from Japanese industry, so the pressure to protect threatened businesses intensifies. And ever more bitter trade wrangles have now reached such a crescendo that they threaten to shatter the world trading order.

At first, import quotas were the chosen instrument for limiting imports of manufactured goods from Japan, even though such products were supposed to be freely traded under GATT agreements. Although these 'voluntary restraint agreements' (VRAs) are usually secretly negotiated by industry groups, they are invariably sanctioned by the United States or European governments, or by the European Community (EC), which is now responsible for the trading pacts of its member nations. As a result, by the end of the 1980s these little reported VRAs hindered imports of hundreds of products, ranging from semiconductors to steel, and from compact disc players to cars. According to Jan Tumlir, former chief economist at GATT, quotas now affect 50 per cent of all world trade.[3]

But even relatively inconspicuous methods of trade restraint such as VRAs appeared distasteful in an era when the EC and the USA spent so much of their energy complaining about Japanese trade practices. So more subtle measures, such as anti-dumping duties, have become the increasingly favoured instruments of protectionism – particularly as they imply action against unfair trade practices, rather than the imposition of import barriers. Moreover, the very impenetrability of the anti-dumping rules provides a perfect smokescreen for politicians who like the rhetoric of free trade, but prefer to be protectionist in practice.

'... deep and palpable unfairness'

Dumping is the practice of selling a product into another country at a price below that prevailing in the home market. The theory of dumping presupposes that selling goods at a lower price in export markets amounts to a predatory practice designed to drive overseas competitors out of business, so providing the exporter with a virtual monopoly, as a result of which it is assumed the exporter can raise prices and recoup earlier losses.

In reality, producers do vary prices in different markets for quite legitimate reasons. Usually, this is no more than a reflection of differing levels of competition. So the basic premise of dumping law – that it is an economic crime for a company to sell the same product for two different prices in two different markets – is absurd. It would be perfectly reasonable, for example, for an ice-cream manufacturer to charge more for his product in Arizona than in northern Canada.

Genuine cases of predatory dumping are much rarer than claimed. Manufacturers who sell off products cheaply in foreign markets usually do so on a very limited scale to shift marginal production or old stock. And although Japanese businesses tend to differ from their western counterparts in that they see nothing unfair in using pricing as one weapon to gain long-term market share, conspiracies to sell below cost and so drive rivals from the market suffer from intrinsic disadvantages, not least the fact that in competitive markets new contenders tend to emerge as soon as a monopolist begins to try to cash in by raising prices. Nonetheless, complaints of dumping have long been a common refrain in industries threatened by low-cost imports.

Most developed countries have for some time maintained regulations allowing them to act against dumping, and in the case of the EC these have been consolidated into Community-wide legislation. The EC's Anti-Dumping Regulation states that a product is considered to have been dumped if its export price to the Community is less than the 'normal value' of the product on its home market. The difference between the two is called the 'dumping margin' and a duty equivalent to that margin can be imposed on the imported product.

EC anti-dumping regulations have in the past generally been used against low-value commodity and semi-finished products from developing and Eastern bloc countries, whose eagerness for hard currency has sometimes led them to sell goods for very low prices. Cases have ranged from East German urea to Czechoslovakian potassium permanganate.

During the 1980s, however, the emphasis of anti-dumping actions swung towards higher-value manufactured goods – particularly the products of Japan's phenomenally successful consumer electronics and information technology industries. Whereas between 1980 and 1982 only eight EC anti-dumping investigations were initiated against Japan and the newly industrialized Asian countries, between 1986 and 1988 this number rose to thirty. Among the raft of high-tech products affected by anti-dumping investigations in the 1980s were video recorders, video tape, electronic typewriters, colour televisions, CD players, photocopiers, computer printers, mobile telephones and microwave ovens.

Anti-dumping regulations, even if fairly drawn up and implemented, are almost always inherently protectionist because they discriminate against importers. Domestic producers can vary their prices or sell at below cost as much as they like without falling foul of the rules because these rules apply only to imports. It is somewhat ironic, for example, that during the late 1950s American car manufacturers managed to beat back initial Japanese attempts to sell small cars in the United States by selling their own stripped-down, low-end models at a loss.

But it was becoming clear by the end of the 1980s that the EC had gone further than this, moulding its anti-dumping regulations not as an instrument for ensuring fair trade, but rather into one aimed at disadvantaging competitive imports. For among the exporters recently caught in the anti-dumping net has been Hong Kong. Bearing in mind the colony's open trading policy, *laissez-faire* economic environment and small domestic market, it is hard to envisage its producers engaging in conspiracies to subsidize dumped exports with profits made from a protected home market. Yet the fact that Hong Kong manufacturers have been found guilty of 'dumping' graphically illustrates a crucial fact, namely that the EC's Byzantine anti-dumping regulations are so drawn up that they result in 'dumping' being found, and anti-dumping duties being imposed, in cases where no dumping has in fact occurred.

Chris Norall is a jovial and articulate 44 year-old American-born lawyer who came to Europe as a child and was educated mainly in England. Although he returned to the USA to obtain a law degree, he came back to marry an Italian girl, settling in Europe in 1973 to practise in Brussels, specializing in EC law in his own partnership, Forrester and Norall. He described to me how the convoluted EC regulations could result in the imposition of anti-dumping duties, even where the manufacturer was selling overseas at a substantially higher price than in its home market.

'What happens is this', Norall said. 'Rather than just comparing prices in Europe and in the exporting country, the Commission investigators "construct" what they consider to be the genuine import price, a calculation necessary in their view because the exporting company usually owns the importing subsidiary and so the import price might be artificial. This "constructive" import price excludes many costs, such as marketing.

'But to work out the manufacturer's home market price and so to establish whether any dumping has occurred, the investigators take quite a different approach. Rather than using a straightforward method of estimating production and distribution costs, the Commission takes the view that the home market sales subsidiary and the parent/manufacturer *should* be treated as a single unit – an opposite approach to that used in assessing the EC price. So all of their costs, and particularly their marketing costs, are treated together.

'The net result is that the marketing costs which are included in the manufacturer's home market calculation are excluded when arriving at prices on the EC market, so almost invariably creating an artificially higher domestic price.

'The result', Norall went on, 'can be quite spectacular. For example,

The Grey Zone

the Japanese are particularly vigorous marketers, as you can tell by watching a televised football match or standing in a central square in any European city and looking at the neon signs. For consumer electronics and office equipment products, these and other marketing costs can easily amount to a third or more of overall costs. Yet just such costs are effectively excluded from the equation used to reach the EC market price. The result? Where there is no dumping, substantial 'dumping' will be found. In a word, the dice are heavily loaded against the exporter.

'Whatever one may think of the merits of Community policy towards Japan,' Norall continued, 'there is something disturbing in the fact that buried at the centre of that policy, embedded in a procedure which, though highly technical, purports to be based on legal principles, is a deep and palpable unfairness.'

But the unfairness does not end there, for the rules have also been drawn up in such a way as greatly to discourage new entrants into the market. For example, the highest duty imposed after an anti-dumping investigation can also be imposed on all new companies, even though they were not named in the original investigation. Moreover, start-up companies which are showing a loss on their early production can also be subject to anti-dumping duties, even if their prices exceed those prevailing in the EC.

It is, of course, not unusual for a new production facility to sustain losses during the early years until an economic level of output is reached or until the brand or product itself gains acceptability. In earlier, kinder times, the Commission showed some willingness to consider adjustments for start-up costs, but now this is no longer the case. 'The message is clear', says Chris Norall. 'If an exporter is starting up a new factory, his exports are bound to be considered "dumped" in the initial period of its operations and no quarter will be given. Let the new exporter beware.'

Copier cartel

It was this rather partisan set of regulations which were invoked by the few remaining European photocopier manufacturers in 1985. Alarmed at what they called 'low-priced' imports from Japan, the five Community producers still in business formed the Committee of European Copier Manufacturers (CECOM). Top managers from each of the manufacturers, many of whom knew each other well from the merry circuit of office equipment trade fairs and other industry events, met together regularly, forming a working group to prepare a complaint to the Commission. It took them less than four months to collect their evidence, which, they claimed, showed both dumping by the Japanese and injury to the European Community copier industry.

As part of their complaint to the Commission, CECOM alleged that, despite a substantial rise in photocopier consumption within the Community, the complainants' market share had fallen from 23 per cent in 1982 to 18 per cent in 1984. When the Commission's anti-dumping investigators duly began their inquiry early in 1986, they soon managed to find evidence of 'dumping' based on the lopsided and convoluted calculations allowed for by the EC regulations. So although, for example, it was established that the Canon NP400, a popular mid-range copier, was selling at a list price of ¥1,298,000 in Japan, and a very similar DM13,400 in West Germany, a massive 'dumping' margin of 42.9 per cent was nonetheless found.

The report of the case in the EC's *Official Journal* later went on to admit that 'the degree of undercutting was in general relatively small in terms of price'. But that did not stop the very same report from concluding just two paragraphs later that 'there was evidence that Community producers had suffered injury through price undercutting by Japanese exporters on the Community market'.[4]

In determining at what level to fix the anti-dumping duty on the Japanese copier makers, the Commission reckoned that prices should be raised to enable Community producers to earn 12 per cent profit on their own sales. Lawyers representing the importers argued that this was excessive in a traditionally low-margin industry, especially as photocopier manufacturers, in common with producers of other types of office equipment, often sell their machines at low margins, compensating themselves with high profits on the consumables which the purchasers are obliged to buy. Wayland Hicks, head of copier development at Xerox Corporation in the USA, estimates, for example, that 60–70 per cent of Canon's copier profits came from supplies such as the toner powder – effectively the ink in copiers.[5]

The Commission, however, saw 'no reason why ... profits should be made only on consumables and supplies', thus imposing their view of how the industry should be run on companies which had been making a success of it for more than a decade. It seemed to the lawyers and industry experts representing the Japanese manufacturers that the Commission was bending over backwards to favour the CECOM case. But there was one further, unpleasant twist to the story.

The Grey Zone

At that time the Japanese manufacturers were selling their machines predominantly through independent dealers, while the Community producers still marketed their equipment largely through relatively expensive, directly employed sales forces. Despite strong protestations from the Japanese, the Commission decided that the target increase in revenues required for the Community producers should be further boosted to take account of their relatively expensive distribution methods. In other words, the Commission was making allowances for the marketing inefficiencies of the Community producers, while penalizing the good practices of the importers.

As a result, a 'dumping' duty of at least 20 per cent was imposed on almost all of the Japanese exporters. And to add insult to injury, when in 1992 the anti-dumping duties were due to end, the Commission declared that it was considering extending the period, which means that the duties are likely stay in place for several years while the bureaucrats make up their minds.

In reaching its verdict, the Commission made no secret of the fact that its aims went rather further than merely objectively determining whether genuine dumping had taken place. 'It is clear', the Commission's report on the photocopier case states, 'that the photocopier industry will continue to form a key part of the office equipment industry as a whole and that the retention and development of the technology currently employed will be essential for the development of future reprographic products ... The imposition of a definitive anti-dumping duty is required to ensure the continued existence of at least certain of the remaining Community producers with the consequent benefits to the Community of employment, technological expertise and local source of supply.'

Ironically, virtually all of the European copier producers had for some time been reliant on Japanese manufacturers for large chunks of their ranges which they either assembled from Japanese kits, or just bought in and labelled under their own names. This was a point not lost on those defending the Japanese manufacturers during the Commission's investigation.

The main instigator of the complaint, Rank Xerox, the European arm of the American-based Xerox Corporation, was in fact the prime culprit in this respect, importing Japanese-produced assembly kits for all of its low-volume range, as well as many of its medium-volume machines. Yet the Commission accepted Rank Xerox's argument for much lower or no dumping duties on such relabelled imports on the grounds that Rank Xerox had been 'obliged' since the late 1970s to purchase such machines from its Japanese associate, Fuji Xerox, for 'self-defensive purposes'.

The report went on to say that 'the ability to bring on to the market a product more quickly than by waiting for Community products to come on stream has enabled the company better to defend its overall position.'[6] It is surely a devastating indictment of Europe's largest copier producer that it should argue that it had found that the only way to beat the Japanese competition was itself to rely on Japanese equipment.

Olivetti of Italy and Holland's Oce were similarly leniently treated with regard to the large numbers of Japanese copiers which they imported to sell relabelled under their own names. The Commission concluded that both companies had attempted to develop fuller ranges of their own models, but were 'thwarted in their attempts to do so because of depressed market prices set by Japanese imports'. The Commission accepted as evidence of these efforts management evaluations of products and a prototype model which had been scheduled for introduction to the market.

I actually remember such prototypes from my days editing the business consumer magazine *What to Buy for Business*. Year after year, as Japanese copier manufacturers displayed ever more impressive offerings on their stands at the giant Hanover trade fair, a pathetic series of non-functioning 'prototypes' were on show at Olivetti's stands. What Olivetti was actually selling was machines made by Mita, Sharp and Canon of Japan. So a fine new principle appeared to have been established, namely that a Japanese machine selling under a Japanese brand name caused 'injury' to European producers, but not if the identical machine was sold under a European or American name.

Hardly mentioned, or apparently even considered, by the EC Commission during its anti-dumping investigation into Japanese copiers was the possibility that the real injury to the European copier industry was a self-inflicted one, caused by the succession of generally low-quality, overpriced European machines which had fallen easy prey to their well-designed, more reliable, lower-cost and better-marketed Japanese rivals. For the copier market, pioneered by America's Xerox Corporation, was to a significant degree handed to Japanese manufacturers by Xerox's complacency and by the failure of a host of other powerful American and European companies to supply the machines the market wanted.

Dry writing

The plain paper copier industry was born when the Haloid Company, a medium-sized New York-based manufacturer of photographic paper, bought the rights to a little noticed copying technology developed in the 1930s by Chester Carlson, a patents clerk and son of an immigrant Swedish barber. Haloid named the new technology 'xerography', Greek for 'dry writing', and in 1959 launched the first automatic plain paper copier, the Xerox 914, later dubbed by *Fortune* magazine as 'the most successful product ever marketed in America'.

The new machine was helped on its way by a superb marketing ploy – instead of selling the machines, they were rented out for $95 a month with 2,000 free copies and a few cents for each additional copy. At a stroke, all the objections to expensive, unproven, new technology were eliminated.

Xerox sales were also helped by a brilliant marketing campaign involving a sales force of smartly turned-out representatives, each of whom was trained in the subtle art of hard sell, together with a series of state-of-the-art television commercials. The most celebrated of these showed a man handing a document to his six-year-old daughter saying: 'Honey, please make a copy of this for me.' The child skips off gaily, waving the paper which she then places in the Xerox 914. Seconds later, she returns the copy to her father. The moral: even a child can operate a Xerox.[7]

Fortunes were made out of Xerox stock – a cab driver who bought one hundred shares when they were selling for less than $10 each in 1954 watched their value rise to more than $1,500,000 by 1970. Xerox had become the American dream. It had broken the record for reaching a billion dollars in sales faster than any other United States company in history; the company was fêted by stockholders and used as a case study of success at Harvard.

Milking it dry

But so secure did Xerox management feel in their achievements that at first they largely ignored potential competition in the photocopier field and instead targeted IBM in a disastrous attempt to enter the computer industry. Moreover, their core copier business was beginning to lose some of its magic. Following the tremendous advances of the 1960s, Xerox rested on its laurels. Only three completely new models were introduced on to the US market during the 1970s, and by the end of the decade Xerox's range consisted largely of machines developed a decade earlier.

In short, profit margins were being maintained at the expense of product development and customer goodwill – especially as ex-rental, reconditioned Xerox machines were being sold to new customers without it being made clear that the equipment was not factory-fresh. Most importantly, Xerox started to concentrate too heavily on the development of prestigious top-end projects, ignoring the lower-value end of the market where its customers were becoming unhappy and resentful – and where the Japanese copier manufacturers were to launch their assault. In the words of Xerox's vice president, Fred Henderson: 'we had this gigantic cash cow and we almost milked it dry.'[8]

No fewer than 147 different plain paper copiers were introduced into the United States market between 1970 and 1980. Almost all were Japanese – and they were different. They were smaller, relatively inexpensive machines which were aggressively sold through low-cost dealer networks, rather than rented out via expensive direct sales forces. Most successful of the Japanese copier companies was the camera maker Canon, whose name is a westernized version of Kwanon, the Shinto goddess of mercy. The company's sales were running at a rate of 250,000 annually by 1980, making Canon number one in copier placements.

Xerox initially responded to the Japanese onslaught with distracted complacency. Distracted, because competition at the very top end of the market, from Kodak and IBM, was Xerox's main concern in the 1970s. Complacent, because Xerox engineers and sales people habitually derided the Japanese 'boxes' – not to be compared with their own superb, high-speed products.

But even where Xerox was making an effort, it was in a very different way to the lean, mean creature which first spawned the seminal Xerox 914. Then, teams had worked seven days a week while the lights regularly burned until midnight – and they liked it. By contrast, Wayland Hicks, who became head of copier development in 1983 at the age of forty, bemoaned the sluggishness and constant bickering of Xerox's new corporate culture thus: 'When a problem comes up, one side blames the other. The engineers say it's a manufacturing problem and the manufacturing guys say: "look at the designs we have to work with." Everyone protects their own interests.'[9]

Moreover, as with its rental policy, Xerox had clung on to its direct sales force-only strategy for too long and turned what had been an asset into a liability. It was not until 1984 that Xerox tentatively began to

The Grey Zone

appoint dealers to supplement its direct sales force. By then, it was almost too late.

Even when Xerox did develop new machines for the low-volume market, the results were far from inspiring. The 'Jap-bashing' Xerox 3300, introduced in the United States late in 1979, was so unreliable that it had to be withdrawn after a week – railcars full of 3300s were laid up on a track near the plant for months. By the time the machine was relaunched in 1982, the damage had been done.

In 1980, moreover, a manufacturing study group at Xerox's headquarters in Rochester, New York, discovered that the Japanese were able to produce copiers at half the price it cost Xerox to make them. The next year a group of Xerox engineers also found that it was taking Xerox twice as long as the Japanese to develop new models.

Canon, meanwhile, was forging ahead, developing a whole new generation of very compact, low-cost machines, the so-called 'personal copiers'. The PC–10 was launched in the USA in 1983 for $995. Costing less than $300 to manufacture on automated assembly lines, the PC–10 sold to dealers for $420, giving them a healthy incentive to push the machine. When, in 1985, distribution was extended to Sears and other mass market outlets, production reached a rate of 400,000 a year and cargo jets had to be chartered to keep up with demand. Xerox's response to the personal copier threat was to push reconditioned versions of their ancient models from the 1960s. Needless to say, they were no match for the new-generation Canon machines.

'It's small, but it's a Xerox'

Ironically, it was Xerox's Japanese associate, Fuji Xerox, which had begun by assembling Xerox copiers in Japan in the 1960s, which largely salvaged the position of its former mentor. For although attempts had been made to discourage Fuji Xerox from designing its own low-end products more geared to Japanese needs, it nonetheless built a prototype which was so successful that from 1969 Fuji Xerox devoted its best development engineers to a project with one simple aim – to produce the smallest plain paper copier in the world. The result of their endeavours, the Fuji Xerox 2200, was born in 1972 under the slogan: 'It's small, but it's a Xerox'.

At first, Xerox Corporation refused to take the 2200. The company's engineers sneered at the little Japanese box and began development of several product concepts with code names ranging from 'SAM' (Simply

Amazing Machine) through to one appropriately called 'Nothing'. All were killed, leaving Xerox without the small machine that might counter the increasing Japanese competition.

Rank Xerox in Europe was the first to crack. By 1977 it was desperate and agreed to import the 2202, an improved version of the 2200. In its first year, 24,000 units of the new machine were sold – more than any previous Rank Xerox product. Xerox Corporation followed two years later by importing the Japanese company's new Fuji Xerox 2300 model, which was so successful that in 1980 700 tons of 2300s had to be airlifted to supplement sea-borne shipments. Ever since, Xerox has been largely dependent on Japanese-designed machines for its small copier models.

In 1980, apart from Rank Xerox, eight European manufacturers were still manufacturing plain paper copiers. Eight years later, seven had dropped out of the market – they included many large companies with excellent facilities, good distribution networks and well-known brand names, such as Agfa Gevaert, the photographic products manufacturer controlled by the West German chemical giant Bayer, and Olympia, the West German typewriter manufacturer. Olivetti of Italy also made a wide range of products in the early 1980s, the flagship of which was the Copia 2000, which became a byword for unreliability; while Gestetner, the British reprographics manufacturer, developed a machine which gained an unsettling reputation for catching fire. Out of the indigenous European producers, only Oce of Holland has survived the onslaught, but even Oce has to supplement its range of large machines with Japanese models for the lower reaches of the market. America has fared little better. Kodak alone survives and prospers at the top end of the market alongside Xerox. Pitney Bowes, IBM and 3M are among the well-known names to have pulled out of copier manufacturing. Of course, Xerox still retains a dominant position in the upper-volume sector, but Canon has for long led it in terms of annual unit sales. Japanese suppliers now make around 70 per cent of the plain paper copiers sold worldwide, while a further 15 per cent are assembled from Japanese kits.

The Japanese have succeeded in the copier market not by dumping or other unfair trade practices, but because they had the design and production skills to make the machines their customers wanted – and they went out and sold those machines aggressively.

Terminated by other reasons

The European Community now uses anti-dumping measures more frequently than any other country or trading bloc. Between 1981 and 1987 it concluded no fewer than 281 investigations. Although only a quarter of these ended with the imposition of duties, half resulted in the acceptance of special undertakings by which importers agreed to raise their prices. Moreover, many of these were accompanied by VRAs which were rarely made public. In many other cases where no duty or price undertaking was imposed, threats of anti-dumping actions have been used as leverage to force secret import restrictions – these are euphemistically referred to by the Commission as 'investigations which have been terminated by other reasons'.

A significant example of the use of the threat of an anti-dumping action to force a pricing agreement occurred in 1989, when the European Community threatened Japanese semiconductor makers with anti-dumping duties for selling microchips at a loss in the mid-1980s – even though virtually every European and American chip maker also sold at a loss during that period of cyclical product glut. In this instance, Japanese chip makers were compelled into a price maintenance agreement to forestall dumping duties.

That the EC's anti-dumping policy is patently unfair has been chronicled by a raft of reports from reputable, independent bodies. In a study for the London-based Royal Institute of International Affairs, for example, Michael Davenport, a former senior economist at the EC Commission, emphasized the essential unjustness of the regulations by highlighting ways in which the system is slanted against importers.[10] Britain's consumer watchdog body, the National Consumer Council, stated in its study: 'The margins of dumping that have been calculated in several cases have far exceeded what is credible ... one suspects that in several cases protection is the true motive behind the attempt to prove dumping.'[11]

GATT itself has recognized the problem and has urged its member nations to update the very nebulous GATT anti-dumping code which is so vague as to allow EC anti-dumping laws to fall technically within its ambit. Yet GATT's proposed changes have been opposed by the EC, which actually wants to modify the GATT anti-dumping code to allow for even more partisan anti-dumping rules.

Making medieval scholastics smile

The United States is also a prolific user of anti-dumping measures which now cover products as varied as photo albums, cement, computer disks, aspirin, paint brushes, bicycles, pears, mirrors and forklift trucks.

US anti-dumping rules are if anything more lopsided and biased than those of the European Community – and have become more discriminatory in recent years. As a result, whereas during the 1950s and 1960s only a tiny minority of US anti-dumping investigations resulted in duties being imposed, revisions to the rules during the 1970s resulted in 'dumping' being found in the overwhelming majority of cases investigated in the 1980s.

As with the EC anti-dumping regulations, the American rules also subtract legitimate costs – such as handling, port charges, freight and insurance – from the US price of an imported product, usually with the result that it appears to be lower than in the exporter's domestic market even when it is in fact higher.

When, for example, in the summer of 1991 Mazda and Toyota were indicted for 'dumping' Japanese-made minivans at below 'fair value' prices, Paul Ingrassia, the head of the *Wall Street Journal*'s Detroit bureau, commented: 'It's hard to say whether the charge is outrageous or just silly'. Ingrassia went on to point out that Chrysler's Dodge Caravan, the best-selling US-made model, actually cost $2,000 less than a Toyota minivan with inferior equipment.[12]

The United States has, moreover, led the Community in using anti-dumping rules against sophisticated Japanese products. Japanese colour TV manufacturers were found to have 'dumped' sets on the US market during the 1970s. Yet most experts believe that underlying the success of Japanese TV manufacturers in the US market was the fact that they left their American rivals standing when consumer demand switched away from large, furniture-styled sets to more compact models. The Japanese were also more adept at marketing and were more efficient producers, and their TVs were more reliable.

Recently, Japanese producers of 3.5" computer micro-disk drives were also found to have 'dumped' their products on the US market by margins of up to 51 per cent. The computer disk drive industry had been almost entirely dominated by American companies in the 1970s. But the market leaders were overhauled by the Japanese in the late 1980s after the new 3.5" micro-disk format was introduced. Although smaller in size, 3.5" drives have a larger storage capacity and are far more rugged than the older format 5.25" floppy disks. Sony, new to the drive market, stole a march on the competition by launching the first 3.5" drive in 1983, and it was other Japanese companies like Hitachi, NEC and Matsushita which were the most nimble in following Sony's lead.

The mass shift to 3.5" drives in 1988 caught many American manufacturers with a glut of old 5.25" drives. Worldwide demand for the smaller drives soared from 4.3 million units in 1986 to 13.5 million drives by 1988, by which time 3.5" drives accounted for 60 per cent of the market, allowing Japanese makers to win significant contracts from personal computer makers. Meanwhile the biggest American drive company, Seagate, suffered substantial sales losses as a result of sticking to the 5.25" format for too long, while Shugart, a former market leader in floppy disk drives, also missed the micro-disk boat and is now an insignificant player. Agility and efficiency, not dumping, lay behind Japanese success.

The US Commerce Department, which is responsible for anti-dumping investigations and enforcement, habitually uses anti-dumping laws to harass foreign companies. The Swedish bearings manufacturer SKF was forced to provide the department with information on over 100 million separate sales during a dumping investigation in 1989. SKF's submission was over 150,000 pages long and weighed three tons.

Even this was not enough. After several revisions and reformattings demanded by officials, SKF ended up providing over 12 tons of documentation. When, largely as a result of strict time constraints imposed by the department, it emerged that a tiny amount of the information provided by a West German SKF subsidiary which accounted for about 1 per cent of sales was incorrect, the Commerce Department treated SKF as though it had failed to provide any information and hit the company with a 180 per cent dumping margin.

The burden of paperwork forced Matsushita, the Japanese consumer electronics giant, to withdraw from a 1989 investigation into small business telephone systems, abandoning $50 million in sales. The final straw was when officials called up on Friday afternoon and demanded that 3,000 Japanese financial documents be translated by Monday morning.

When a Swedish glue manufacturer, responding to a request for information on other countries to which it was selling glue, replied that it was not selling elsewhere, officials raised the dumping duty on the company from 2 per cent to over 90 per cent on the grounds that the company had not provided the information requested. It took a case in the Court of Appeals to point out that the answer 'no' is not a refusal to provide information if there is none to provide.

US anti-dumping regulations allow Commerce Department officials to limit their examinations to sales data for larger companies in a dumping investigation, but then to impose any dumping duties on smaller companies regardless of the prices they are charging. So hundreds of Hong Kong sweater producers pay dumping duties because an investigation in 1989 found that one company was dumping. When, on the other hand, a few small Taiwanese sweater producers could not respond in time to the bureaucrats' request for huge amounts of information, hundreds of Taiwanese producers were penalized with a 21.94 per cent duty.

The Commerce Department can also compare the average foreign price over a six-month period with individual US sale prices. Most companies vary the prices of their goods, but if this results in any single US sale occurring at a price below the average foreign price, dumping is deemed to have been found. It was this ploy that allowed the US Commerce Department's guardians of fair trade to catch the Japanese Juki typewriter company, even though the vast majority of its US sales were at or above the so-called fair value. Similarly, a Canadian raspberry grower was penalized for a price difference between his US and Canadian sales of 0.002 per cent.

Toshiba were caught out because the company sold cellular mobile phones in Japan directly to small local dealers, while its US sales went directly to one large wholesaler who then sold on to dealers. The Commerce Department refused to make any adjustment to take account of the legitimate price difference between the two types of sale and found a dumping margin.

But perhaps the Commerce Department's best wheeze is the double jeopardy trick which trapped Brazilian steel wheel producers. To ascertain whether the manufacturers were obtaining their steel at a fair price, Commerce compared it to the price at which South Korean producers sold similar steel to the USA. But this price was unrealistically high because Korean steel exports to the USA were restricted by an import quota which naturally raised price levels. So US steel import restrictions first inflated the price of Korean steel in the US market, and then the Commerce Department cited that price to justify penalizing the Brazilians.

United States rules even allowed TV sets donated to charity by a Japanese manufacturer to be considered as sales at $0.00, so lowering the company's average US price and raising its dumping margin. No wonder that one American trade expert quipped that the US dumping rules would 'have probably made many medieval scholastics smile in heaven'.[13]

During the 1980s the US Commerce Department reached a 'not guilty' verdict in only 5 per cent of its investigations into dumping, penalizing more than 3,000 foreign companies in the process.[14] But in many ways the United States is now moving on from simply using trade barriers such as VRAs and spurious anti-dumping duties. Increasingly, America advocates managed trade. This involves not only fixing importers' prices at levels where they represent less of a threat to domestic producers, but also making deals that the exporting country buys a set quantity of goods from the USA – regardless of the inherent competitiveness of its products. And blazing the trail in the direction of managed trade is none other than the formerly flourishing semiconductor industry, once the very embodiment of the independent, free-booting, all-American business ethos.

Notes

1 Michael Davenport, *The Charybdis of Anti-Dumping: A New Form of EC Industrial Policy?*, Royal Institute of International Affairs, London, 1989.

2 *Newsweek*, 14 August 1989.

3 Jan Tumlir, *Protectionism*, American Enterprise Institute, Washington, 1985.

4 *Official Journal of the European Communities*, vol. 28, 2 August 1985.

5 Gary Jacobson and John Hillkirk, *Xerox: American Samurai*, Macmillan, New York, 1986.

6 *Official Journal of the European Communities*, vol. 28, 2 August 1985.

7 J.H.Dessauer, *My Years with Xerox: The Billions Nobody Wanted*, Doubleday, New York, 1971

8 Quoted in Jacobson and Hillkirk, op. cit.

9 Ibid.

10 Davenport, op. cit.

11 *International Trade and the Consumer: Consumer Electronics and the EC's Anti-Dumping Policy*, National Consumer Council, London, 1990.

12 *Asian Wall Street Journal*, 18 June 1991.

13 James Bovard, *The Fair Trade Fraud*, St Martin's Press, New York, 1991. Many of the examples in this section are quoted in Bovard, who provides a superb critique of US anti-dumping policy.

14 Ibid.

2 Managing Trade

Free trade, one of the greatest blessings which a government can confer on a people, is in almost every country unpopular.

Thomas Babington Macaulay[1]

In the late 1970s, Silicon Valley's scientists, technicians and young whizz kids were the toasts of the nation and seven of the top ten microchip makers were American. A decade later, one of the most dramatic industrial reversals of all time was complete. For by 1988 Japan's NEC had grabbed the position of top semiconductor maker, while the former leader, Texas Instruments, had fallen to number five. Six other Japanese chip makers had also entered the top ten, giving Japanese companies nearly half of the overall world market in microchips and more like 90 per cent of global D-Ram memory chip sales.

Convinced that the Japanese had beaten the great American industrial success story of the 1970s only by guile and government support, the US Semiconductor Industry Association (SIA) filed a complaint in June 1985. The SIA claimed that Japanese manufacturers had dumped microchips on to the American market at below cost in order to gain market share and force American producers out of business. The complaint also asserted that, because many Japanese semiconductor manufacturers also make computers, televisions, video recorders and other consumer electronics products which use their own microchips, this limited sales opportunities for American semiconductor makers, which tend to be specialist producers only making microchips.

If the Japanese had dumped chips in the mid-1980s by selling them at below cost, then so had virtually every other manufacturer in Europe and the United States. For what had actually happened was that most manufacturers had misread the market in 1985. Personal computer sales had been expected to double, but they actually increased by less than a third. As a result, purchases of memory chips fell dramatically and chip makers cut prices drastically to offload inventory. Even new-generation 256K D-Rams, which had initially been priced at around $45 each, fell to less than $3. So in the oversupplied market of the mid-1980s, few chip makers, whatever their country of origin, sold semiconductors at a profit – that is in the nature of this cyclical, glut-to-famine industry.

The argument that Japanese electronics conglomerates gained an unfair advantage and were better able to weather the storm by using their semiconductors in their own products is more interesting. Certainly, the large, integrated Japanese electronics companies, which make components for use in their own products as well as for sale to other companies, benefited from offsetting poor demand by sales to their own consumer and business electronics subsidiaries. But there are also examples of semiconductor manufacturers in the West who consume many, if not all, of their own microchips internally – in particular, AT&T and IBM of the USA, Philips of the Netherlands, France's Thomson and Siemens of Germany.

There were at one stage more American integrated electronics companies, such as General Electric, RCA and Westinghouse, which were initially leaders in semiconductor manufacturing, but they simply proved to be less competitive than the new breed of specialized 'merchant' microchip firms, such as Intel, which now predominate in the US industry. Moreover, whereas the Japanese integrated electronics manufacturers also market their chips aggressively to other companies. IBM has chosen only to manufacture semiconductors for its own internal use, while AT&T sells only a third of its production to other firms.

Many Japanese companies which produce consumer and business electronics have also only in recent years diversified into semiconductors and other electronic parts to become integrated electronics companies. These include Sony, which began making components for its own internal use, but now also sells $2 billion worth of its semiconductors and components to other manufacturers. That American producers of consumer or business electronics, such as Apple or Zenith, have not gone down the same route and developed more components in-house is hardly the fault of the Japanese.

All of this indicates that to suggest that the structure of Japan's electronics industry has somehow given it an 'unfair' advantage is specious and represents the worst kind of special pleading – especially when it is borne in mind that in Japan, unlike in the West, there are no longer any government restrictions on imports of foreign-made semiconductors and import tariffs are zero.

Rather, the real reasons behind Japan's advantage in semiconductors and broad swathes of the information technology industry lie beyond such self-serving excuses in the fundamental factors underpinning Japan's competitiveness – factors which allowed the Japanese semiconductor manufacturers to outstrip their American competitors startlingly quickly.

'We screwed up'

The American industry's problems really became apparent in 1980 when no fewer than six Japanese companies launched new-generation 64K D-Ram memory chips while the American products were still under development. By 1981, world markets were inundated with a flood of Japanese 64K D-Rams, at prices far below Silicon Valley's. During that year, the market price for a 64K D-Ram fell from $30 per device to $15, before plummeting in early 1982 to $5 a chip. By that time, Japanese companies had cleaned up three-quarters of the world market.

A year later, the American industry suffered yet another blow when Fujitsu brought out samples of its new 256K chip – way ahead of any American products. Over the next few years, almost all of the American D-Ram makers pulled out of the business.

This success was not achieved by unfair trade or dumping, but because Japanese producers were quicker off the mark in designing products. Japanese quality has also all too often been superior to that of western companies. In 1982 the American scientific instruments and minicomputer maker Hewlett Packard tested over 30,000 memory chips from three American and three Japanese suppliers. They found that the best US supplier had a failure rate six times that of the worst Japanese supplier.

Even the Pentagon felt compelled to crack down on major US semiconductor producers in 1984 and 1985 for inadequate testing of components supplied to military contractors. Moreover, the president of Intel's Japanese unit, William Howe, himself accepted that American producers often did not treat their customers as well as they might: 'We tended to get a little arrogant', he said, admitting 'It was pretty bad.'[2] Or in the more graphic words of Tim Propeck, director of product marketing at Mostek, a leading American chip maker: 'We screwed up.'[3]

One reason for the better Japanese quality was that the Japanese concentrated on increasing yields of good chips during the earlier stage of the manufacturing process – the etching of the circuitry on to round wafers of silicon. As the tiniest speck of dust can ruin a chip, the Japanese invested in ultra-clean manufacturing facilities and automated production which dramatically increased yields to close to 80 per cent, compared to the 50 per cent or so being achieved by American manufacturers.[4]

Despite these considerations, the US International Trade Commission ruled in favour of the SIA complaint and in 1986 the United States imposed initial duties on imports of Japanese semiconductors. To forestall further threatened penalties, the Japanese accepted the July 1986 Semiconductor Accord by which Japanese manufacturers not only agreed to raise their prices in the American market to ease pressure on American producers, but also informally agreed to increase their purchases of American-made chips, which then accounted for only 10.5 per cent of the Japanese market.

A year later, however, the SIA complained that the Japanese were not complying with the deal. So on 17 April 1987 the American government imposed a retaliatory tariff of up to 100 per cent on sales to the USA of $300 million worth of Japanese electronics goods, although this was later reduced to $164 million. The dispute rumbled on until 1991, when a further accord was made, this time with an open agreement by the Japanese to import 20 per cent of their semiconductor requirements.

Super 301

America's ability to enter into such managed trade agreements has been significantly boosted by the 1988 Trade Act, whose 482 pages are almost entirely devoted to complex procedural changes which enhance the capacity of the USA to deal with 'unfair' trading practices. Unfortunately, in current trade parlance this more often than not means trade in foreign products whose competitiveness is greater than American equivalents.

Among the procedures introduced in the 1988 Trade Act is the so-called Super 301 clause, which requires the US trade representative to identify priority unfair trade practices – and in extreme cases to point the finger at individual countries which maintain substantial trade barriers. If no agreement is reached, unilateral retaliatory action can be taken under Super 301. Needless to say, Super 301 is hugely popular with those Americans who believe that the only remedy required for

US economic ills is to 'tough it out' with its trading partners. But although in theory the provisions of Super 301 might sound perfectly fair, in practice they are both illegal and unjust.

Illegal, because the United States is a member of GATT, and unilateral action runs counter to basic GATT principles as well as violating its specific provisions. These based on the premise that GATT should act as an adjudicator in trade disputes, preventing the unfair imposition of penalties by a country which unreasonably feels itself to be aggrieved. Unjust, because the United States possesses enormous leverage which allows it to bully trading partners into agreements.

Permeating this reinforced United States trade legislation is the belief that fair access to markets should be judged on the basis of results. In other words, the new legislation contains a presumption that if the USA is running a trade deficit with another country, unfair trade practices rather than the poor competitiveness of many American products must be the reason.

The assumptions underlying current US trade policy are potentially extremely damaging because they encourage the growth of bilateral, managed trade deals, whereby the threat of action forces individual trading partners into satisfying American demands by agreeing to import specific quantities of US goods. This United States pressure is often bought off by simply taking trade away from other countries and giving it to American suppliers.

The way in which more efficient competitors can lose out to this type of trade bullying was graphically illustrated when, in 1990, the Japanese military were told by their government to hold up a $750 million deal to purchase twenty-seven British Aerospace 125–800 small jets, which had won a tender for search and rescue aircraft on price and performance.

According to a senior diplomat working in Japan at the time, what had happened was that in response to senior American politicians who were urging the Japanese to boost imports from America, the Japanese military suggested that they might be interested in buying Boeing AWAC early-warning planes. But Boeing would not reopen its production lines for the order, so the Americans focused on the search and rescue deal and attempts were made to muscle out the BAe 125 in favour of the Cessna Citation, causing the contract to be stalled. In this instance British Aerospace ultimately prevailed, but high-level browbeating by the Americans almost won the day.

Aero-engine maker Rolls-Royce was less fortunate. Air India decided to switch an order for Rolls-Royce's large Trent turbofan engines for its Boeing 747 aircraft in favour of American Pratt and Whitney powerplants in suspicious circumstances after US pressure was brought to bear on India to buy more American goods – pressure which included a Super 301 action against India.

American insistence has also been successful in other areas. By pressurizing the South Koreans to open up to foreign insurance companies, for example, the United States actually ensured the entry of just two companies – both of which were American. And when, following demands from the United States, South Korea announced a plan to cut its trade surplus with the USA, what it actually intended to do was to switch the majority of its imports of agricultural products away from countries like Argentina and China and buy them instead from America.

Similarly, pressure exerted by the United States for the opening of Japan's beef market aimed to increase quotas for US producers, rather than generally to liberalize the Japanese import regime;[5] while in 1989 the Taiwanese government restricted contracts for rolling stock and signalling equipment for its new Tamshui line rapid transit system to US companies to ease trade tensions with its biggest customer.

So there has to be a strong suspicion that recent American trade legislation has to do less with genuine dissatisfaction at the inability of GATT to resolve complex trade disputes, than with allowing the United States to introduce protectionist measures in the guise of ensuring free and fair trade. If the American commitment to liberal trade were genuine, the USA would work for a strengthened GATT. In reality, every recent opportunity to give GATT real teeth has been opposed by the United States.

The paradox is that, at the very moment that the triumph of capitalism over communism seems complete, the power which did the most to ensure that success is relapsing at a quickening pace into the very anti-market policies of managed trade which served the Soviet Union and its former Eastern bloc allies so poorly. That this is happening is due both to the intensifying heat of competition from Japan and the emergent east Asian economies, and to the strong and widespread conviction that Japan has won its economic triumph by unfair and underhand means which can be countered only by a tough response.

Notes

1 *Essays on Mitford's History of Greece*, 1824.
2 *Wall Street Journal*, 6 July 1988.

3 Quoted in Marvin J.Wolf, *The Japanese Conspiracy*, New English Library, London, 1985.

4 Clyde Prestowitz, *Trading Places: How We Allowed Japan to Take the Lead,* Basic Books, New York, 1988.

5 Jagdish Bhagwati, *Protectionism*, The MIT Press, Cambridge, Mass., 1988.

3 Getting Tough

I refer to the tendencies in men to blame their own misfortunes and those of their cultures on others: to exercise judgement they need for themselves on the lives of others; to search for a villain to explain everything that goes wrong in their private and collective courses. It is easy to be high-minded about the lives of others and afterwards to feel one has been high-minded in one's own.

Laurens Van Der Post, *The Night of the New Moon*

According to a *Washington Post*/ABC News Poll, nearly half of Americans questioned felt that Japan was more of a threat to America than the USSR. It seems that many of the captains and generals of American industry agree. Take Jerry Sanders, one of the classic Silicon Valley self-made men and the president of a leading American semiconductor manufacturer, Advanced Micro Devices. 'Clearly,' he says, 'our industry has been deprived of hundreds of millions of dollars – more like into the low numbers of billions – of profits, because of Japanese predatory pricing, resulting from their protected home market and their subsidies.'[1]

Then there is Chrysler's boss, Lee Iacocca, who after a strenuous round of lobbying on Capitol Hill complained to *Automotive News*, the car industry's trade publication: 'They don't know there is a war on. They don't have the foggiest idea.'

No less a man than Donald Trump, former billionaire property developer, grumbled to his fellow business people in Manhattan: 'We're the biggest suckers in the world. If we get any kinder or gentler we won't have any America left. Japan is ripping us off like no one has ever ripped us before' Mr Trump's solution to the problem is to exact 'a pound of flesh' in the form of a 20 per cent import tax.[2]

Needless to say, there are also those in the American photocopier industry who are bitter about the way they have been beaten by the Japanese. Paul Charlap of the American copier company Savin, which imported vast quantities of Japanese-made copiers to sell under its own name, is quoted as saying: 'The only good Jap is a dead Jap. They lie, they cheat and they steal. It's all smiles, all show and display to hide their evil intent ... They couldn't give a goddamn about the rest of the world. They care about one thing: the Japanese.'[3]

During one particularly acrimonious trade dispute, American members of Congress, never backward in promoting themselves in support of a populist cause – especially one with a good photo opportunity potential – ceremoniously consigned Toshiba video recorders to a flaming bonfire. Later, members were also to be seen with their sleeves rolled up for the cameras, wielding sledgehammers and smashing Japanese computers.

For nowhere is the sting of Japanese competition so keenly felt as in the United States, whose economic pre-eminence was so ungraciously curtailed by the Japanese upstarts. But worse may be to come. For now, having conquered the American car and semiconductor industries, the Japanese are preparing for an assault on the jewel in the crown of American high-tech manufacturing – its computer industry.

Already IBM is beginning to feel the pressure. 'Stress and turmoil' are the words chosen by IBM chairman, John Akers, to describe the state of the US computer market. The main Japanese computer producers are showing signs of the type of exponential growth which, in an earlier era, catapulted a group of tiny, unknown car makers into global giants. In the late 1980s the worldwide computer systems revenue of the main Japanese computer manufacturers rose at a 45 per cent compound annual rate, while sales by American suppliers grew by only 10 per cent a year.[4] A few more years of such growth differentials will put the Japanese industry neck and neck with America's – already Japanese companies occupy third, fourth and sixth positions in the world computer makers' league.

Them or us

The idea of the Japanese computer industry overtaking that of the United States horrifies the neo-mercantilists, who view all international economics in terms of 'them or us' and are forever fretting about whether or not America is still number one. These people use the same language as the old cold warriors – except that now the threat comes from Japan rather than the Soviets. They include in their ranks the labour unions, politicians from both main parties, academics and industrialists from corporations most threatened by Japanese competition.

The Democrats and labour unions have traditionally opposed industry and the right's lobbying for military programmes, but have always themselves been inclined to the corporatist ideal of government subsidies and trade barriers to protect ailing industries and promote 'strategic' ones. Now these formerly opposed groups have been united by the 'Japanese threat', which provides the external danger needed to justify their joint pleas for government assistance. Together, they have formed a powerful alliance which cuts across the political spectrum, for the first time uniting the right-wing and powerful industrial interests with the left.

There are also, of course, many Americans who would not consider themselves as protectionist, but who genuinely believe that they have 'got to get tough' with Japan over trade, arguing that 'it's the only language they understand'. Unfortunately, the result of such attitudes is an increasing unfairness and inconsistency in American policy towards Japan.

The new Super 301 legislation provides a very good example. The 1989 US government *Report on Foreign Trade Barriers* lists a huge number of impediments erected by a variety of countries against American exports. Among those countries mentioned is Australia, censured for duties in excess of 15 per cent on manufactured goods – considerably higher than average levels for other industrialized countries.

Needless to say, the EC, with which the American trade deficit was $12.8 billion in 1988, comes in for something of a pasting for tariffs on a wide variety of products, the 'buy national' policies of EC member governments, and grants and subsidies for virtually all agricultural products, severely disadvantaging American exports.

South Korea, with which the USA had a trade deficit of $9.9 billion, is also reprimanded, as is Taiwan, which ran a surplus of $14.1 billion with the United States. Even tiny Switzerland is not ignored, faulted for its system of beef import quotas, as well as for the effective exclusion of US manufacturers from supplying equipment for the country's electricity utilities.

Under the 1988 Trade Act, the US trade representative, Mrs Carla Hills, was obliged to use this report to draw up a list of priority unfair trading countries for special treatment and possible retaliatory sanctions under Super 301. At first it looked as though a fairly large list would be produced, probably including the EC, Taiwan and South Korea. Indeed, virtually any of the countries covered by the report could have served as a good victim for Super 301. Yet all were ignored when the list was finally published – with the exception of three.

For in the end, Japan was bracketed with two of the very worst offenders, Brazil and India (where the average tax on imports is 143 per cent), for possible retaliatory 100 per cent duties on selected exports to the United States if they failed to remove specified trade barriers within eighteen months.

The *Report on Foreign Trade Barriers*, with some reason, criticized Japan for having maintained high tariffs on agricultural products and for the Japanese government's unwillingness to buy American supercomputers. Plans to develop a domestically produced military helicopter were also censored.

But on the other hand, the report admitted that Japan was the United States' second largest export market in 1988 and praised it for having average tariff rates on industrial products which were among the lowest in the world. The report also commended Japan for the impartial system of telecommunications equipment approval set up by the Japanese Ministry of Post and Telecommunications which, unlike in almost all other countries, allows for the approval of imported telecommunications equipment without discrimination in favour of domestic producers.

Indeed, Japan came out of the report relatively well. Its import restrictions were far less onerous than those of many other countries, while many of the criticisms made about Japanese practices could just as easily have been made about the United States itself. After all, the American government also buys almost entirely home-produced supercomputers, while it is not unknown for the US Defense Department to co-operate with American aerospace manufacturers to produce helicopters and military planes. Yet it was Japan and not the EC, South Korea, Taiwan or any one of a number of other suitable countries that was chosen to accompany India and Brazil on the blacklist.

Behind this decision lay a good deal of internal US administration politics. On the one side was the 'get-tough' lobby led by Secretary of Commerce, Robert Mosbacher, and Mrs Hills. On the other side was the 'free trade' school that included Richard Darman, the director of the Office of Management and Budget, and Michael Boskin, chairman of the Council of Economic Advisors. 'Get-Tough' Hills had already established her credentials when she came into office in January 1989 claiming that she would wield a 'crow bar' to pry open foreign markets. Darman and Boskin, on the other hand, argued that unilateral retaliation would undermine the post-war economic order and could set off a trade war.

Mosbacher and Hills won. For despite advice from State Department officials to go easy on Japan, together with cables from the new US ambassador to Japan, Michael Armacost, which warned that lambasting Japan as a trade villain would provoke 'an emotional outburst' in Tokyo, President Bush, beset by angry members of Congress and Senators, decided to go ahead and take action by including Japan on the blacklist.[5]

Part of the problem was that, having whipped up just enough anti-Japanese hysteria to cover for their own shortcomings and policy failures, American politicians had to be seen to be doing something. But these political imperatives did not prevent the US administration's action from being viewed as inconsistent and unfair in Tokyo, especially as it came shortly after another extraordinarily erratic action which had already dented Japan's faith in the reliability of its main ally.

'S' is for 'sucker'

'The "S" in FSX stands for "sucker"', brayed an angry Congressman. A new US dispute with Japan had begun. In November 1988, Japan had signed an agreement with the United States to share in the development of a new fighter. Under the deal, General Dynamics was to be given 40 per cent of the $1.3 billion worth of work to develop a prototype of a new version of its F–16 fighter, to be called the Fighter Support Experimental, or FSX. Mitsubishi Heavy Industries and its Japanese subcontractors would get the rest of the work, and the Japanese government guaranteed to buy about 170 of the fighters in the mid-1990s.

At the time, the deal was seen as a triumph of American policy. Despite hard lobbying from Japanese aerospace companies, the Pentagon had dissuaded the Japanese from developing a fighter on their own. The bunting had hardly been taken down, however, when Washington's Japan-bashers moved into action. Tormented by a vision that the American aerospace industry would go the same way as their TV and semiconductor industries, five Senators wrote to President Bush demanding a review of the deal, maintaining that the Japanese should simply have bought American F–16s off the shelf.

In fact, few major industrial countries import ready-made military aircraft. Instead, they either make their own or at the very least negotiate for local assembly or offset deals to guarantee some security of supply in the event of hostilities – an imperative sanctioned by GATT. This, after all, was precisely what the United States Navy did when it made a rare decision to purchase a foreign aircraft – the British AV8B Harrier jump-jet – but insisted on American assembly of the plane. In any case, the United States already dominated the Japanese defence market overwhelmingly, accounting for 98 per cent of Japan's arms imports.

Despite these considerations and the fact that the State Department and the Pentagon were keen to go ahead with the transaction, which they felt was extremely advantageous from America's point of view, the administration caved in to the pressure and returned the deal to the melting pot for much of 1989. By the time President Bush eventually allowed the project to go ahead late in the summer, a great deal of damage had been done to US-Japanese relations.

Even then the deal almost stalled when it emerged that, far from the Japanese being the main beneficiaries of technology exchanges as had been asserted by the congressional Japanophobes, General Dynamics would in fact gain greatly from Mitsubishi Heavy Industries' advanced composite wing material technology, for which the Japanese company demanded payment.[6] Eventually the Japanese government agreed to shoulder the cost of transferring the technology to American manufacturers lest Japan should be seen to be taking away the last bastion of America's industrial might. But by then the deal had less to do with military or even industrial factors than with political considerations.

Sweeping up around Japanese computers

This type of inconsistency unfortunately now permeates American dealings with Japan. Fujitsu's attempt to take over semiconductor maker Fairchild in 1987 was, for example, blocked for reasons of 'national security', even though Fairchild's existing owner was a French company, Schlumberger, which had acquired it in 1979. Salt was rubbed into the wound when two years later another French company, Matra, was allowed to acquire Fairchild Industries, a key defence electronics and space activities company, while Veba of Germany was permitted to buy a Monsanto subsidiary involved in the sensitive defence electronics sector.

Likewise, Sony's purchase of Columbia Pictures late in 1989 provoked agitated comments that Japan had bought 'America's soul'. Yet the fact that such all-American businesses as Dunkin' Donuts, Brooks Brothers, Holiday Inns, Smith & Wesson, Burger King, Haagen Dazs, Hilton International, Ball Park Hot Dogs and Pepperidge Farm are all British-owned raises hardly a whimper of protest.

When, moreover, in 1989 French computer maker Groupe Bull bought up Zenith's PC business, France's Usinor-Salicor acquired the second largest stainless steel producer in America, and French aluminium producer Pechiney took over American National Can, the largest packaging group in the world, there was barely a murmur – despite the fact that all of the French companies concerned are state-controlled and heavily subsidized by the French government, partly for the very purpose of buying up foreign companies.

These inequities would be enough to try the tolerance of the most patient of nations, but in the case of Japan they are exacerbated by a newly shrill and aggressive note which has entered into American dealings with Japan over the past few years. For American politicians, ever eager to play to the gallery, have been refining the subtle art of Jap-bashing since Walter Mondale proved himself less a national leader than a follower of populist whims when in 1982 he complained: 'We've been running up the white flag when we should be running up the American flag ... what do we want our kids to do? Sweep up around the Japanese computers?'[7]

An intellectual impetus for such anti-Japanese populism has, moreover, been increasingly supplied by an influential new generation of books on Japan which assert that the Japanese system is so fundamentally different from western models, and that the Japanese are such irredeemably unfair players in the international economic game, that the United States and Europe are justified in protecting their industries and meting out such special treatment.[8]

'... half pique and half contempt'

In some respects, claims that Japan trades unfairly, however ill-founded, should come as no surprise. For nations in industrial decline generally use accusations of foul play against others both as an excuse for eroding competitiveness and as a smoke screen for the erection of their own trade barriers. This happened in Britain during the 1870s and 1880s with the rise of the National Fair Trade League, the National Society for the Defence of British Industry and the Reciprocity Fair Trade Association, each of which called for import restrictions.

Behind these demands for an end to Britain's relative embrace of free trade principles lay the fact that, while in the mid-nineteenth century Britain accounted for one-third of industrial production, between 1870 and 1913 its share halved. Over the same period the United States expanded its share of global output from less than a quarter to more than a third and was outproducing Britain in pig iron by a ratio of three to one.

In fact, Britain's decline and the rise of the United States in the late nineteenth century offer some interesting parallels which can help put current American disputes with Japan into context. For then, many in Britain harboured a resentment towards the upstart colonists similar to that which many Americans today feel towards Japan. The great free trader and liberal Richard Cobden wrote just after the middle of the century: 'A considerable portion of our countrymen have not yet reconciled themselves to the belief that the American colonies of 1780 are now become a first-rate independent power', going on to say that many people 'possess a feeling of half pique and half contempt towards the United States'.[9]

Since the war, the United States has in turn seen its share of world output halve, while Japan's share of global GDP has increased from 1.6 per cent to 10 per cent. In 1967 US companies controlled more than 80 per cent of world computer production and around three-quarters of semiconductor output. There were then also twenty-five US-owned manufacturers of colour televisions. Now there is only one and no indigenous American company manufactures consumer electronics products in volume.

Although, moreover, the electronics industry remains the United States' largest manufacturing employer, in 1984, for the first time, America imported more electronic goods than it exported. A year later, the USA was running a trade deficit of close to $140 billion, of which $50 billion was with Japan. Never has the world's leading financial and industrial power fallen so precipitously from a position of having an export and capital surplus and industrial dominance, to the predicament of being the world's largest debtor with an inability to compete effectively in a large number of industrial sectors.

As America's performance has dwindled, so demands for protection have increased, just as they did in Britain in the late nineteenth century. For whatever its rhetoric, the Reagan administration was far finer in word than deed and became the most protectionist administration since the 1930s. The new Bush regime, under huge pressure from Congress and the Senate, has proved little better, so that there is now a real risk of a decline into the type of conditions which brought about the Smoot-Hawley Act in 1930. This protectionist legislation, designed to safeguard American industry and jobs against foreign competition, ended in retaliatory measures against the USA from twenty-five of its trading partners, with the result that by 1933 American exports had declined by about 60 per cent.

Any hope that America has learned from this and is prepared to examine the real causes of Japanese success in order to breathe new life into its economy is seriously diminished by the paranoid reaction to Japan's success and the increasingly strident protectionist backlash. It is always easier to blame foreigners for your problems – especially when they are orientals who are naturally assumed to harbour devious or sinister motives.

This helps to explain the inconclusive soul-searching in the USA about the loss of national competitiveness, the deep and disturbed fear of Japan's economic success and huge trade surplus, and the dread that Japan's progress threatens American leadership and even its national security.

From the Japanese viewpoint, there is more than a little irony in all of this. For in the seventeenth century it was Japan which found it necessary to close its doors to western trade for fear of the effects of the marked superiority of western technology. From 1636 the shogun forbade Japanese dockyards to construct ocean-going vessels, ordered merchants to trade only within China, revoked the citizenship of Japanese living abroad and promised death to any such who dared to return. When a Portuguese vessel unwisely called in 1640, it was sent home with a message in the form of the decapitated corpses of sixty-one of its crewmen. Only a small Dutch trading post was allowed, cooped up in the tiny, artificial, fan-shaped island of Deshima in Nagasaki harbour.

But so debilitated did Japan become from lack of contact with the West that by the mid-nineteenth century a handful of American gunboats were able to prise open its ports to trade, imposing, moreover, a largely free trade regime through a series of 'unequal treaties' which prevented the Japanese from erecting tariffs of more than 5 per cent on imported goods for fifty years (a few years later, the US Congress sharply raised American tariffs on Japanese goods). The result was that many traditional industries were destroyed by the sudden influx of western products and Japan ran trade deficits with the West for a very long period.

Of course, the stimulus afforded by competition from the West also prompted the rapid modernization and upgrading of Japanese industry. Yet now that Japan has become competitive, it is the Americans who have suddenly lost their appetite for free trade and are begging the Japanese to restrain their exports as relays of industrialists and special pleaders troop to Capitol Hill to beg for protection against what they claim to be the unfair business practices of the Japanese. They are buoyed by a widespread public perception that the Japanese have not played by the rules. How justified is this?

Notes

1 Quoted in Marvin J. Wolf, *The Japanese Conspiracy*, New English Library, London, 1985.

2 *Sunday Telegraph*, 19 November 1989.

3 Gary Jacobsen and John Hillkirk, *Xerox: American Samurai*, Macmillan, New York, 1986.

4 Source: 'Datamation', quoted in *Business Week*, 23 October 1989.

5 The story of the political background was told in *Newsweek*, 5 June 1989.

6 *Wall Street Journal*, 28 November 1989.

7 *New York Times*, 13 October 1982.

8 See Karel van Wolferen, *The Enigma of Japanese Power*, Macmillan, London, 1989; Clyde Prestowitz, *Trading Places: How We Allowed Japan to take the Lead*, Basic Books, New York, 1988; and Wolf, op. cit.

9 *The Political Writings of Richard Cobden*, Cassell, London, 1886.

4 Scotch and Snow

Japan's export performance has been underpinned by strong price competitiveness, high quality and an outstanding ability to adapt to change in world demand ... there is also little evidence in general to support the contention that import impediments (either formal or informal) imposed by the Government are a decisive factor in Japan's trade surpluses.

OECD Economic Survey on Japan, 1988/9

One of the most widely held beliefs about the Japanese is that they are super-exporters who protect their home market to give themselves a secure base from which to launch withering assaults on western industries. Apart from formal trade barriers, so the received wisdom goes, the Japanese are adept at using informal 'administrative guidance' to hinder imports, on top of which their labyrinthine distribution system acts as a disincentive to importers. Further, the Japanese people themselves have a deep cultural bias against foreign goods.

How do these assumptions stack up? Despite their reputation for being highly successful exporters, the Japanese in fact fare pretty badly by international comparison. As trade tensions gained momentum in 1991, figures produced by the Organization for Economic Co-operation and Development (OECD), the research and advisory grouping of the main industrial nations, showed the following:

- Out of twenty-three industrial countries, Japan managed to come only twenty-second in terms of the share of its gross domestic product (GDP) accounted for by exports.

- Moreover, at 9.4 per cent of GDP, Japan's export figure was less than half that of Canada, West Germany, Sweden, Switzerland, Denmark, Iceland, New Zealand, Austria, Denmark, Norway and even Portugal.

- Japan's export ratio was also far lower than the figure for Britain – even excluding Britain's oil exports.

- Japan's figure was also only a fifth of the totals for Belgium and Ireland, both of which export more than half of their GDP.

The objection could of course be made that as Japan's GDP is so large, it is irrelevant that the country exports only a low proportion of GDP. So exports per head of population may be a fairer guide. But even then:

- Japan ranked only seventeenth out of twenty-three industrial nations, beating Turkey, Portugal, Spain, Greece, Australia and New Zealand, but being outsold by countries as diverse as Switzerland, Britain and Ireland.

- Canadians, Austrians, Germans, Swedes, Finns, Irish, Icelanders and Danes exported about twice as much per head as the Japanese.

- The Swiss, Dutch, Norwegians, Austrians and Belgians sold three times as much abroad per head as the Japanese.[1]

Nor, taking into account the large size of its population, is Japan even substantially responsible for the huge trade deficits run by the United States since the early 1980s. In 1984, for example, Japan, with a population of just over 120 million, ran a bilateral surplus with the United States of $36.795 billion, while Canada, with only 25 million people, exported no less than $20.387 billion more to the USA than it imported.

Further, in terms of overall sales Japan was soundly beaten in export markets by the United States, which sent $422 billion worth of goods overseas in 1991 compared to Japan's $315 billion. West Germany also outsold Japan, managing $403 billion worth of overseas sales despite having a population only half the size of Japan's.[2] Yet few politicians or commentators complain about German surpluses. It is also worth pointing out one largely ignored fact – namely that Japan runs a large deficit on its services, in areas such as shipping, transport, travel and insurance. This deficit was a massive $16 billion in 1990 according to IMF figures.

Some people argue that, although Japan's exports may not be as high as they are sometimes made out to be, its imports are also very low – in fact Japan comes twenty-second in the OECD imports per capita table and bottom on the basis of imports as a percentage of GDP. The reasons for this are complex. Trade barriers play a part, but so do other factors. First, Japan has a relatively large and rich domestic market – as a rule, the larger the home market, the lower the imports in relation to GNP. This is because larger economies tend to supply more goods internally whereas smaller ones, such as Holland and Belgium, cannot do so as easily and so both import and export more as a proportion of their overall production.

Then there is the competitiveness of Japan's industry and economy, which undoubtedly makes life difficult for western goods. In this last respect, Japan's low propensity to import is not so very different from that of the United States in the 1950s when the USA was at the height of its economic power.

It is also said that low Japanese domestic demand caused by Japanese government policies has inhibited imports. Although there is an undoubted element of truth in this, the other side of the coin is that many western countries – and particularly the United States – have consumed too much and hence sucked in imports. At least in recent years the Japanese have taken steps to increase their domestic demand, while America appears to have done little to address the problems of a society living beyond its means.

Japan has also been criticized for the fact that it has traditionally imported more commodities than manufactured goods – oil alone accounts for about a fifth of Japan's total import bill and the country is the world's largest importer of fuel and food. In 1985 the Japanese imported only $347 of manufactures per head, compared to $1,078 in the USA – in fact, Japan's total imports of manufactured goods that year were lower than those of the Netherlands. Its exports, on the other hand, are predominantly in the manufactured sector.

This, however, might be expected of a country with few natural resources apart from its inhabitants. Japan has little to export except what it makes, and it has to import virtually all of its essential raw materials. There is not an ounce of cotton in Japanese textiles, not a scrap of metal in Japanese cars, railcars or bridges, and not a drop of oil which Japan does not have to buy in from distant countries. Japan also imports all of its nickel, tin, phosphates and bauxite, half of its food and a high proportion of its coal, coke, lead and potash.

As overall imports grow, however, the situation is changing rapidly and purchases of foreign manufactured goods are rising fast. By 1988, 50 per cent of Japan's imports were of manufactured goods, compared with only 20 per cent in 1980. Sales of imported manufactured goods, moreover, rose by 80 per cent between 1985 and 1989. Indeed, just as French prime minister Mrs Cresson was launching her bitter attack on

Japan in the summer of 1991 for having a hermetically sealed market, the French luxury products group LVMH was announcing that close to a quarter of its annual £2 billion sales were in Japan, while the French car maker Peugeot was on target to increase its sales in Japan by a fifth, despite a fall in the overall Japanese car market.

Many commentators have regarded the preponderance of certain products in Japan's exports as part of a concerted policy by Japanese companies – guided by government policies – of targeting western industries. It is certainly true that Japan's exports are concentrated disproportionately in sensitive and highly visible areas. In the early 1970s they consisted of ships, steel, radios, TVs, tape recorders, synthetic cloth, toys and cameras. Now it is vehicles, office information and telecommunications products, electronic components, machine tools and consumer electronics.

It is easy for westerners to grow purple in the face about the success Japan has achieved in export markets for these products and to impute Japanese targeting of certain industries to all kinds of evil motives. But all the Japanese have done is perfectly sensibly to concentrate in export markets on those areas where their comparative advantage over western producers is greatest. Put simply, the Japanese have sold what has been easiest for them to sell.

Also worth noting is the enormous help given to Japanese exporters by western companies, which have often made the conscious decision to concede the superiority of Japanese manufactures. Japanese photocopiers, cars, personal computers, electronic typewriters, pickup trucks, printers, fax machines, televisions, music centres and machine tools have all been distributed in vast quantities bearing well-known American and European brand names such as Xerox, IBM, Chevrolet, Dodge, Ford, RCA, Olivetti, Gestetner, Philips and Siemens, to name but a few. Indeed, in 1985 about one-third of total Japanese sales to the USA were of products branded with American names.

A hungry attitude

Then there is the hungry Japanese attitude towards exporting. The Clean Air Act, passed by the US government in the early 1970s, had severe implications for car manufacturers, especially foreign ones, for it meant that they would have to adapt their cars specially for the American market. At that time, the Toyota chairman, Eiji Toyoda, was told by the chairman of Renault of France: 'I refuse to pay any attention to a country that does such idiotic things. Renault is going to stop exports to the US'. And it did. The French car maker simply gave up selling Renaults in America until the late 1970s, when it resumed sales with only limited success. Toyota, on the other hand, fitted its cars with catalytic converters and managed to carve out a huge and profitable market in America.[3]

Toyota's export effort in the United States was subsequently assisted by the lethargy of its western rivals. Except for Volkswagen, none of the European manufacturers was prepared to make the heavy investment in marketing and distribution necessary for the huge American market, while Detroit failed to develop a really competitive subcompact car and even Volkswagen was slow in replacing the Beetle in the early 1970s. Japanese manufacturers had no such inhibitions and were able to capture a large part of the booming US small car market.

Consider, too, the fact that in 1989 *Car and Driver* magazine recognized nine out of the ten best cars sold in America to be Japanese, while a California research company's survey of customer satisfaction for 1991 put Toyota and Nissan equal top – the best-placed American range was Cadillac in eighth position. Perhaps these facts help to explain why in three successive years up to 1991 Americans chose to make the Honda Accord the best seller on the US market.

It is also worth contrasting the differing attitudes of various western countries and companies towards selling in Japan itself. When asked in a magazine interview whether he was interested in the Japanese market, Raymond Levy, the boss of Renault, replied: 'It's not really an important market. ... France and northern Europe are our priorities.'[4] Mercedes Benz, on the other hand, has made great efforts to sell its cars in Japan to which the German company now sends almost 10 per cent of its output.

In the 1970s American automobile manufacturers were, in fact, fairly successful in Japan, managing to market about 20,000 cars a year to the Japanese market at a time when few European manufacturers were interested in selling there. By the mid-1980s, however, sales of American cars to Japan had plummeted to a mere 2,000 annually. Over the same period, shipments of European cars soared – by 1990 sales were growing at an annual rate of around 60 per cent and in 1991 they totalled 168,000. If 'trade barriers' prevented American car makers from selling in Japan, why did they not also stop BMW, Rover, Mercedes, Jaguar and Volkswagen? Germans buy far fewer American cars than the Japanese, yet Germany is not accused of having trade barriers against US automobile exports. The truth is that American luxury cars have become less and less competitive compared to their rivals, but it is far easier for American politicians to blame it on 'unfair' trade practices.

One paradoxical advantage enjoyed by American cars was the fact that, although Japan is a right-hand-drive country, in the post-war years many Japanese actually preferred left-side steering models because driving an import was a status symbol – an interesting counterpoint to those who claim that the Japanese have a cultural bias against imports. But whereas European manufacturers such as Mercedes Benz and BMW now offer Japanese customers a choice of right- or left-drive models, US car makers have never bothered to make right-side steering models for those Japanese who want them – even though Honda manages to export right-hand-drive cars from Ohio to Japan.

Ironically, when early in 1992 Ford finally announced that it had decided to export right-hand-drive vehicles from America to Japan and other right-hand-drive countries for the first time since the early 1900s, it emerged that the model in question – a sporty coupé called the Ford Probe – was none other than the Mazda MX-6, built for Ford by Mazda at its plant at Flat Rock, Michigan.

Japan, it is true, is still a difficult market in which to sell – but largely on account of its competitiveness and quality orientation. Many people persist in making the error of confusing this with protectionism. Yet Japan now compares very favourably in the openness of its market with most countries. In 1971 Japan was joint equal top of the developed countries with France when it came to import quotas. By 1981, however, Japan was below most of the industrial nations in the number of such barriers.[5]

Japan does nonetheless still undeniably maintain trade barriers, particularly in areas such as farm products. So how important a factor have these been in restricting overall imports to Japan? Perhaps the best arbiter of whether or not remaining Japanese trade restrictions have been the real cause of American trade deficits is the United States Federal Trade Commission itself. It released a study on protectionism which included an admission that the US trade deficit has been largely caused not by unfair foreign trade barriers, but by internal American factors such as the high dollar and rapid growth in the USA during the 1980s which sucked in imports.

Another report, this time by the American Chamber of Commerce in Japan, concluded in 1992 that Japanese government policies were among the least significant obstacles which US companies face in their attempts to break into the Japanese market. The survey of 340 leading American companies with Japanese operations placed the high cost of land and housing, difficulties in recruiting skilled staff, mistakes made by the companies themselves and the fact that many US businesses do not try hard enough as far more notable factors than trade barriers or government policies.[6]

This may explain why former US trade representative William Brock confessed to having a 'nightmare' in which 'the Japanese do all the things we ask them to do – and nothing changes' – a point which was later stressed when Brock conceded that in his judgement two-thirds to three-quarters of the US trade deficit with Japan 'is our own fault'.[7]

Structural impediments

Walk down almost any street in a Japanese town or city and one of the first things to strike you will be the multitude of small 'mom and pop' stores, usually run by elderly and retired people who are willing to accept both long hours and low incomes. Japan does have plenty of sizeable department stores, but the number of supermarkets is still small by comparison with many western countries.

It is certainly remarkable that the country with the world's most productive manufacturing industry should maintain one of the least efficient retailing and distribution systems. Japan, with half the US population, actually has more stores and twice the proportion of wholesalers.[8] Japan's retailers are now at the centre of trade disputes with western countries, their labyrinthine and often picturesque distribution system being described by the Confederation of British Industry (CBI) as 'the strongest barrier to the mass marketing of European products in Japan'.[9]

Many people who are prepared to admit that most of Japan's formal trade barriers have now been dismantled nonetheless maintain that the Japanese retain a series of more subtle import restrictions. Referring to these as 'non-tariff barriers', they cite Japan's retailing system, semi-official 'administrative guidances' which make life difficult for importers, and the apparent unwillingness of the Japanese to buy western goods as the main obstacles to foreign sales. Such importance is now attached to these problems that they have spawned a series of US–Japanese talks – the so-called Structural Impediments Initiative.

In the early 1980s Michael Perry was in charge of Nippon Lever, the Japanese arm of the giant Anglo-Dutch detergent and personal products company Unilever, which has enjoyed great success in the Japanese market with products such as Timotei shampoo and Lipton tea. Perry has more experience of Japan's distribution and retailing system than most. Yet he adamantly states: 'At no time in our experience was there a shred of evidence to support the view that the Japanese distribution system was used to discriminate against foreign manufacturers. Sure, it is complex, multi-layered and inefficient. It made life tough for us – but that was true for everybody else as well.'

In fact, some western companies have gained advantage by successfully bypassing the distribution system. These include Coca Cola, which was warned in the early 1960s that its normal sales methods would prove unworkable in Japan. Undeterred, it ignored local distributors and set up its own network of bottlers. Today, Coca Cola's distribution system is among the most efficient in Japan and more profitable than its American one.

Moreover, Japan is not unique in having an intricate distribution system. West Germany uses its *Baunutzungs Verordnung* law to protect small shopkeepers by virtually prohibiting any new retail outlets above 10,000 square metres in size, while Italy and to a lesser extent France have similar regulations.

Further, a retail structure which puts massive purchasing power into the hands of large chains of stores is no guarantor of success. It can make access to shelf space harder, as evidenced by frequent complaints from manufacturers about the overwhelming power of Britain's large supermarket groups. As it is, a combination of pressure from the large store groups and consumers in Japan is already resulting in a slow but steady erosion of its small store sector, which may eventually result in a structure closer to that of Britain or America. But this may help Japanese industry more than western importers. For by liberalizing Japan's inefficient and rigid distribution structure, more resources will be freed to fortify Japan's overall economic strength.

Another of the 'structural impediments' to selling in Japan is the supposed Japanese hostility to imported goods. In fact, more often than not the Japanese are suckers for impressive western brand names – Chanel 19 is Japan's best-selling scent, Tokyo's fashionable ladies wrap themselves in Hermes scarves and there are often queues outside the Luis Vuitton shop. Even relatively downmarket but quintessentially western outlets, like McDonald's and Pizza Hut, do very well in Japan.

There is, however, an element of ambivalence in the Japanese attitude to buying western goods which gives at least some justification to those who persist in thinking that the Japanese are not open to western goods or influence. Sometimes, of course, the Japanese are simply nationalistic in their purchasing. To an extent this is due to the fact that the Japanese still perceive Japan as being a poor country with the result that many feel an obligation to buy locally made goods.

In addition, although much of Japan's early culture came second hand from China, its geographical isolation allowed the country both to impose its own modifications on these newly imported ideas and to preserve a large measure of self-identity. It thus developed the means to learn from and adapt foreign ideas without losing its own cultural singularity. So a tenacious pride in Japan's own forms and methods has developed, allied with an extraordinary openness to outside influences – a unique combination.

The net result of this complex of factors is that, although on the one hand the Japanese are very open to and respectful of good-quality western goods and influences, there is also a very strong attachment to local products and traditions, born of a combination of genuine pride as well as the perceived need to buy Japanese in order that the nation might survive.

It is commonly assumed that the citizens of most western countries have, by contrast, a very open attitude to imports. This is more true, perhaps, of Americans than, say, the French who have been known to drum businessmen with Japanese car dealerships out of the local Rotary club. Indeed, Americans can be over-influenced in their quality judgements by the fact that a product is advertised as imported. But even their cultural attitudes are not invariably well disposed towards foreign goods.

The Ford Mustang, when launched in the 1960s, was one of the great symbols of the prowess of the American motor industry. Based on standard saloon car components, the two-door Mustang gave its owners sports car feel and performance for the cost of an average family motor. It spawned a whole host of imitators and became one of the great American automotive legends.

But the Mustang has also come to symbolize the decline of that industry, for though the first Mustangs have become sought-after collectors' items, subsequent models bearing the proud name have become progressively flabbier and more mundane. The last model was, in fact, so ordinary and uninspiring that Ford decided to buy in the coupé version of the Japanese Mazda 626 as its replacement and badge it with the Mustang name.

When word of this leaked out to automobile aficionados, however, a huge outcry ensued. For despite the fact that the Mustang-badged Mazdas were to be assembled in the USA, and although the impressive high-tech Japanese car was a huge advance on the previous American model, many Americans felt Ford's move to be a grave insult to their national pride and self-esteem. Such was the protest that Ford rapidly dropped the idea in favour of continuing its production of the old model, selling the US assembled Mazdas under a more anonymous and less emotive name.

A rich man's drink

Ask a British industrialist or politician for an example of Japanese protectionism and he or she will unhesitatingly quote Scotch whisky. James Moorhouse, a British Conservative Member of the European Parliament, for example, states in his pamphlet *Righting the Balance: A New Agenda for Euro-Japanese Trade*, that: 'A standard bottle [of Scotch] will normally be marketed at around $100, deluxe variants for much more', claiming that Japanese duty discriminates against Scotch and prices it out of the market.

How does this statement square with prices in Japanese shops? The answer is that it does not. Scotch in Japan costs no more than it does in Britain. It is just an example of the type of hearsay so beloved by those who are convinced that the Japanese have triumphed only through a protectionist conspiracy. What is true is that the duty levied on Scotch whisky in Japan was, until recently, higher than on some other locally produced spirits, and this was what lay behind a widely misreported dispute between the Scotch whisky industry and the Japanese government.

Most western countries tax alcoholic drinks according to their strength. The Japanese, however, have traditionally, and arguably more logically, imposed duty on alcohol largely according to price and quality rather than strength, on the progressive principle that if you can afford a more expensive drink, you can also manage to make a larger contribution to the nation's coffers. Thus a poor person's drink, such as crude sake (rice wine) or the even rougher shochu (a type of vodka made from barley and potatoes) was taxed less heavily than the rich person's premium grade whisky – or, indeed, higher-quality sake.

There is, perhaps, the grain of an argument in the assertion that this tax system constituted an import barrier, designed to protect the many small Japanese shochu producers. But nothing prevented Scotch importers from selling rougher grades of their products at prices closer to that of shochu. Yet although bulk Scotch producers happily sold their cheaper spirit to Japanese companies for blending, the main Scotch distillers took the decision to avoid selling very downmarket Scotch in the Japanese market in order to protect their prestige image.

Far from representing a problem, the price premium of Scotch over lower-grade tipples has been a significant advantage to the whisky producers. Why? Because in Japan, the more expensively you drink, the higher your status. When, for example, the lower-priced Johnnie Walker Red Label appeared alongside the premium Black brand, it failed to inspire the Japanese drinker.

When in 1979, moreover, import procedures were liberalized, allowing unofficial 'parallel importers' to undercut the exclusive accredited shippers, so forcing the main agents to reduce prices to meet the new competition, Scotch whisky sales fell because the price reduction had effectively lowered its value as a gift.

Nonetheless, after a complaint on behalf of the Scotch distillers from the EC Commission, GATT ruled in 1988 that the Japanese tax system was in fact unfair. In this instance, its ruling that the Japanese tax system did constitute an import barrier had to be a marginal one, although the Japanese government acceded to the verdict and agreed to equalize spirit duties.

If the tax system really had significantly forced up Scotch prices and been an impediment to sales, these tax changes which were introduced early in 1989 should have resulted in price reductions. But despite a ¥688 (£2.75) tax cut on a bottle of Bell's, the importers in fact maintained the retail price at ¥3,200 (£13). So ironically, the result of years of hard lobbying looked like being no price reduction at all on some brands – at least until Japan's National Tax Administration Agency, presumably hardly able to contain its glee, ordered the importers to cut their prices by the amount of the tax reduction.

In fairness, one main agent did decide to cut the price of Johnnie Walker Black Label by no less than ¥2,000 to ¥6,000 (£24). But as the tax break was only ¥607, this illustrates the fat margins the importers had enjoyed and the somewhat dubious nature of their complaints against the tax system.[10]

The conclusions should be obvious. First, Japan's idiosyncratic system of taxing spirits actually made very little difference to Scotch prices. Rather, the main reason for high Scotch prices was the margins maintained by the accredited agents, as evidenced by both the low prices charged by parallel importers and the large reduction which the Johnnie Walker agents were able to make when they decided to cut prices as part of a campaign against the unofficial importers.

Moreover, high prices were probably an advantage in the status-conscious Japanese market. Indeed, the position of Scotch is probably far more threatened by downward price pressure caused by the tax cuts and pirate importers than by any import barriers, supposed or otherwise – which may be why a new fifteen-year-old blend of Johnnie Walker called Gold Label is now being launched, selling for ¥10,000 (£40) a bottle and available only in Japan to prevent parallel importing.

Wrong snow

In August 1986 the Japanese Consumer Product Safety Association suddenly announced that standards for ski equipment would be changed with immediate effect. A special voluntary quality label, called the SG-mark, would henceforth be reserved for products that met the specific requirements of Japanese conditions. The move subsequently took on a somewhat ridiculous dimension when a spokesman absurdly stated that the new standard was needed because of the distinctly different properties of Japanese snow.

Needless to say, the hapless official's comments were gleefully seized upon by western reporters. For although there was no question of a ban on foreign skis, western manufacturers felt that meeting the new conditions would entail either interfering with their production lines, or cutting down on exports in a market where foreign firms accounted for about half of the $500 million ski equipment sales. Western governments were urged by the ski makers to make representations to GATT, and after much-publicized discussions Japan reluctantly agreed to withdraw the new standards with effect from late 1987.

On the face of it, this is a blatant, if bizarre, example of Japanese protectionism. But there is more to this story, for little mention was made in the press of a dispute which had arisen between the two main western standards bodies, ISO and DIN, on ski quality. The Japanese, rather than wait for this to be resolved, had simply decided to introduce their own standard, which was not compulsory, but to which foreign manufacturers were welcome to accede – in the same way that Japanese manufacturers might be expected to comply with western standards if they wanted to sell to Europe or to North America.

In the context of Japan's export surpluses and growing trade tensions, its decision to promote a Japanese ski mark was, at worst, a foolish one, but probably no more than that. Unfortunately, the ski saga has now entered the realms of mythology, and is periodically trotted out by

Scotch and snow

journalists and politicians as yet another example of devious Japanese trade practices.

The problem is that one-sided media comment on disputes such as these helps to provide a convenient scapegoat on which western business leaders and politicians can vent frustration for their failures. Such reporting also furnishes useful ammunition for the powerful industrial lobbies seeking protection from Japanese competition. Moreover, each dispute enters the national consciousness and public opinion becomes ever more steeped in assumptions of Japanese deceit, helping to set a scene of animosity and distrust for the next round and encouraging journalists in their quest for yet more examples of oriental trickery.

In his book *Second to None: American Companies in Japan*[11] the former senior editor of *Time* magazine, Robert Christopher, quotes Kneale Ashworth, the head of the Japanese subsidiary of American personal products group Johnson & Johnson. 'Not long ago,' Ashworth told Christopher, 'a reporter for the *New York Times* came to see me, sat himself down ... and said: "Tell me about non-tariff barriers that Johnson and Johnson face here in Japan." When I told him we didn't face any, he said: "I beg your pardon." So I said again: "We don't face any non-tariff barriers. We've got lots of problems, but that isn't one of them." With that, he shut his notebook and got up to leave. I was a bit surprised and asked him: "Don't you want to hear the good news?" He said: "No, I just want to hear about non-tariff barriers" – and away he went.'

Notes

1 Source: OECD figures for 1991.

2 Source: GATT.

3 Eiji Toyoda, *Toyota: Fifty Years in Motion*, Kodansha International, Tokyo, 1987.

4 Quoted in *Car*, January 1990.

5 S. Okita, 'The role of the trade ombudsman in liberalizing Japan's market', in *World Economy*, 1984.

6 *Trade and Investment in Japan: The Current Environment*, American Chamber of Commerce in Japan.

7 Quoted in Robert Christopher, *Second to None: American Companies in Japan*, Tuttle, Tokyo, 1987.

8 Source: Japan Chamber of Commerce and Industry.

9 *Relations between the Community and Japan*, House of Lords Select Committee on the European Communities, 13th Report, June 1989.

10 *Financial Times*, 9 March 1989.

11 Christopher, op. cit.

5 Survival of the Fattest

As their thoughts are commonly exercised rather about the interest ... of their own particular branch of business, than about that of society, their judgement, even when given with the greatest candour (which it has not been upon every occasion), is more to be depended on with regard to the former of those two objects, than with regard to the latter ... Any proposal for the regulation of commerce which comes from this order ought to be listened to with great precaution.

Adam Smith, on merchants and manufacturers[1]

'Let's not talk about free trade. Let's talk about fair trade. America is the only country which has practised free trade and abided by its agreements', shrilled Congresswoman Bentley at a cowering Japanese government spokesman during a TV interview. So how free and fair has the United States been when it comes to trade?

The answer is not very. For not only have American trade barriers increased sharply over the past decade, but there has always been a strong protectionist tendency in the United States which has been only partly disguised by the free-market rhetoric of American leaders. In the post-World War II era, for example, Presidents Eisenhower and Kennedy launched America into a new sphere of protectionism, first with 'voluntary' restraints on Japanese exports of cotton textiles in the 1950s and then with mandatory controls on all textile imports.

Following on from that, President Johnson ushered in the apparatus for restricting foreign meat imports; and steel imports were restrained under President Nixon, who also considered the ice-cream industry to be strategically vital. So when in 1970 the USA was hit by what an agriculture under-secretary called a 'flood' of imported ice-cream (amounting to 1 per cent of US consumption), a quota was imposed which slashed imports by 95 per cent.

President Ford built on this achievement by tightening steel import quotas. Textile and footwear imports were further limited under President Carter. But it was under President Reagan that post-war American protectionism really took off. For this leading champion of the free market first conceded to further pressure from the textile and steel industries, and then added automobiles to the long list of foreign products which were denied free access to the American market, ushering in an era when almost any industry threatened by foreign competition knew that it had good friends in Washington.

Injuring the 'Big Three'

On 12 June 1980 the United Auto Workers union (UAW) filed a petition with the United States International Trade Commission (USTIC) – the government body which adjudicates on trade issues – claiming that the domestic motor industry was being seriously injured by foreign imports. The Ford Motor Company subsequently joined the union as a co-petitioner for import relief.

On 10 November 1980 the USITC determined that automobiles and light trucks were not being imported into the USA in such a way as to be a substantial cause of injury to the domestic industry. Rather, the USITC found that the failure of the 'Big Three' American manufacturers to adjust sufficiently to increased demand for smaller, more fuel-efficient vehicles was a major cause of their problems.

So the auto industry appealed to the president for trade restrictions and embarked on a feverish round of lobbying members of Congress and Senators, many of whom where indebted to the auto industry for campaign contributions and retainers. Although the president initially resisted the pressure, by early 1981 legislation to restrict Japanese imports was gaining broad support in Congress.

In April 1981, following meetings with US trade officials, the Japanese trade ministry, MITI, agreed under pressure to 'voluntary' restraints on automobile exports to the USA to allow the American industry time to become competitive. In May of the same year an agreement was finally reached restraining Japanese imports to 1.68 million units for the subsequent year. A later agreement also restricted imports of four-wheel drives to 82,500 units.

At the end of the first year of restriction, and under further severe pressure, Japan agreed to renew the so-called voluntary restraint agreement (VRA) for a further year; this was repeated again in 1983 and

Survival of the Fattest

1984. When, however, Ford, Chrysler, American Motors and the UAW urged the Reagan administration to extend the VRA for a fifth year, MITI protested, citing record profits by the large US automakers and the sharp reduction in unemployment in the American auto industry.

Nonetheless, the Japanese were again coerced into holding auto exports for 1985 to 2.3 million units. This restriction remained in force until 1988 when it was succeeded by another, even more shadowy export restraint agreement. Meanwhile American pickup truck producers are still protected by a massive 25 per cent tariff – more in line with tariff levels in Third World than industrialized countries.

'Hypocrites, or dishonest, or fools'

Other import quotas initiated during the Reagan years included 'voluntary' limits on imports of machine tools from Taiwan, Japan, West Germany and even Switzerland. Although these agreements are 'voluntary', when in 1987 Taiwan exceeded its quota the US Customs Service threatened to seize and impound Taiwanese machine tools. The situation was only resolved when Taiwan 'voluntarily' agreed to compensate for overshipments by reducing exports even further for a three-year period.

One year later, a Taiwanese company began shipping machine tool parts to an Israeli manufacturer, who combined them with locally made components and exported the finished product to the United States. At first US Customs ruled that the machine tools were Israeli as enough of the value originated there. But the Commerce Department thought differently and counted the machine tools against the Taiwanese quota, retrospectively – and presumably voluntarily. As a result, the Taiwanese company stopped shipping the parts and the Israeli company has gone out of business.

At first West Germany voluntarily decided to tough it out and refused to co-operate with the import quota programme. So the United States unilaterally declared maximum market share levels for German machine tools. Meanwhile other European countries remain under threat of 'remedial action' if they take the word 'voluntary' too seriously and try to increase their US market share.

'Voluntary' restraints on steel imports resulted in the USA imposing a ban on all shipments of European steel pipe in 1984 because the EC refused 'voluntarily' to reduce its pipe exports by 50 per cent – even though the USITC had determined that European pipe imports were not injuring US producers.

Other relatively new restrictions limit imports of South Korean video recorders, microwave ovens, colour TVs and semiconductors. The strategic economic interests of the world's leading economy also necessitate import quotas on bras, tampons, typing ribbons, tablecloths, tents, twine and ties. Then there are tariffs on more than 8,000 products, many of them penal, such as the 151 per cent impost on watches, 458 per cent on tobacco stems and 67 per cent on shoes.

Just in case some damagingly cheap foreign product should still slip through the net, there is the *de facto* protection of anti-dumping duties on a huge raft of products from ball bearings to computer displays. If that does not quite do the trick, there are increasing numbers of managed trade agreements covering key products such as semiconductors.

American politicians are long on the rhetoric of free and fair trade, but short on its realization; far sighted when it comes to the deficiencies of others, but myopic about their own shortcomings. The *National Trade Estimate: Foreign Trade Barriers*, the annual list of foreign trade barriers produced by the US Trade Representative, has been described by one Congressman as 'a chamber of horrors that greets US businesses as they seek to export American goods and services around the world'.[2]

The horrors outlined in the 1990 edition included the Canadian import quota on United States ice-cream – but there was no mention of the fact that, while Canada at least does allow some imports (347,000 kilograms), the USA prohibits Canada from sending a single scoop the other way. The European Community is censured for tariffs on US farm products such as avocados, wood and trucks. The EC duty on wood is 10 per cent while the US duty is 20 per cent. European truck tariffs range from 5 per cent to 22 per cent; the US tariff is 25 per cent. The American tariff on imported avocados is 21.6 per cent, compared to the EC tariff of 4 per cent.[3]

In short, it may by now be becoming apparent to the perceptive reader that, however impressive the United States' free-trade pronouncements – and the heartfelt convictions of Congresswoman Bentley – in practice America has been extensively protectionist for many years. It is, moreover, adding trade barriers at an accelerating rate. In the words of American author Jim Bovard, those who contend that the American market is open are 'hypocrites, or dishonest, or fools'.[4]

Land of the free

Although rarely reported in the press, import quotas are at least a fairly straightforward form of protection, in contrast to the so-called covert, non-tariff barriers which the Japanese are held by many people to maintain. Of course, by contrast the United States is an open market and American politicians loudly and fondly proclaim their devotion to free trade. Former US trade negotiator Clyde Prestowitz assures us in his book *Trading Places: How We Allowed Japan to Take the Lead*: 'The United States has been relatively easy to penetrate. Its open society makes for an open market that has welcomed foreign goods.'[5]

In 1988, for example, the USA imposed a customs user fee on imports, and was the only major country to levy such a charge. The fee raised $536 million in taxes on imports in the first ten months of operation before being declared illegal by GATT.

The United States also prohibits imports of firearms and munitions unless the importer can demonstrate that the imports are for specific uses and obtains a licence from the US Treasury – something which US manufacturers do not have to do.

The US Merchant Marine Act of 1920 requires that only US-registered vessels be used in American territorial waters for activities such as dredging, towing and salvaging. As only American-built vessels are eligible for US registration for these purposes, foreign-constructed vessels are effectively prohibited from such work. United States law also requires that vessels registered in the USA for coastal commerce should be built in the USA. The same applies to US-flagged vessels fishing in American waters. The total market from which foreign-built vessels are thus effectively excluded is worth about $1.3 billion a year.

Should an American ship require repairs while in a foreign port, the owners are required on their return to pay a 50 per cent duty on the cost. This is designed to benefit domestic ship repair yards. But most US yards are so occupied with lavish military contracts that one American flag carrier was recently told that it would have to wait at least nine months before any domestic yard could even begin the work.[6]

Nor is it unknown for the American government to resort to 'administrative guidance' to discourage imports. The Massachusetts Institute of Technology ruled out buying a supercomputer made by Japan's NEC following a US Commerce Department official's warning that it might attract anti-dumping charges if the price were too low.[7]

Even seemingly reasonable regulations have, on occasions, been used as non-tariff barriers to imports. Plants entering the USA are governed by quarantine regulations designed to protect American agriculture against the importation of foreign diseases and pests. The process is, however, often a very laborious one which the US government has failed to improve, allegedly due to inadequate staffing. In fact, pressure from American growers against amending the regulations, which they see as a valuable impediment against imports, is a major factor in the procrastination.

This may be why one survey of non-tariff barriers by the World Bank showed that in Japan they covered 9 per cent of all goods, while in America they affected 34.3 per cent. France was even worse, with non-tariff barriers covering 44.2 per cent of goods, and even the Netherlands came in with a figure of 21.4 per cent.

Overall, Japan's totals were the third lowest of the sixteen industrialized countries in the survey.[8] This was reinforced early in 1990 by David Henderson, head of economics at the OECD, who said that during the 1980s the United States had the worst record for devising new non-tariff barriers.[9] When it comes to niggling import restrictions, there is little that the free-trading United States can learn from Japan.

Co-operation and understanding

Maybe the Japanese have something to learn from the United States. When in 1971 President Nixon wanted additional restraints on imports of Japanese textiles, he first threatened to perpetuate the US military occupation of Okinawa if the Japanese government did not co-operate; and he then threatened to penalize Japan under the World War I Trading with the Enemy Act.[10] When Japan finally succumbed, the White House announced: 'President Nixon wants to express his personal appreciation for the co-operation and understanding of our negotiating partners.'

In 1984 imports of luggage and handbags were suddenly made subject to import quotas on the grounds that they had small pieces of cotton or polyester in their covers and so should be subject to import restrictions covering textiles. US Customs also prohibited the import of tennis shoes from Indonesia in 1989 because the boxes contained a spare pair of laces which were deemed to be an item of clothing requiring a separate import licence. Even superannuated, cast-iron, red British telephone booths were refused entry to the 'land of the free' when the all-seeing US Customs Service reclassified them as fabricated steel, requiring a steel import quota licence.

Survival of the Fattest

Early in 1989 the US Customs Service suddenly redefined the meaning of sugar to include Canadian blended corn sweeteners and banned all Canadian blended imports as they exceeded the sugar import quota. The first time Canadian companies learned of this was when their trucks were turned back at the USA–Canada border. $25 million of imports were wiped out at dead of night by the stroke of a bureaucrat's pen.

At least American legislators can occasionally rise above the special interest pleading of inefficient industries. In 1984 Congress generously ruled that the Customs Service should not impose tariffs on articles returned from outer space, provided 'such articles were previously launched into space from the customs territory of the United States aboard a spacecraft operated by, or under the control of, United States persons and owned by US citizens'.[11]

Back on the ground, public procurement policy offers another rich vein of non-tariff protectionist possibilities. At federal, state and local government levels the Buy America Act is used to limit imports. This legislation states that if US companies' products or services are no more than 6 per cent more expensive than foreign ones, they should get the contract; but in the mass transit sector, the rate increases to 25 per cent, meaning that, all other things being equal, a foreign bus or locomotive manufacturer can be up to a quarter cheaper than an American company and still not make the sale – which is why you see no foreign-made buses in American cities.

The Department of Defense is also prohibited from purchasing certain products from foreign sources and must give preference to US manufacturers for reasons of 'national security'. Yet among the affected products which cannot be said to have a genuine bearing on national security are coal and coke, textiles, stainless steel, valves, anchor chains, vehicles and bearings.

Work on federal construction contracts by Japanese companies accounted for less than 0.25 per cent out of a total expenditure of $435 billion in 1989. This places into perspective frequent American charges that US companies are excluded from Japanese government public works contracts.[12]

The United States is also increasingly tending to ignore the rulings of GATT itself – as when GATT ruled illegal a US increase in taxation on crude oil in 1987 which was applied at a higher rate on imported oil. Several other similar GATT cases against the USA are still outstanding. The United States is also more and more disregarding basic GATT obligations. At the outset of the Uruguay round of trade talks in 1986, participating countries agreed not to introduce new trade barriers during the course of the negotiations – the 'standstill' commitment. By March 1990, however, there were a large number of notifications of breaches of this undertaking, most of which referred to the United States.

Gentlemen agreeing

Each year throughout the late 1970s and 1980s, officers and staff of the British Society of Motor Manufacturers and Traders (SMMT) met their Japanese counterparts from the Automobile Manufacturers Association (JAMA) in either Britain or Japan. When in Britain, they usually stayed for a pleasant couple of days' golf at Gleneagles. The purpose of these gatherings was to discuss the so-called Gentleman's Agreement, an import quota dating from 1977, by which the Japanese motor manufacturers agreed to limit exports of cars and light commercial vehicles to Britain to no more than 11 per cent of the market.

As sales of Japanese cars in unrestricted European countries such as Denmark, Finland, Ireland, Holland and Belgium account for between a quarter and a half of the market, it is clear that this agreement limits the Japanese to much less than half the sales which they might achieve in a free market.

The Japanese originally accepted these restraints under a government threat of more formal restrictions. At the same time, they also acceded to an 'industry to industry understanding' which prohibits shipments of heavy commercial vehicles. As a result, when in the early 1980s attempts were made to sell Japanese Hino trucks which were assembled in the Republic of Ireland into the British market, they had to be withdrawn. The import quotas for Japanese cars and trucks which exist in France, Spain, Portugal and Italy are even tougher – Italy, for example, has an import limit for Japanese cars of only 2,550 a year.

Anti-Japanese trade barriers in Europe parallel – and in some cases exceed – those in the United States. In addition to import quotas on Japanese cars:

- France has restricted imports of Japanese toys, machine tools, small motor cycles, tape recorders, radios, colour TVs and video recorders as well as Taiwanese and Korean footwear.

- Italy has limited sales of Japanese video recorders, car radios, cameras, leather shoes, silk, colour TVs, motorcycles, four-wheel-drive vehicles and trucks in addition to Korean and Taiwanese shoes.

Survival of the Fattest

- Spain has barred imported Japanese and South Korean machine tools and video cassette players.

- Germany has restrained imports of Japanese colour TVs since 1973.

- Overall, in 1989 individual member states of the European Community maintained more than 150 import quotas on Japanese goods alone – and the number is growing.

Even Britain – one of the more free-trade-oriented of the EC nations – has maintained import quotas on imports of black and white TVs from Singapore, South Korea, Taiwan and Thailand; on lathes and machine tools from Japan; on colour TVs from Japan, Singapore, South Korea and Taiwan; on music centres from Japan, South Korea and Taiwan; on video recorders from South Korea; on pottery from Japan and Taiwan; on stainless steel cutlery from Japan and South Korea; on forklift trucks from Japan; and on footwear from Taiwan. Many of these British import quotas were in force throughout the late 1960s and 1970s. Although some were abandoned in the mid and late 1980s, several remain in force.

Increasingly, however, the EC itself has taken over responsibility for the Community's trade policy and has enforced numerous recent EC-wide import quotas against non-EC goods. Community-sanctioned import restraints now cover Japanese machine tools, numerically controlled lathes and machining centres, forklift trucks, colour TV tubes, video recorders, colour televisions and compact disc players; as well as Korean footwear, video recorders and microwave ovens. In addition, the EC has imposed high tariffs on many sensitive products in the electronics sector.

Until 1988 the European Community even maintained internal national steel production and trading quotas between its member countries, supposedly to allow for orderly capacity reductions to restructure the market. Despite the dismantling of these internal quotas, a series of limitations on imports of non-EC steel, originally imposed in the 1970s, remain in force. These include quotas and provisions, euphemistically referred to as 'consulting arrangements' and 'price monitoring systems', to ensure that importers do not bring steel in below a certain price. Among the exporting countries affected are South Korea, Finland, Norway and, of course, Japan.

Indeed, the fact that, some three decades after the so-called Common Market[13] was inaugurated, European Community countries still have not fully opened up their own internal market to free trade between member countries – let alone to outsiders – puts complaints about Japanese trade barriers into perspective. Even with the much-vaunted '1992' initiative to do away with trade barriers between EC member states, a fully open internal market is unlikely to be achieved by the target date. EC member states' transport ministers, for example, are still squabbling over plans to allow completely free access for road hauliers to each country's roads.

Under the current system, most EC countries insist on internal haulage being carried out by their own nationals, with the result that many of the trucks criss-crossing the Community are empty on their return journey – an estimated 30 per cent of the trucks crossing the West German/Dutch border carry no loads – costing about £150 million a year and needlessly adding to congestion and pollution. France and West Germany were counted among the nations wishing to retain restrictions, while Britain stood in the van of the liberalizers. In the end, Germany actually took unilateral action and imposed a special toll of up to £4,000 for trucks using major roads – craftily exempting their own hauliers by reducing annual road tax on German lorries by a similar amount so that the toll affects only foreigners.

Nor is European public procurement policy any fairer than that of the United States. Most European countries have systematically favoured domestic suppliers for public-sector contracts. From 1993 the EC is introducing a procedure whereby member governments can dismiss any bids where at least 50 per cent of the value of the goods is not Community made. Other niggling non-tariff barriers abound in Europe. For example, France requires labelling of pesticides used on imported fruit and vegetables – including those from other EC countries – but exempts French produce from these conditions.

Standards and regulations are also systematically used to favour domestic suppliers, such as when in 1983 Britain banned imports of UHT milk ostensibly on health grounds, but in reality to protect fresh milk distributors from low-priced competition. In 1986 the European Community rejected Muse, a Japanese standard for a new generation of razor-sharp high-definition television (HDTV), despite the fact that there was no real alternative and the Japanese had been working on Muse for fifteen years. Instead, the EC Commission has been pushing a different and far less well-developed technology – in the teeth of opposition from European broadcasters – primarily to protect the interests of Europe's main TV producers, Philips and Thomson.

Bearing in mind that so much western comment on Japanese trade practices is based on the premise that they are sneaky and underhand, it is worth noting how many western trade barriers fall into the same category. For one thing, 'voluntary' restraint agreements which fix prices and market shares are actually illegal under US anti-trust and European competition laws. But European governments and the United States get round this illegality by asking the Japanese administration to order their firms to comply, so technically placing the deals outside their control.

Recently, for example, the EC Commission declared that it would not use its own competition laws against its new EC-wide vehicle import quota with Japan. As the Commission can play the roles of both lawmaker and lawbreaker, it feels that it has the luxury of choosing not to obey its own laws.

But perhaps the most blatant example of double standards occurred in 1991. One of the commonest complaints against the Japanese during the 1980s was that their system of taxing large cars at a higher rate than smaller ones was a 'non-tariff barrier' against large, and particularly American, models.

There might just have been something in the argument that the Japanese were justified in giving tax breaks on small cars in a country where space is at a premium – and city dwellers often have to prove ownership of a parking space before they can buy a car. After all, many other less crowded countries followed a similar policy of taxing larger cars more heavily, including Belgium, Denmark, Greece, Italy, the Netherlands, Portugal and Ireland, without incurring criticism. Yet no sooner had the Japanese succumbed to the pressure and reduced sales tax on larger cars than the United States itself slapped a 10 per cent 'luxury' tax on cars costing more than $30,000!

Notes

1 Adam Smith, *The Wealth of Nations*, 1776.

2 Rep. John Dingell, *Congressional Record*, 28 April 1987.

3 James Bovard, *The Fair Trade Fraud*, St Martin's Press, New York, 1991.

4 Quoted in the *Financial Times*, 11 February 1992.

5 Clyde Prestowitz, *Trading Places: How We Allowed Japan to Take the Lead*, Basic Books, New York, 1988.

6 US Trade Representative, Trade Policy Staff Committee, Hearing on Uruguay Round Tariff Reduction Proposals, 31 October 1989. Quoted in Bovard, op. cit.

7 *Fortune*, 21 December 1987.

8 J. Nogues, A. Olechowski and L.A. Winters, 'The extent of non-tariff barriers to imports

of industrial countries', World Bank Staff Working Paper, Washington, 1986.

9 *Financial Times*, 2 July 1990.

10 William Cline, *The Future of World Trade in Textiles and Apparel*, Institute for International Economics, Washington, 1987

11 Quoted in Bovard, op. cit.

12 Source: US Commerce Department figures, quoted in the *New York Times*, 3 June 1991.

13 The original name of the six-nation organization inaugurated by the Treaty of Rome in 1956, which was later superseded by the European Economic Community, followed by the twelve-member European Community.

6 The Protection Racket

Defeated soldiers in their own defence have to protest that their adversary was something out of the ordinary, that he had all the advantages of preparation, equipment, and terrain, and that they themselves suffered from every corresponding hardship. The harder they have run away, the more they must exaggerate the unfair superiority of the enemy.

Field-Marshal Slim, Allied Commander in Burma, 1942-5[1]

The long catalogue of American and European trade barriers should place into perspective the chorus of allegations from western politicians, writers and industrialists that Japan is uniquely hostile to imports. The truth is that Japan has not in the past been significantly more protectionist than many other countries and is now rather less so.

The treatment of Scotch whisky, for example, is one of the most celebrated cases of supposed Japanese protectionism. Yet some of Britain's European Community partners have discriminated far more against Scotch than the Japanese. Until recently, France taxed mainly domestically produced grape-based spirits at a far lower rate than imported grain spirits, as well as placing stricter conditions on the advertising of Scotch than on cognac.

Italian tax also discriminated against Scotch and gin in favour of local spirits, while West Germany for many years prevented the import of French crème de cassis on the grounds that it had an alcohol content too high to be classified as a wine, but too low to be considered a liqueur. For a time Bonn even blocked the import of still mineral waters on the grounds that bubbles were needed to kill micro-organisms. Germany also until recently prevented the import of foreign beers that contained additives permissible in other EC countries.

Canada has also been involved in numerous trade disputes about alcoholic products with the United States. Until 1992 Canada's provincial liquor boards had a monopoly on the import of foreign alcoholic drinks, which privately owned liquor stores were prohibited from selling. The government liquor boards refused to stock many imported items and, where they did, charged far higher mark-ups on foreign brands than they did on domestic products. This practice particularly hit imports of American beer and was the subject of a successful complaint to GATT which the Canadian government refused to comply with.

Canada also imposes a requirement that American car exports to Canada should equal production in the Canadian plants of the 'Big Three' US car makers. Canada also restricts imports of ice-cream from the United States. Yet Americans do not consider Canadians to be unfair traders – even though on many occasions in recent years Canada's per capita bilateral trade deficit with its southern neighbour has been far greater than Japan's. So why has Japan so singularly attracted the wrath of the West?

Cultural affinity may be one reason for the more benign view of the Canadians. Canada, moreover, is not a particularly successful economy and therefore is not perceived as a threat – resentment of the top dog is rarely far from the surface of many trade disputes between the West and Japan.

Another reason why many people sincerely maintain the belief that the Japanese are unfair traders is that large sections of the western media pounce on any example of Japanese protectionism and blow it up out of all proportion, yet American and European trade barriers are little reported. So while most westerners are aware of disputes with Japan over Scotch, skis, non-tariff barriers and so on, very few actually realize that their own countries restrict imports of cars, motorbikes, televisions, textiles, steel, semiconductors, machine tools, trucks and many other products.

Level playing fields

Of course, American business and political leaders have also been more comfortable in the work of erecting trade barriers when they have managed to convince themselves – and others – that these actions are in response to unfair trade by competitors. This, of course, is sometimes actually the case. But such industrialists and politicians also have an interest in playing up Japan's misdemeanours and keeping quiet about their own.

There are a number of reasons for this. Nothing is more natural than to blame foreigners for your own failures – something which politicians are particularly adept at. Making whipping boys of the Japanese has had the comforting effect of absolving the American and European political and industrial establishments from their own responsibility for declining industries and trade deficits. Of course, the process is made all the more easy when the foreigners in question are from a distant land which few westerners know well and to whom it has been relatively simple to impute the most devious motives.

Secondly, bashing the Japanese has also been a very good way to help secure re-election – a ploy which is particularly effective in those American states which produce cars or other items in direct competition with Japanese goods. Indeed, it is now virtually obligatory for congressional and senatorial candidates to prove their strong sense of patriotism to their electorate with anti-Japanese, pro-protectionist sentiments – which was how Senators Danforth and Packwood became household names. The ploy can be especially useful in close elections. In August 1985, for example, a Texan Democrat used the imports issue to triumph in a very tight race for a congressional seat.

More recently, President Bush succumbed to the temptation and indulged in a little vicarious Japan bashing early in 1992 – election year – when he took a group of prominent American industrialists on a trip to Japan. Ostensibly, his aim was to secure better access for US products; a more likely reason was to divert responsibility for America's deep-seated economic ills away from his administration.

Industrialists play the same kind of game. British business people for example, love to tell the public that they would be able to compete in Japan or other markets 'if only there were level playing fields'. Some say that, while the British are 'playing cricket', the Japanese are playing harder games by different rules. The implication is that it is always the foreigner – usually the Japanese – who is not playing by the rules, while the poor old British lose out.

Ironically, far from being a gentle and mellow game cricket can be a tough sport – which is appropriate enough because the game these industrialists are playing is indeed a rough one. For the third and crucial point is that, by maintaining that the Japanese do not trade fairly, such people are not only making excuses for their own failure to produce and market competitive products, but more often than not also using supposed unfair trade practices to lobby for subsidies or protection for themselves. Put simply, the more that industrialists can convince the public of how disagreeable the Japanese are, the more likely they are to win hand-outs and protection from their governments.

It should, therefore, come as no surprise that anguished cries for 'fair trade' more often than not come from industrialists who themselves have had more than their fair share of protection and subsidies – like Francis Lorentz, chairman of French computer maker Groupe Bull, and Hans Dieter of Siemens-Nixdorf of Germany, who used a computer conference late in 1991 to argue that Japanese competitors enjoyed special privileges in their home market. They urged the European Community to establish a 'level playing field' for computer manufacturers.[2] Yet Groupe Bull and Siemens-Nixdorf must themselves be among the most pampered computer manufacturers in history, benefiting from decades of cosy government procurement, research subsidies and capital grants.

Likewise, the twenty-one American industrialists who accompanied President Bush on his trip to Japan early in 1992 were a pretty cosseted bunch of professional scapegoat seekers. Those in the electronics industry who did not rely significantly on government contracts for most of their profits were adept pleaders for protection – none more so than the representatives of the 'Big Three' automobile producers, who over the years have signally failed to create a flexible, well-trained workforce, underestimated the importance of quality and paid themselves too much. The fact that the average chief executive of an American corporation earns 125 times the annual remuneration of a manufacturing worker, compared to just 16 times in Japan, was not lost on the Japanese businessmen assigned to meet the US delegation.

So noisy complaints about Japanese protectionism, real or imagined, are a key weapon in the battle to limit competition from Japanese imports. There is nothing new in this. Economists have long pointed out that business people who are often loud in their praise for the general principles of free trade frequently find it inappropriate to apply it too rigorously in their own particular case. As Adam Smith succinctly observed some two centuries ago: 'when one or more producers gather together, they talk about ways to restrict trade'.

Industrialists lobbying for protection usually find ready allies in the trade unions – indeed, in the United States the large industrial labour unions are among the keenest advocates of trade barriers to protect the jobs of their members. During the 1980s the American unions have devoted considerable efforts to retaking control of the Senate for the Democratic Party. Very simply, this has meant that a great many new Democratic senators owe a strong allegiance and loyalty to organized labour. So when a union like the Teamsters, the biggest in the USA, runs million-dollar advertising campaigns urging people to 'Buy American', it can be imagined what they will be saying to every Democratic Senator whose election they supported.

And if industrialists and union leaders can claim that the industry in need of protection is 'strategic', all the better. Of course, it is easy for any industry to claim it is strategic – and most usually do. One European trade expert once said that the only industry he could think of where noone tried to make the claim was musical instruments.

The electronics industry is singularly expert at playing the 'strategic' card. Hardly had the smoke from the Gulf War cleared, for example, than US semiconductor industry leaders showed up in Washington to solicit for more government favours. Their letter to President Bush read: 'We are proud of America's men and women in the Gulf. We are also proud of the role of American technology in this effort ... Our industry supplies the American semiconductors which make these high-technology weapons possible.'

The implication was clear – American high-tech weaponry needs US-made semiconductors, so the government should support the industry. It must have embarrassed the seasoned lobbyists of the American semiconductor industry when it emerged soon after that many of the electronic components used in the sophisticated US arsenal were already Japanese – which did not, of course, prevent the war from being won.

Of course, in most cases the elaborateness of the special pleader's justification for a trade restraint is directly proportional to its unsustainability and cost to consumers and the economy as a whole. But industrial lobbies have almost always been more powerful and vociferous than those of the more diffuse consumer groups which are harmed by trade restraints, and which are neither as vocal nor as politically influential as industrial and trade union lobbies. Furthermore, those consumers also have also often been infected by anti-Japanese sentiment.

'Throwing a banana into a cage of monkeys'

Sadly, the devil often has the best tunes. Protecting jobs plus a mistrust of foreigners has provided trade barriers with a compelling populist appeal. Free trade, on the other hand, has rarely been a cause to fire up the masses.

Just about the only time in history when free trade became a popular cause was during the campaign in the middle of the last century to abolish the Corn Laws which protected English agricultural landlords from imported corn. Public meetings addressed by the great free-trade reformer Richard Cobden drew tens of thousands of people in the industrial towns of the north. When, owing to his concentration on the free-trade campaign, Cobden went bankrupt, a public subscription raised the then massive sum of £75,000. And when Cobden subsequently lost it all speculating on Mississippi land, another appeal raised a further £40,000.

Almost invariably, however, it has been the protectionist lobby which has won hands down, even where the reality is that foreign competitors have simply been more competent and efficient – which is so often the case.

One major advantage enjoyed by the proponents of trade-limiting measures is that they confer large benefits to small groups of people in protected industries and slight losses to large numbers of consumers who are, anyway, rarely aware of what is going on. Once a benefit has been conferred on a group in society, moreover, it does not readily surrender it.

I have myself seen this many times when groups of MPs, backed up by trade unions and management, lobby government ministers for trade restrictions on imports to protect whatever domestically made product is under threat. The MPs representing the affected constituencies make a huge noise in Parliament – the rest say nothing, and indeed it is doubtful whether they receive a single letter from consumers likely to be affected by whatever import barrier is proposed.

The government probably realizes that protection can only delay structural economic adjustment and harm the economy in the long run. But no politician seeking re-election likes to be seen to be damaging the interests of any particular group, and if the government refuses to act, ministers can be blamed for factory closures and job losses. If the MPs in question represent marginal constituencies, and especially if an election is close at hand, it is a brave government minister who holds out.

Politicians well know that they will get more accolades – and campaign contributions – for maintaining and augmenting trade barriers than for abolishing them. This is particularly true in the United States where as far back as 1886 the economist Henry George noted: 'To introduce a tariff bill into a congress or parliament is like throwing a banana into a cage of monkeys.'

'Just plain lousy'

The increasingly shrill denunciations of the Japanese by western industrialists should, however, be heeded with a keen awareness of the interest such commentators have in limiting competition. For industrialists are adept at masking their own special pleading with the shimmering veneer of higher purpose. Speaking at an electronics conference, Mr Caillot, chairman of the French Electronics Industry Association and president of the French electronics firm Thomson, even managed to invoke the need to secure what he called 'Europe's political, economic, cultural and social freedom' in urging tough limits on new Japanese plants in Europe. What he really wanted to secure, of course, was his job and salary. But it seems to work. Thomson is one of the most heavily state-subsidized and protected electronics companies in the world.

Chrysler's Lee Iaccoca is also rather good at this. He has consistently blamed his company's difficulties on 'unfair' Japanese competition, which he uses to justify his perpetual lobbying for protection. In his autobiography, for example, Iaccoca writes: 'The field where this game is being played is not level. Instead, it's strongly tilted in favour of Japan. As a result we are playing with one hand tied behind our back.'[3]

Yet the splashy advertising that Chrysler was running in 1991 was headlined: 'In 1981, the quality of American cars was just plain lousy. All of us', the advertisement continues, 'built a lot of lousy cars in the early '80s and we paid the price. We lost a lot of our market to import competition. But that forced us to wake up and start building better cars and trucks.' This, of course, begs a number of questions:

- Was it 'unfair' Japanese competition which took sales from Chrysler in the early 1980s, or the 'lousy cars' which the American company was building?

- If Chrysler's cars were 'lousy' in 1981 – and who better to tell us that than the boss himself – why did the company deserve protection?

- If 'import competition' – limited though it was by import quotas – forced Chrysler to 'wake up' and make better cars, would more competition not have made them even more efficient?

- And if Chrysler really is now building competitive products, why does Mr Iaccoca keep running to Washington to plead for yet more protection?

Iaccoca also claims in his book to be an ardent free-marketeer:

'Ideologically, I've always been a free-enterpriser, a believer in survival of the fittest', he says, before going on to criticize the Japanese government for supposedly helping its car industry. 'To begin with, Japanese industry is not playing by itself. It's backed to the hilt in its close relationship to the Japanese government in the form of MITI ... its overall impact on Japanese industry has been incredible', he writes.

Yet in addition to enjoying the protection of import restrictions, the virtually bankrupt Chrysler was itself rescued by the US government in 1980 with $1.5 million in loan guarantees, making Iacocca an instant American folk hero in the process. So who is really the unfair trader? Chrysler, protected from too much foreign competition and rescued from bankruptcy by the US government when it made 'lousy cars'? Or the Japanese?

Japan's best customers

You might think that, if the Japanese are as dreadful as they are customarily painted by so many western business people, they would prefer to have as little to do with them as possible. Not a bit of it. For what above all demonstrates the insincerity of many of the industrialists and the self-serving nature of their Japan-bashing is the fact that they themselves have been among the best customers for Japanese goods.

Chrysler itself has imported millions of Japanese-made Mitsubishi cars and trucks to the USA since the early 1970s. It sells these vehicles under its all-American brand names – almost always in direct competition with its own US-produced cars and trucks. The American car maker has also imported millions of Mitsubishi engines to power its US-made cars, and it plans for many of its forthcoming models to use Japanese powerplants. But there is more:

- Between 1970 and 1990 the big three American car makers imported no fewer than 6.5 million Japanese cars and trucks to sell through their own dealer networks. The rate of these so-called 'captive imports' has been accelerating and by 1992 was running well in excess of 500,000 vehicles annually.'[4]

- Chrysler and General Motors have entered into joint ventures with Mitsubishi[5] and Toyota respectively to make Japanese-designed cars in Japanese-run plants in the USA. The American car makers sell hundreds of thousands of vehicles from these plants under their own names, through their own dealer networks, in competition with their own all-American products.

- Ford also buys in large numbers of vehicles from Mazda's wholly owned US plant to sell under the Ford name in the United States and Europe. The American number-two car maker also obtains high-tech multi-valve engines from Yamaha and is using the Japanese company's design skills for a new range of small engines for the European market. Moreover, despite being a prime mover in the battle to persuade the European Community to place strict limits not only on Japanese imports but also on production from Japanese-owned plants, Ford plans to buy in products from a joint venture plant in Germany with Mazda.

- Rather than developing four-wheel-drive vehicles in Europe, or importing their American 4x4 models, Ford and General Motors have chosen to sell four-wheel-drives bought in from Isuzu's UK plant and Nissan's Spanish factory.

- Ford has also elected to use its Asian dealer networks for the most part to sell Japanese-made Mazdas under the Ford badge – in preference to selling American or European-produced Fords.

- General Motors is another vigorous lobbyer against Japanese car plants in Europe, yet has itself ceded its British commercial vehicle factories to the Japanese producer, Isuzu, from which the American auto giant buys vans and trucks for sale under its own brand names.

It would seem that the US car makers view an imported car or truck as bad, unless they themselves sell it under their own badge. Then it is good.

But it is not just the Big Three American automobile manufacturers which display such blatant double standards. The same is true of many other companies, like copier makers Rank Xerox and Olivetti, which cheerfully imported tens of thousands of Japanese machines themselves, yet lobbied hard for protection from Japanese competition. Having achieved that end, they continue to assemble Japanese copiers in Europe.

In addition to copiers, Olivetti makes computers, as does France's Groupe Bull. Both continually press for trade barriers against Japanese electronics companies and have even asked for Britain's computer maker ICL to be barred from European collaborative research programmes because the company is now owned by Japan's Fujitsu. Yet Olivetti and Bull happily sell high-value mainframe computers from Japanese manufacturers through their own distribution networks.

The European consumer electronics industry plays the same game. Many of the factories of European television makers Thomson and Philips are located in the Far East, from where they import sets into Europe. So when they complained, during an anti-dumping investigation, of the expansion of colour TV imports from Asia, a large part of the protested imports actually came from plants which Thomson and Philips themselves owned in Singapore and Taiwan.

Yet it was not these European-owned Asian plants, but South Korean manufacturers who were penalized by anti-dumping duties. As a result, European companies can bring in as many low-cost TVs from their Asian factories as they want, while Korean producers have to pay high duties.

Thomson has also lobbied hard for import quotas on Japanese video recorders, yet its European plant is run jointly with Japan's JVC, as is its main component factory. Even Thomson's Singapore plant is a joint venture with Toshiba.

But perhaps a special prize for hypocrisy should go to Volkswagen. For on the very day that the German company announced both that profits were up by 33 per cent and that it would need more capacity to keep up with growing sales opportunities in Europe, its chief executive, Carl Hahn, issued the EC Commission with a warning that it should be vigilant on the accessibility of the Community for Japanese cars.[6] Yet only six months earlier the company had trumpeted the creation of 750 new jobs to boost production for the Japanese market, where VW sales had risen by a quarter.[7] Moreover, Mr Hahn's dislike for Japanese competition did not stop his company from concluding a deal to assemble Toyota pickup trucks in Germany for sale under the VW badge.

Of course, what these western manufacturers want is the best of all worlds. They want to limit competition from the Japanese and other Far Eastern producers, so raising the prices they can charge. But they also want to profit from low-cost, reliable Japanese products which they buy in large numbers to sell at inflated prices under their own brand names. Where that option is limited because of quantitative restrictions on imports, they procure goods from Japanese-owned plants in the West, assemble Japanese products themselves, or at least buy in the Japanese technology which they tell us would be so harmful if freely deployed by the Japanese themselves.

The net result of this breathless round of lobbying is fat profits and an easier life for European and American companies, together with less choice and higher prices for their customers. This offers an important clue as to why Japanese manufacturers so often collude in this process. At first it might seem unlikely that the Japanese would acquiesce in their goods being kept out of western markets, but the truth is that European and American protectionism offers the Japanese some important advantages.

First and foremost, restricted importers have the consolation that decreased sales volumes will be significantly compensated for by higher prices and profit margins. For much of the increased profitability in protected markets accrues to the importers, who are able to obtain premium prices for their goods which are in short supply as a result of import restraints.

This effect is especially apparent with Japanese cars, which invariably sell in restricted markets at a premium. At its launch, the top version of Toyota's best-selling MR2 mid-engined sports car cost around £8,000 in Tokyo; the same car was priced at close to £11,000 before tax in Britain. US prices for Japanese cars before import restrictions were imposed in the early 1980s averaged 9 per cent more than comparable models in Japan; by 1985, American prices were 35 per cent higher.[8] These bloated prices paid by consumers for import-restricted products therefore usually go straight into the pockets of foreign industry.

So far from creaming their own domestic market to dump at low prices abroad, as they are so often accused of doing, Japanese industry if anything does quite the opposite. The reality is that trade barriers in the West have allowed the Japanese to make huge profits out of western consumers. Gouging rather than dumping is the true economic crime of the past decade. Yet who can really blame Japanese manufacturers for taking advantage of the absurd policies of western governments?

The long-term disadvantages for western industry which arise from protectionism also go some way towards explaining the sometimes ambivalent Japanese response to such moves in the West. For genuine concern about possible exclusion from vital export markets is tempered by the realization that the more protectionist western countries become, the more they are effectively cutting their own throats. For the reduced competition brought about by import barriers almost invariably blunts the competitive edge of western manufacturers, which become increasingly reliant on their own, high-priced domestic market – and less and less able to compete with the Japanese in third markets where they meet them on equal terms. How many new European or American cars do you now see in Africa, for example?

So the whole protection game is often little more than a cynical ruse. Industrialists use self-serving complaints about the Japanese to cover for their own lack of competitiveness and threats of job losses to blackmail politicians. Politicians eagerly snap up the bait, using 'unfair competition' from Japan to acquit themselves of any blame for industrial problems. The Japanese, meanwhile, often fail to protest too strongly because of the advantages they gain. Everyone seems to benefit from the racket except those least able to pay – the people who have to buy the products.

Notes

1 Field-Marshal Sir William Slim, *Defeat into Victory*, Cassell, London, 1956.

2 *Financial Times*, 4 October 1991.

3 Lee Iacocca, *Iacocca: An Autobiography*, Sidgwick and Jackson, London, 1985.

4 Source: Ward's Automotive Reports and the Motor Vehicle Manufacturers' Association of the United States.

5 Chrysler sold its share in the joint venture to Mitsubishi in 1992, but will continue to buy vehicles from the plant to sell through its dealer network.

6 *Financial Times*, 10 May 1990.

7 *Wall Street Journal*, 11 October 1989.

8 Alan Oxley, *The Challenge of Free Trade*, Harvester Wheatsheaf, New York, 1990.

7 An Overanxious Mother

The principal role of the government of Japan at the operating, business level of industrial change and growth has been to facilitate and accelerate the workings of the market, to speed the process of reduction of declining sectors, and to work to clear the way for market forces to have full play in emerging growth sectors.

James Abegglen, consultant and Japanese industry expert

Close to the bright green splash of Hibaya Park, which relieves the grey density of central Tokyo, rises a gaunt, modern, seventeen-storey block made of grimy white stone, situated in the heart of the Kumagasaki government office district, a sprawl of monotonous buildings stretching around the moats which guard Emperor Akahito's sixteenth-century palace.

This is the headquarters of MITI, Japan's Ministry of International Trade and Industry, whose very name sets the minds of western business people and politicians racing, conjuring up images of sinister conspiracies to dominate world industry, hatched over cups of green tea in secluded rooms which foreigners are unlikely ever to penetrate. Many western commentators maintain that MITI's support of Japanese industry has been a significant and unfair factor in Japan's economic success. Indeed, so emotive has MITI become to many westerners that it has been variously described as the 'puppet master with invisible strings' and 'a spiderless web'.

Enter the portals of this supposed nerve centre of the Japanese conspiracy for world domination and, striding down the dimly lit, linoleum-floored corridors, you catch glimpses of harassed bureaucrats sitting at utilitarian, steel desks, toiling among mountains of papers and files. Every now and then you are passed by a functionary, staggering beneath a heap of files. Is this really the place where the West's economic defeat was planned and directed?

Economic totalitarianism

Many observers certainly think so. Take this description by an American journalist in his top-selling book on Japan: 'Behind their [the Japanese] massive penetration of foreign markets is a system of business activity which can best be described as "economic totalitarianism", a government-directed enterprise in which all the energies of Japan have been mobilized to overwhelm world competition. It is a national conspiracy directed from a central command post, a squat building in Central Tokyo, the headquarters of MITI.'[1]

Such is the intensity of interest in MITI and its works that it has spawned an extensive library of writing, one of the recurring themes of which is that state intervention in Japanese industry goes back to the early, formative years of industrialization in the second half of the last century. New businesses striving to match western competitors, the theory goes, needed hand holding by the government, with the result that mutually supportive attitudes have become deeply ingrained in the Japanese political-industrial system.

It is certainly the case that much of Japan's early industrialization took place under the close tutelage of the state. Following the overthrow of the shogun and the installation of a modernizing regime of young samurai in the so-called Meiji Revolution of 1868, the new government inaugurated steamship lines, took over and developed shipyards, opened cotton mills and imported machinery to be sold to entrepreneurs on an instalment plan. Model silk factories were also founded by the state, along with a brewery at Sapporo.

The close bonds of mutual reliance between government and industry were further strengthened when in the late 1870s growing indebtedness forced the government to sell off state assets at give-away prices to merchant traders such as Mitsui, Ono and Shimada. Other groups, such as Mitsubishi and Kawasaki, both founded by former samurai, also owe their foundation largely to state patronage and lucrative government contracts.

There is, moreover, no doubt that MITI's widespread reputation for being a powerful and competent bureaucratic force is to a large extent justified. The chief reasons for its effectiveness, and that of the Japanese bureaucracy as a whole, lie in the quality of the people it employs and its tightly cohesive structure. For Japan's leading bureaucrats have invariably attended the top universities – and MITI's officials are among the brightest and the best.

Each year more than 32,000 university graduates take the exam which could gain them entry into the top civil service jobs in Japan. On average, fewer than 2,000 pass. Of these, about 600 apply to MITI and fewer than fifty are selected. Around three-quarters of them will have come from the Tokyo University's Law Faculty, which provides a broad-based training in politics, law and public administration – and where, more likely than not, they will also have rubbed shoulders with Japan's future political and industrial leaders.[2] A high proportion of MITI people, moreover, find their way into top business and political jobs towards the end of their careers – indeed, since the mid-1950s only four Japanese prime ministers have not been former bureaucrats – ensuring unrivalled cohesion between the country's political, bureaucratic and industrial élites.

One of the most vaunted success stories of MITI guidance is shipbuilding, which was successfully encouraged by very low-interest loans, backed by an official programme of orders for Japanese ship builders which lasted up until 1962. More recent MITI initiatives have included collaborative research programmes in the 1970s and 1980s, which are credited with the success of the Japanese computer and semiconductor industries.

A toothless old dog

These much-publicized achievements have given rise to an image of effortless command, of a monolithic Japan Inc. where a compliant business community sways to the whims of a wise and far-sighted bureaucracy. But as the Japanese economy has developed in complexity, so MITI has become relatively less effective, so that it is now sometimes even referred to as '*kyoyku mama*' – 'an overanxious mother', or even 'a faithful but toothless old dog'.

Moreover, even in its heyday, MITI's attempts to reorganize and encourage Japanese industry frequently met with fierce opposition and failure. In 1955, for example, when MITI attempted to create a mass car market within Japan by nurturing a small, low-cost 'people's car' along Volkswagen lines, the scheme was leaked to the press and created such a storm of protest from existing and would-be car makers that it had to be abandoned.

An Overanxious Mother

Shortly after, in 1957, when Toyota began marketing a new diesel truck, MITI called in Eiji Toyoda – now the company's chairman – and told him to stop the project on the grounds that Isuzu was already in that market. Toyoda refused and set up a separate franchise network to distribute his diesel trucks, which were ultimately very successful.[3]

Indeed, MITI's attempts to interfere with the car industry were consistently rebutted. Despite offering the inducement of a special, subsidized loan fund to reward firms which complied with its plans, several industry reorganization schemes aimed at reducing the number of Japanese automobile makers through mergers were rebutted by the industry and private banks – to the much-publicized embarrassment of MITI.

Ironically, Nissan did absorb struggling Prince Motors in 1966, but this particular merger had actually been opposed by MITI. Eventually, Toyota and Nissan, the two largest firms, took over a handful of the weaker automobile makers, but Isuzu, Mazda, Honda and Mitsubishi remained – and despite official frowns were soon joined by yet more new entrants in the form of Subaru, Suzuki and Daihatsu.

The car industry again caused MITI problems when, shortly afterwards, Mitsubishi decided to join with Chrysler of the USA in the formation of a new car company – a decision taken without reference to MITI and at a time when the ministry believed it had sewn up a Mitsubishi–Isuzu merger.[4] The fact that one of Japan's most successful industries has flourished in spite of almost totally ignoring MITI's attempts at guidance should call into question the common assumption that MITI has been central to Japan's economic achievement.

MITI's attempts to encourage mergers among steel, machine tool and chemical companies also failed after a great deal of opposition. Bids to restructure the aluminium industry were similarly unsuccessful, as were efforts to consolidate the computer industry in the 1970s. Sharp led the calculator manufacturers in opposition to MITI's bid to shut off semiconductor imports – a move aimed at helping the infant Japanese microchip industry, but which would have greatly harmed the calculator manufacturers. Attempts by MITI to persuade steel companies to restrict their production in order to increase prices in 1965 failed owing to the opposition of just one firm, Sumitomo.

One of MITI's most significant failures occurred in the oil industry, which has been tightly regulated, and often state controlled, in many western countries. When in 1955 MITI created a state oil company called JAPEX, it was hamstrung by opposition from Japanese oil interests, and at best the company accounted for only 2 per cent of the market. MITI tried again in the 1960s to consolidate private oil firms into a state oil concern, but failed. For its third attempt to expand its influence in the oil industry, MITI used a state holding company to buy shares in private oil groups, but this plan was vetoed by the Ministry of Finance. In the end MITI had to settle for a state oil development company which provided exploration and drilling support to the private sector.

Nor did MITI always get its predictions of up-and-coming industries right. It was only after a decade of successful private-sector endeavour in robotics that the first MITI development programme was initiated. On other occasions, the bureaucrats simply misjudged situations, as when Sony had to postpone efforts to import transistor technology for two years because MITI officials thought that the company would be unable to make good use of the technology.

Notions of a harmonious Japan Inc. should also be judged against a background of almost continual squabbling between different arms of the bureaucracy. In 1951, for example, many bureaucrats advised the Bank of Japan to refuse a loan to create the first modern post-war steel plant – a MITI-inspired project – on the grounds that Japan could not hope to compete against America's steel industry.

Problems over the Narita International Airport in the 1970s, which, owing to public resistance, had stood idle for a decade, were further compounded by jurisdictional disputes between ministries. More recently, the Ministry of Finance and the Bank of Japan indulged in very public squabbling over whether or not to raise Japan's interest rates in order to support the yen – a row which was one factor in the destabilization of Japan's stock market early in 1990.

Japan's Fair Trade Commission, although weaker than its model agency in the United States, has also been a thorn in MITI's side, opposing MITI-sponsored cartels, most famously in the Black Cartel case. Japan's twelve leading oil companies, together with seventeen senior executives, were indicted by the Fair Trade Commission for operating an illegal cartel, which involved price fixing and withholding products from the market in order to drive up prices. In 1980 the High Court ruled in favour of the Commission and against MITI.

MITI's plans have not invariably met with success even when they have enjoyed strong political support. The Ministry lost one battle in 1963 when it promoted a law to empower itself to set up cartels in certain industries. Despite backing from Prime Minister Ikeda, the measure failed in the Diet owing to opposition from business and the Ministry of Finance. Ironically, MITI's most consistent successes have not been in 'targeting' western industries with relentless export campaigns, but rather in co-ordinating export restraints at the behest of the American and European governments.

Industrial policy

Nonetheless, the view that Japan owes a great deal of its economic success to MITI's guidance is widespread. In part this is because interventionism is always popular with politicians and bureaucrats – not least because it increases their power. When attributed to others, moreover, it excuses relative economic failure at home. State industrial policies are, further, often favoured by business people, for they both explain away their own lack of success and hold out the prospect of subsidies, protected markets and an easy life at home.

Industrial strategies are also appealing to the public because they provide simple answers to complex problems – and these simple solutions appeal both to would-be imitators and to detractors of Japan's economic performance. Possibly these are the reasons why the idea of an economic conspiracy based around an interventionist MITI has held such sway in the West over the past few years.

Indeed, the attribution of economic dominance primarily to such uncomplicated, easily digested factors is nothing new. In 1967 the United States was, perhaps, at the zenith of its economic, political and military power. With 6 per cent of the world's population, America's industries produced twice as much as the whole of Europe combined and accounted for a third of the world's output.

'A highly organized economic system, based on enormously large units, nourished by an industrial–academic–governmental complex and stimulated, financed and guided by the national government' was how the foreword to one of the most successful books on America's success – *The American Challenge* by the French publisher and radical politician Jean-Jacques Servan-Schreiber, which became a European best seller when it was published in 1967 – described not Japan, but the United States.[5] The book's conclusion was that a major factor in America's economic dominance was the close relationship between its industry and government. Then, commentators searched for easy, saleable explanations for America's success – as they now do for Japan's.

Among his evidence, Servan-Schreiber cited the fact that the US electronics industry did 63 per cent of its business with the government, compared to only 12 per cent in Europe. He also pointed out that the

US government accounted for 85 per cent of total American research and development. All of which illustrates two things: first, the propensity of commentators to ascribe economic success to such policies of state intervention in industry; and secondly, that western countries have been as interventionist as oriental ones.

'... pinching money from a blind man's tin'

On 3 April 1989 banner headlines all over Europe proudly proclaimed the fact that Airbus Industrie, the European aircraft manufacturing consortium, had won yet another huge order for twenty of its new A-330 long-range jetliners from the Hong Kong airline Cathay Pacific. It seemed almost like a fairytale success story for the European aerospace industry, which for so long had played second fiddle to that of the United States. Most galling to Airbus' main rival, Boeing, must have been the fact that one of America's top flag-carrying airlines, TWA, had also just ordered forty of the aircraft, all on top of a substantial sale of the smaller, mid-range A-320 to America's Northwest Airlines just a year earlier.

But despite its increasing sales success, Airbus – jointly owned by British Aerospace, France's Aerospatiale, Casa of Spain and Deutsche Aerospace – has never sold an aircraft at a profit. It has, moreover, swallowed up a massive $13.9 billion[6] in unpaid loans and guarantees without ever having produced any proper accounts. For Airbus is primarily financed by the national governments of the consortium's companies, which cover the losses sustained in the manufacture of the various parts of Airbus aircraft. Since 1967, for example, West German support for Airbus alone has totalled $5.6 billion.[7]

In addition to Airbus, the main British and French aerospace manufacturers have consistently been awarded lucrative contracts for military aircraft and engines which have helped to subsidize their commercial operations. Even so, not one of the many post-war British or French commercial airliners, planes such as the Caravelle and Trident, would have flown without substantial additional government aid, including the purchase of such aircraft by state-owned airlines.

Between 1945 and 1974 total British government contributions to a swarm of exotically named aircraft, ranging from the Brabazon to the Hermes and the Comet to the Britannia, totalled £741.2 million at 1974 prices, from which investment the state received a return of only £54.5 million.[8] The loss on the joint Anglo-French supersonic aircraft

Concorde alone is believed to have reached £1 billion (at 1970 prices).

So generous has the British government been to the national aerospace industry that in 1967 Britain's minister of technology, Anthony Wedgwood-Benn, recounted at a dinner how ministers of aviation had been 'the most hated and feared ministers in the Government. While their colleagues were grateful for anything they could wring from the Chancellor of the Exchequer, Ministers of Aviation ran off with sums of money that made the great train robbers look like schoolboys pinching money from a blind man's tin.'[9]

Many of the smaller European nations have been just as extravagant. The Swedish government, for example, granted Saab-Scania a $187.5 million loan for the development of the Saab 2000 airliner in 1989; the Italian government has given huge subsidies to its state-owned aerospace companies, Aeritalia and Augusta; and the Dutch government was closely involved in bailing out Fokker in 1988.

But aerospace is only one of the most popular and high-profile fields of government industrial intervention in Europe. Office equipment has also been considered as a strategic industry, worthy of state support. In Britain in the late 1970s, for example, the government's National Enterprise Board (NEB) set up state-owned Nexos with the avowed aim of taking on IBM by marketing largely British office equipment made by a series of NEB-backed satellite companies. Ironically, the most successful product in Nexos's brief and inglorious life was a Japanese fax machine with which Nexos so heavily overstocked that, when it went under, the whole of its inventory of 1,000 machines was sold back to the importer for just £1.

The British, Italian, French and German governments have also channelled huge sums into their computer, telecommunications, electronics and semiconductor industries since the 1950s, cosseting them with government contracts and protecting them from foreign competition. Take, for example, Britain's main computer manufacturer ICL, which was formed in 1968 as a result of a state-sponsored merger of smaller firms. Not only did the company get substantial R & D funding throughout the 1970s, but it also benefited from helpful government procurement policies. The Central Computer Agency, which was responsible for government purchases of computer equipment, consistently gave 90 per cent of its orders to ICL until the mid-1980s. When in 1981 the company nonetheless went through a rocky patch, the government stepped in with a £200m loan guarantee.

The largest European semiconductor producer, the Franco-Italian SGS-Thomson group, was formed in 1987 out of two state-controlled semiconductor companies which had both been the recipients of significant government subsidies over a very long period. The new joint company has continued the tradition by making further losses each year, all underwritten by the French government and an Italian state holding company.

This is in line with a long-established European practice of supporting high-tech industry. As far back as 1966, France had its Plan Calcul, designed to counter the American 'threat' by forming a major French flagship computer company, since when the French electronics industry has received many billions of dollars in government aid.

The West German computer maker Siemens has also benefited greatly from sympathetic government procurement policies and research subsidies. In 1976, for example, the West German government put up $300 million for a six-year research project designed to aid its information technology industry. Later, a $1 billion programme was announced for research into the information technology, computer and robotics fields.

A number of other nationally based state programmes to support and develop local high-tech industries have been supplemented in recent years by EC-wide schemes, such as the £860 million EC Esprit programme – half-funded by the EC – and the Eureka programme, to which around £320m is committed by the Community each year. In short, a huge raft of European electronics companies owe their existence predominantly to subsidies and protection from their own governments and the EC.

The car industry has also been targeted for intervention by most western European governments. Here the French have been the main culprits. Apart from being substantially protected from Japanese imports, state-owned Renault has absorbed an enormous sum of government money, believed to be close to FFr100 million (£10 billion). Renault has used the money both to cover losses and to expand into automobile-related areas such as robotics for car factories and Formula One racing. One ill-starred venture even involved them entering the coffee market in a countertrade deal with Colombia, involving the exchange of cars for coffee. Renault bought two brand-new instant coffee plants which utilized a new process from a Belgian conman, only to discover that the technology did not work – by which time the coffee had gone off.

Britain's car industry has also been subject to extensive intervention – and not always with happy results. In 1968 the Labour government, through its Industrial Reorganization Corporation, encouraged the two main indigenous car manufacturers, Leyland and BMC, to merge in a market rationalization move. But the group had to be taken into state ownership in 1976 after running into difficulties. Apart from being protected from Japanese imports, the company was given subsidies amounting to £2 billion before being sold back into the private sector in 1988.

Even West Germany has intervened in its generally successful auto industry by bailing out Volkswagen and taking a substantial stake in the company when it ran into difficulties in the early 1970s, following its failure to develop new models to replace the venerable Beetle.

The more sophisticated industries have not monopolized this state largess, however. According to one report by an EC Commissioner, the EC coal industry accounts for £7 billion in state subsidies a year, while the manufacturing sector as a whole receives no less than £1,200 per employee in state aid. Steel and shipbuilding are the other most favoured industries, getting £4 billion and £900 million respectively.

But the report goes on to show that, even excluding the most subsidized areas, each EC manufacturing worker is supported to the tune of £1,050.[10] The EC itself has authorized member governments to pay 'production assistance' worth 26 per cent of the contract value to its shipbuilders to bridge the cost gap with Korean and Japanese yards. Moreover, a survey by Italy's independent accounting watchdog, the Corte dei Conti, alleged that in 1988 Italy's pampered companies had pocketed £20 billion of the state's money.

State-owned industries have been particularly good at soaking up public finds in Europe. Britain's nationalized industries were receiving support worth £3 billion a year by the late 1970s,[11] while Italy's state industry holding company, IRI, which has interests in steel, shipbuilding, defence and heavy industries, has consistently made losses of over $1 billion a year, accumulating debts of nearly £50 billion. The French government's response to a £600 million loss for 1990 by its computer maker, Bull, was to pump in £400 million in additional capital.

Indirect subsidies such as export credits – which insure firms against non-payment for exports – are also widely used to help national industries. According to OECD figures, its twenty-four member nations had $225 billion in export credits outstanding in 1990 – much of which will be lost and the tab picked up by taxpayers. Britain's Export Credit Guarantee Department, for example, lost £600 million in 1990/1, while the French government wrote off £900 million in export credits over the same period. The United States Export–Import Bank did even better, standing to lose $5 billion – 40 per cent of its outstanding loan guarantees – by 1989.[12] Even little Switzerland has its Export Risk

An Overanxious Mother

Guarantee programme, which lost nearly £100 million in both 1987 and 1988 and has built up an accumulated debt to the Swiss government of SFr1.6 billion (£650 million).

Most developed nations are also guilty of tying their overseas aid to the purchase of domestically produced goods. All of the 175 million condoms supplied up to 1990 to Africa by the American aid organization USAID were made in the USA, as required by its procurement rules – despite the fact that these cost three times as much as those bought on the world market by other organizations. As a result, USAID had to cut back its role as the main supplier of condoms to Africa.[13]

Impeding foreign investment is another common means by which European governments protect and nurture their industries. All the major European governments have intervened at one time or another to prevent companies being bought up by foreign concerns – even the fairly free-market-oriented Thatcher government prevented General Motors from buying the four-wheel-drive vehicle producer Land Rover. But Sweden has gone further than most, enshrining the principle in a law which prevents foreign investors from acquiring more than 20 per cent of the voting rights in a Swedish-owned company without government approval, a rule which was only abandoned by an incoming non-socialist government in 1992.

A new Orient Express

When during his State of the Union address in 1986 President Reagan talked of a plane which would be 'a new Orient Express that could, by the end of the 1990s, take off from Dulles Airport and accelerate up to twenty-five times the speed of sound, attaining low Earth orbit or flying to Tokyo within two hours', his audience broke into a spontaneous ripple of applause. President Reagan was outlining plans for a hypersonic plane now known as the National Aerospace Plane – NASP for short. In the land of free enterprise, under an aggressively free-market president, every cent of the project was to be state funded.

Since President Reagan's far-sighted address, Congress has provided nearly $1 billion[14] in cash for the NASP project, which involves developing a space plane about the size of a Boeing 727 airliner which will take off from an ordinary runway, before accelerating and leaping into orbit at Mach 25, twenty-five times the speed of sound. The craft will be a major departure from current space vehicles in that it will be powered by air-breathing engines for its flight through the atmosphere before moving on to conventional rocket motors.

It may well be that the NASP will never make its dramatic leap into orbit or transport well-heeled travellers from Washington to Tokyo in a mere two hours, for many in President Bush's administration are getting cold feet about the project's ultimate viability. But NASP shows the type of support often given to American industry by its government. For not only do US aircraft manufacturers such as Lockheed and McDonnell-Douglas gain lucrative contracts from such projects, but they also stand to benefit from any NASP technology which might be developed.

NASP, however, is in many ways untypical of American industrial support in that it is fairly overtly aimed at the civilian commercial market. More generally, US support for industry has tended to be disguised in the garb of military spending. Although, for example, the Pentagon's Defence Advanced Projects Agency (Darpa) is a military research body with a budget of more than $1 billion in 1990, it funds a variety of primarily commercial research projects including super-fast computers and lightweight satellites.

Other recent development programmes which have also secured substantial commercial benefits for American electronics producers include the $1 billion Very High Speed Integrated Circuit (VHSIC) project. This resulted in Motorola and TRW producing a 1.5-inch square silicon 'superchip' containing 4 million transistors – effectively a supercomputer on a chip – which will find a wide variety of applications where high speed, small size and great computing power and reliability are needed, such as in computer-aided design, medical diagnostics, plant process control and complex imaging.

Moreover, the United States has for many years run expensive research programmes operated by the Department of Defense as well as by the National Aeronautics and Space Administration (NASA) which, although primarily military, have had important commercial spin-offs. These have included the $5 billion C–5A Galaxy Airforce Transport plane programme in the 1960s, which spawned both the Boeing 747 jumbo jet and the DC–10. General Electric and Pratt and Whitney were also helped by the project to major advances in engine technology. Before that, the Boeing 707 was originally developed as the KC 135 in-flight refuelling tanker for the US Air Force.

The United States computer and semiconductor industries have also benefited greatly from enormous government procurement programmes. More than half of the production of American semiconductor companies, for example, went to the US military in the 1960s, while in the early 1980s the US government spent $15 billion annually on computer hardware – far more than total Japanese production at that time – and virtually all of it went to American suppliers.

However, in recent years United States support for its industry has become increasingly overt and unrelated to military needs. Apart from the NASP programme, NASA has aided General Electric in the development of its new 90,000lb-thrust GE90 big fan engine with a diameter as large as that of a Boeing 737, which is aimed at the next generation of twin-engined long-range aircraft. Federal support is being given to a $260 programme to help the big three automobile makers develop batteries for electric cars; while one of the large federal-sponsored research programmes, the superconductor collider project, is funded to the tune of $8 billion.

In short, American government help for its industry is enormous and growing. Consider the following:

- Overall US state funding for R & D in 1987 was $60 billion, of which $41 billion was estimated to be defence related, leaving a healthy $19 billion of state funding for purely commercial research programmes – the type of state support customarily viewed by American politicians and industrialists as 'unfair' in competitor nations.[15]

- Overall, the US government spends 100 times more than the British government's R & D programme, despite having an economy only six times the size.

- Aside from military research, the proportion of United States civil research which is government financed is higher at 33.9 per cent than in many European countries – and far higher than in Japan, which funds a mere 2 per cent of its industry's research.

- In 1985 no less than 76.2 per cent of the US aerospace industry's R & D was supplied by the state, compared to only 9.3 per cent in Japan.

- At the same time, 40.3 per cent of American electrical industry research was government funded, as opposed to only 1 per cent in Japan.[16]

Japan Inc?

To assert, therefore, that Japan's tremendous economic success has been overwhelmingly due to the cohesive relationship between its industry and the bureaucracy – a tight state–industry embrace which has spawned the monolithic and impenetrable 'Japan Inc.', wisely nurturing, protecting and guiding its enterprises towards near world domination in a process sometimes referred to as 'state-sponsored capitalism' – is conveniently to ignore the fact that western countries have been at least as guilty in the game of state intervention in industry as Japan.

The impact of MITI on those industries which it has encouraged and which have been successful is open to some doubt. In the 1960s, European missions went to Japan to investigate the miracle of progress in its shipbuilding industry. They concluded that complaints that Japan's advantage was partly based on state support and concealed subsidies had no real substance. A subsequent thorough OECD inquiry concluded that subsidies to Japanese shipbuilders did not exceed 10 per cent of their total costs, which was far less than their overall cost advantage – and a lower level of subsidy than in many Western countries.[17]

MITI's involvement in semiconductors and computers has also been considered crucial. Yet its programme in the early 1970s to support the development of large-scale integrated circuitry involved only $100 million over seven years, divided among a number of companies – a minuscule amount by the standards of electronics industry R & D, or compared to subsidies provided by other governments.

The enormously successful Japanese machine tool industry was also the subject of a long-term MITI programme, yet an in-depth study carried out by an American academic demonstrated the following:

- Pressure from Japanese machine tool users in the early 1950s resulted in subsidies for machine tool purchases being extended to imported products – MITI had wanted to limit them to domestically produced machine tools.

- Attempts to subsidize research into computerized controllers for machine tools in the late 1950s foundered because Japanese companies preferred to buy in foreign technology.

- Not one of MITI's marketing or production plans came close to being realized – attempts to build economies of scale through mergers of existing companies and restrictions on market entry by new firms completely failed as Japanese machinery makers flooded

An Overanxious Mother

into high-tech equipment sectors, while established firms flatly refused to co-ordinate or consolidate production.

- Attempts to boost exports were largely limited to help with foreign trade shows and surveys of foreign markets, support which was anyway largely ignored by Japanese producers.

- From 1956 to 1965, when MITI was most closely involved with the machine tool industry, subsidies totalled little more than $35 million – less than 5 per cent of total Japanese machine tool industry investment in the period. The US Department of Defense Manufacturing Technology Program, by contrast, disbursed $745 million between 1977 and 1981.[18]

Moreover, the list of industries in Japan which grew without the benefit of any specific or significant MITI support policy is extensive and includes sewing machines, cameras, bicycles, motorbikes, transistor radios, colour televisions, tape recorders, magnetic tape, audio equipment, watches, calculators, textile equipment, farm machinery, robots and photocopiers.

The fact is that, while myths about the subtle powers of shadowy bureaucrats may be soothing concepts for westerners bewildered by Japan's rapid advance, state economic planning has been too much a common denominator between virtually all nations – industrialized and developing – to be the reason for Japan's achievement. Indeed, if economic success were substantially determined by industrial interventionism, Brazil and India would be among the world's most powerful economies.

Notes

1 Marvin J.Wolf, *The Japanese Conspiracy*, New English Library, London, 1985.

2 E.F.Vogel, *Japan as Number One*, Harvard University Press, Cambridge, Mass. 1979.

3 Eiji Toyoda, *Toyota: 50 Years in Motions*, Kodansha, Tokyo, 1987.

4 Richard Boyd, 'Government–industry relations in Japan: access, communication, and competitive collaboration', in S.Wilkes and M.Wright (eds), *Comparative Government–Industry Relations: Western Europe, the United States and Japan*, Clarendon Press, Oxford, 1987.

5 J. Servan-Schreiber, *The American Challenge*, Penguin, London, 1969.

6 This estimate is based on a report by accountants Coopers and Lybrand. Because Airbus does not maintain proper accounts, the precise figure is unknown.

7 Office of the US Trade Representative, *1989 National Trade Estimate Report on Foreign Trade Barriers*, Washington.

8 Keith Hayward, *Government and British Civil Aerospace*, Manchester University Press, Manchester, 1983.

9 *Flight*, 6 July 1967. Quoted in Hayward, op. cit.

10 *A Bonfire of Subsidies? A Review of State Aids in the European Community*, EC Commission, Brussels, 1989.

11 *Economies in Transition: Structural Adjustment in OECD Countries*, OECD, Paris, 1989.

12 US General Accounting Office, *Export–Import Bank's 1988 and 1989 Financial Statements*, July 1990.

13 *Financial Times*, 23 January 1992

14 *Congressional Quarterly Report*, 6 January 1990.

15 Commission of the European Communities Directorate-General I, *Report on US Barriers to Trade*, Brussels, 1989.

16 Robert Ford and Wim Suyker, *Industrial Subsidies in the OECD Economies*, OECD, Paris, 1990.

17 Robert Guillain, *The Japanese Challenge*, Hamish Hamilton, London, 1970.

18 David Friedman, *The Misunderstood Miracle*, Cornell University Press, 1988.

8 Industrial Policy

For every complex problem, there is a solution which is neat, plausible and wrong.
H.L.Mencken (1880–1956)

Some American commentators who accept that the United States' huge military programmes have been a source of indirect subsidy to US industry, providing commercially valuable spin-offs, nonetheless assert that such defence-based intervention in industry is not as effective as the more direct commercially oriented support which, they say, predominates in Japan or Europe – and which they now propose as the cure for American industrial ills.

Support directed primarily towards military objectives, they argue, tends to involve batch production of relatively small runs of expensive, highly specified products with little commercial application. Generous US Air Force research subsidies for numerically controlled machine tool manufacturers in the 1950s, for example, geared the industry to sophisticated and complicated equipment, leaving it at a severe disadvantage against cheaper and more flexible models from overseas. Having high-tech companies too dependent on defence contracts also inclines them away from commercial markets – Northrop, Lockheed and Martin Marietta all rely on the Pentagon for more than three-quarters of their sales.

The dreams of politicians

But the argument that the United States should, therefore, move in the direction of some imagined 'Japanese-style' or 'European-style' blueprint is fundamentally flawed. Leaving aside the fact that US government industrial support is already frequently directly commercial, even where clothed in the garb of military programmes, interventionist industrial policies are unlikely to be effective. This is not because free, unfettered markets are perfect, but rather because well-meaning interference in markets by politicians and bureaucrats to try to perfect the market mechanism is likely to do more harm than good.

There are several reasons for this. First, too often industrial policies promote types of economic activity which is inherently unsuited to a particular country. An extreme example is Nigeria's $6 billion steel programme. The main mill was built 250 kilometres inland, far from ports, despite the fact that all of the coking coal has to be shipped in – a classic example of a government-sponsored industrial development which has not the slightest hope of succeeding. Thirteen years after the project began, the plant is operating at just 13 per cent of capacity – its cost would have paid for Nigeria's annual steel requirements twenty times over.

Other state-sponsored projects hopelessly out of line with the underlying capabilities of the sponsoring nation include the Indian rocket programme and Brazil's attempts to build up a computer industry. Misplaced national pride and the dreams of politicians too often substitute for heard-headed commercial reality in the formulation of such state-directed industrial policies.

Even relatively advanced countries make the error of attempting to promote industries that are beyond either their research or their productive capabilities – or often both. Decades of massive state aid to European computer, semiconductor and consumer electronics industries have failed to produce world-class competitors because, even where appropriate research and development resources have been available, efficient production and effective marketing have too often been lacking.

It is significant that perhaps one of the most successful and consistently profitable of the European computer companies in recent years is Britain's ICL. During the 1960s and 1970s the company was subject to continual government-inspired mergers, preferential public procurement, research grants – and rescue plans as it lurched from crisis to crisis. A hands-off approach was adopted in the 1980s, however, with the result that the company had to examine where its real competitive advantage lay. Even a takeover by Japan's Fujitsu, which would have created hand-wringing angst on the continent, was not considered a suitable issue for government intervention.

As a result, although ICL is a slimmer company than some of its European rivals, it has found markets where it can grow and prosper. ICL is, for example, now a world leader in retail systems and gains more than half its revenues from software and services, rather than competing head on in every area of hardware, as it was previously encouraged to do by politicians. The Fujitsu takeover has, moreover, left the company managed locally, with its respected research capacity intact, but in a far stronger position to develop profitable global markets in areas where it can succeed.

In short, a more market-based approach has delivered what is possible, rather than what politicians would ideally like. ICL's larger European competitors, meanwhile, have slipped into ever greater losses and dissipate much of their energy carrying begging bowls back and forth from their national governments to the European Commission, while politicians come up with ever more ambitious restructuring and collaboration programmes.

Another problem with intervention in industry is that it tends to be driven by political and social rather than commercial objectives. During the 1960s, regional development policies led the British government to encourage the siting of new vehicle plants in the north-west of England and in Scotland, well away from the traditional centre of car manufacturing in the Midlands. As a result, components and engines had to be shipped expensively across the country and eventually two of the three plants built under this initiative proved uneconomic and had to close.

The British steel industry has also suffered greatly from such wellmeaning but ultimately disastrous political meddling. When in the late 1950s the steelmaker Colville's wanted to build a large strip mill in north Wales, close to a deep-water port to facilitate the import of ore and the export of the finished product, the government insisted for reasons of regional policy that it split the plant between two sites, one of which was in Scotland, far from its main markets and well inland.

Subsequently, wishful thinking by politicians led to unattainable targets and overinvestment. In 1973 the government decided on a major expansion plan to raise output in the nationalized British Steel Corporation from 23 to 28 million tonnes. Even this was not enough for the trade unions, so the target was upgraded to 36 million tonnes, which proved to be hopelessly optimistic – the market just was not there and British Steel ended up saddled with massive and expensive overcapacity, becoming the world's largest loss-making company by the early 1980s.

State-sponsored mergers have also too often contained little industrial logic and have actually created more problems than they solved. When the British Industrial Reorganization Corporation encouraged the merger of Britain's two major car manufacturers, BMC and Leyland, in 1968, the new group became so absorbed with the tremendous difficulty of integrating the two companies' model ranges that basic industrial problems were left unattended. As a result, potentially profitable and successful parts of the group, such as Jaguar and the Leyland trucks division, were steadily dragged down by less prosperous parts.

National champions

One further problem with government-led mergers is that too little attention is paid to the importance of competition. For although industry consolidation schemes may contain some theoretical economic logic, in that they are designed to achieve economies of scale and so create strong competitors, they almost always also have the effect of reducing competition. Forging world-class companies with good economies of scale through the selective and toughening process of international competition is one thing; attempting artificially to create internationally competitive companies via the choices of bureaucrats and politicians rarely works in practice – especially if competition is further decreased by trade barriers.

Yet the tendency to undermine competition by promoting 'national champion' companies with protected, near monopolies of the home market and secure government contracts is a striking feature of postwar western industrial strategies. The idea is to give such favoured companies a secure base from which to attack world markets. But too often industrial standard bearers have preferred the cosy security and fat profits of their home markets over venturing into the leaner, meaner world of exports. Such policies have, moreover, led to unnecessary duplication, as in the European telecommunications industry where for too long relatively small producers existed in protected national environments, preventing the emergence of truly global competitors.

Nor have MITI and other Japanese government departments, such as the Ministry of Posts and Telecommunications (MPT), been completely free of the bureaucrat's typical aversion to competition, which they often consider to be unruly and difficult to control. The Japanese construction equipment maker Komatsu was protected from both internal and external competition for some time, during which period its products were poor in quality and its manufacturing inefficient. Only when the government allowed Mitsubishi to form a joint venture with the American manufacturer Caterpillar was Komatsu forced to innovate and upgrade in a process which made the company a viable global competitor.

Generally, however, MITI and the MPT have been more aware than their western counterparts of the role of competition and have tried to keep more than one competitor in play. In telecommunications, for example, three major Japanese public exchange manufacturers compete vigorously against one another.

There have, however, been difficulties even where government policies are positively geared towards maintaining competition. MITI's industrial policies in the 1950s were aimed at preventing the domination of the aluminium, PVC and caustic soda industries by large competitors. All of the main companies were made to expand their capacity at about the same rate. The result was that companies were saddled with high-cost, small-scale facilities which have continued to stunt the development of these firms to this day. Preserving competition in a way which prevents the most efficient competitors from growing is likely to do more harm than good. Or to put it another way, maintaining several competitors by political edict is not the same thing as real competition – especially if each company has its own guaranteed share of the market.

A more positive form of competition-oriented state intervention is that designed to prevent monopolies or trusts. All major industrial nations have anti-monopoly and anti-trust laws. These are usually allied to strong regulatory bodies dedicated to ensuring that competition is maintained by preventing undesirable corporate takeovers, or deterring companies from establishing too dominant a position in particular markets.

Although some free-market purists might question the morality of restricting companies which have legitimately achieved a powerful position by efficiently making and marketing successful products, most accept the greater good achieved by the maintenance of competition. Yet even with this most market-oriented type of intervention, mistakes have been made by heavy-handed laws and regulators.

The copier pioneer Xerox was hit during the early 1970s by management-sapping anti-trust actions initiated by American rivals. Yet despite the protection of the world's toughest anti-trust laws, none of these ever really developed into serious competitors. Ultimately, it was not anti-trust actions but more nimble and efficient Japanese copier makers which ended Xerox's near-monopoly – which would seem to call into question the common assertion that monopolists can always destroy new competitors by undercutting them until they go out of business.

More often than not, monopolists eventually grow flabby and complacent and, as in the case of Xerox, create a high-price umbrella under which fresh competitors take shelter and flourish. The only really sustainable monopolies have been where public-sector companies are protected by state edict from competition, such as those publicly owned utility monopolies which persist in many countries.

Those American legislators who have been most determined in their initiation and enforcement of anti-trust legislation should also ask themselves whether consumers and the economy as a whole really benefited from the long-standing ban on IBM entering the telecommunication market and on AT&T marketing computers, a ban which persisted until the mid-1980s.

Food stamps for the rich

Another problem with state intervention is that government grants and subsidies too often go to those with the greatest lobbying power. The US Export-Import Bank controls the United States' major export subsidy programme, providing over $4 billion annually in loans and loan guarantees to boost US exports. These loans have cost American taxpayers billions of dollars. Yet studies have shown that they have had little effect on exports, and over the past decade 70 per cent of the loans have gone to fewer than twenty large corporations, including General Motors, Boeing and Westinghouse[1] – the scheme was aptly dubbed 'food stamps for the rich' by leading US economist David Stockman.

This may be why many leaders of medium-sized businesses are not totally enamoured of state-sponsored research programmes. T.J.Rodgers, the founder of Cypress Semiconductor, a fairly new American semiconductor maker with a turnover of $200 million a year, is one of Silicon Valley's most outspoken entrepreneurs. During congressional testimony, Rodgers strongly argued against aid for government-sponsored semiconductor research consortia, explaining that they were set up to benefit a small number of ailing 'fat cats', rather than the industry as a whole.[2]

This is a critical point. The directing of resources into one company or industry invariably takes place at the expense of others. During the late 1950s and 1960s, MITI insisted on companies applying for permission to import some types of technology to facilitate its plans to aid the development of certain industries. One of the victims of this policy was Sony, whose development was impaired by the difficulty it experienced in obtaining permission to buy transistor technology from the United States. Mazda was also harmed by MITI's refusal to allow it to import radiator technology in 1968 because the company had opposed the ministry's consolidation plans designed to create two large vehicle producers based on Toyota and Nissan. So a basic question which should also always be asked of any interventionist industrial policy is, what could the resources directed into certain favoured industries have achieved elsewhere if it had been left to market forces?

Moreover, the beggar-my-neighbour aspect of state subsidies tends to mean that the more one country indulges in such policies, the more others will tend to join in, so cancelling out any potential advantages. Steel, once again, offers a good example of this process. The establishment of some form of steel industry has traditionally been regarded by most developing countries as indispensable to any nation with serious pretensions to industrialization. So countries like Brazil and India have piled in, more than doubling the number of steel producing nations between 1950 and 1985 – a process which has only been encouraged by steel plant equipment suppliers from developed nations, who are themselves often subsidized with state-provided export credits.

Meanwhile in developed countries the steel industry has also been regarded as having a particular industrial machismo. So national governments in countries like Britain, Italy and France have subsidised expansions in capacity regardless of realistic market expectations.

The result has been a huge merry-go-round of subsidies, interference and protection, with distortion being piled upon distortion, leading to a hopelessly ill-proportioned, warped international steel industry, caught in a vicious spiral of massive overcapacity. Developing countries unload unprofitable steel from unsustainable plants in a desperate attempt to service the debts incurred in their construction, in turn prompting developed countries to erect ever tougher trade barriers to shield their domestic producers' own massive overcapacity.

Even the much-vaunted Airbus programme, the glory of European state co-ordinated and subsidized industrial co-operation, is subject to doubts. Although Airbus does successfully compete with Boeing in the medium-range airliner market, one in-depth study concluded that on top of huge losses Airbus still had a negative discounted net value, and that the main beneficiaries of the programme had not been European aerospace industry, but rather international airlines which had gained from lower-cost planes as a result of the competition to Boeing.[3]

Preventing great harm

It is at least arguable, however, that state intervention in industry has been generally less harmful in Japan than in most western countries. There is one major reason for this, and a number of subsidiary ones. Above all, the extent to which intervention has succeeded and been of significance in the development of the Japanese economy has been almost entirely due to the fact that, unlike European intervention, the Japanese variety has generally been geared to run with the grain of market forces, rather than against it.

Put simply, MITI, and Japanese bureaucrats and politicians in general, have well understood that the nature of successful economic development is for countries to upgrade from labour-intensive, low-added-value products (the 'soft technologies', such as textiles) on to medium-technology, less labour-intensive, higher-added-value products (the 'hard technologies', such as steel, heavy engineering and shipbuilding), before graduating to sophisticated, capital- and technology-intensive products such as computers and software – often called the 'knowledge industries'.

This evolution allows productivity steadily to increase, permitting higher wages and improved living standards, while the economy continually stays ahead of advancing rivals. So as the Japanese have seen newer or developing economies like South Korea and Taiwan steadily gaining ground on their older industries, MITI has tended to cushion their abandonment while encouraging business to move on to areas of higher development.

The Japanese footwear industry provides a good example of how this works in practice. In 1970, Japan was a major exporter and had a hugely favourable trade balance in footwear. But shoes are a low-technology, labour-intensive industry and MITI largely resisted pressure to protect the Japanese industry. So during the 1970s, shoe imports into Japan, mainly from Taiwan and South Korea, increased by 30 per cent a year while exports declined 17 per cent annually, until by the end of the decade Japan was running a large footwear trade deficit.

As a result, while the share of Japan's exports taken by basic industries such as shoes and textiles slipped from 15 per cent to 5 per cent between 1965 and 1985, iron and steel took over, peaking at 20 per cent of exports in the mid-1970s. But a decade later this had in turn declined to only 6 per cent by which time steel had been overtaken by newly rising industries such as vehicles, which had accounted for only 5 per cent of exports in 1965, a figure which had grown to 20 per cent the mid-1980s. In the process, textile industry leader Toyobo lost its pre-eminent position as Japan's largest company to shipbuilder Mitsubishi Heavy Industries in the 1960s, which itself was succeeded by Nippon Steel in the 1970s, which was in turn supplanted by Toyota in 1983.

The Japanese, moreover, have generally recognized the interdependence of developing and developed economies. By allowing up-and-coming countries to move into industries which it had largely vacated, Japan has ensured that such economies have been better able to afford to buy its more advanced products, which often include major components and assemblies at the higher-technology end of those industries which Japan had largely relinquished. An obvious example is marine engines. Although South Korea almost caught up with Japanese ship production in the late 1980s, most of the engines going into vessels built in South Korea, together with many of the more complex assemblies and equipment, are still either Japanese or assembled under licence to Japanese companies.

MITI's role, therefore, has been one of keeping a step ahead of market forces, by setting high standards for new plants and concentrating resources in areas where it thinks Japan might be internationally competitive. As a result, unlike its counterparts in Europe, MITI has generally not been preoccupied with bailing out ailing public-sector industries. It has rather concerned itself with positive changes in the industrial structure of the economy.

With some exceptions, declining industries, or those operating in fields in which MITI officials considered that Japan could not be competitive, were either assisted into diversification or encouraged to merge or even to go out of business. Thus, far from being an example of state socialism, as some have alleged, the Japanese government has accepted the ultimate value and inevitability of market forces, largely limiting its own role to hastening industrial adjustment to the trends.

According to the American expert on Japanese industry James Abegglen, this management of declining sectors, rather than the promotion of sunrise industries, is MITI's greatest contribution to the Japanese economy. It may be the case, he says, that:

it is in the power of governments to prevent great harm but not to do great good. In contrast to the governments of the Western economies, it is the Japanese government's policy toward declining industries that is most impressive. The government is capable of a real recognition of the need for and desirability of industrial structural change. Money is not spent in efforts to shore up declining industries. Tariffs are not raised to defend declining industries. Instead, assistance is given to the prompt and effective closing down of capacity.[4]

Western interventionism, by contrast, has often been out of line with market forces. For while it is true that much state support has gone to advanced industries, such as aerospace and electronics, the more complex political imperatives of western economies – with their massive traditional industrial sectors employing vast numbers of workers represented by powerful political lobbies – has ensured that a great deal of state aid has been targeted on keeping alive the type of industries which the Japanese have vacated.

Perhaps the classic example of this difference in approach lies in the textile and clothing industry, an essential springboard to industrialization in a developing economy; but, owing to its relative labour intensity and low added value, not one which should form a large component of an advanced economy. Yet textiles have long been subject to both protection and subsidies in the West. In the 1920s and 1930s, most western countries imposed higher tariffs on textile imports than they did on other manufactures, and this system continued after the war, with the United States insisting on restrictions on cotton textile exports from Japan in 1955, followed by the 1961 and 1962 Short and Long Term Arrangements on cotton textiles which further limited imports. By 1963 the USA had set up import restrictions against seventeen countries and territories. Most of the main Western European economies maintained similar restraints, which were all consolidated into the international Multi-Fibre Arrangement (MFA) of 1974.

Originally considered a temporary measure to give western textile industries a four-year 'breathing space' to restructure and meet low-cost competition from developing countries, the MFA has nonetheless been renewed every four years following shrill and effective lobbying from the textile manufacturers and unions – which is, perhaps, understandable bearing in mind that much textile production tends to be concentrated in areas of high unemployment. By 1991 MFA quotas covered close to 70 per cent of the $200 billion a year trade in textile products.

Japan's textile industry was, of course, a major component in its early industrial development. Japan had already become a major exporter of

Industrial Policy

synthetics in the 1930s, and textiles formed the basis of Japan's post-war recovery. But although subject to import restraints abroad, Japan has offered its own textile manufacturers only scant protection from imports from developing countries. As a result, between 1980 and 1987 Japanese textile production fell by 7 per cent, import penetration more than doubled to 37 per cent, and Japan's share of world textile exports fell to only 3.8 per cent, slipping below South Korea's 7 per cent and Italy's 10.1 per cent.[5] In fact, by 1985 Japan was running a deficit in its textile trade.

Although Japanese textile companies have in recent years lobbied more actively for the protection which was available under the MFA – the provisions of which Japan, alone among the developed countries, had never implemented – they have been vigorously resisted by MITI which has particularly wanted to see Japan move out of the lower-value end of the textile market and into other areas. In fact, Japan has been well in advance of the West in calling for the rapid abolition of the MFA during the Uruguay round of GATT trade talks.

Instead, MITI has organized a series of schemes to cut capacity in the textile industry. These, together with the pressure applied to Japanese textile manufacturers by the relative absence of protection, have not only improved their competitiveness but also tended to push them into the upper end of the textile market where they are less in direct competition with producers whose labour costs are low. Kanebo, for example, is now earning big profits from new products such as its line of scented fabrics, used in a brand of underwear called Casablanca which is supposed to exude a romantic aroma.

Japanese textile companies have also been forced to diversify out of textiles and clothing. In the 1970s many of Japan's major textile firms moved into chemicals, construction and car components. As a result, by 1978 more than a third of the sales of the six leading synthetics producers were non-textile, compared to only a tenth in 1968. Teijin, the company that pioneered the production of artificial fibres in Japan in 1918, now dominates the global market for magnetic tape together with another venerable Japanese textile company, Toray, which has also moved into advanced materials.

Meanwhile, in the West, many textile and clothing firms still produce goods in the lower sector of the market where profits are slim and where, in many instances, they even find it difficult to recruit employees prepared to work for the low wages on offer in what is inevitably a relatively unproductive industry.

Textiles, however, is not the only declining industry which has been supported through state intervention. OECD figures show how disproportionately European countries have concentrated industrial subsidies on declining sectors of the economy. In France from 1981 to 1986 state support accounted for almost 60 per cent of the output of the steel and shipbuilding industries.[6]

Ineffectual tinkering

Even where state intervention in the West has been geared towards the encouragement of the industries of the future, such efforts have often been hamstrung by confused objectives, political meddling and conflicting imperatives, not to mention the unsuitability of some advanced industries to economies incapable of sustaining them. Take Britain's nuclear power industry, for example. Political rather than commercial considerations resulted in the decision in 1965 to go ahead with home-grown advanced gas-cooled reactor technology, despite offers of cheaper boiling water and pressurized water reactors from General Electric and Westinghouse of the USA. As a result, Britain has since then been burdened with an expensive nuclear generating capacity which has consistently overrun its costs, underperformed its technical specifications and drained Britain's industry of some its best scientists.

But although Japanese interventionism has been more rational than that in the West, state-directed industrial policies are neither the key to Japanese success nor the answer to western industrial problems. Indeed, though it has been fashionable for journalists and politicians to focus on the role of MITI in the Japanese economy, it should be borne in mind that examples of failed interventionism far outweigh the successes.

On top of the central planning of industry operated, but now in the process of abandonment, by the former Eastern bloc nations and the Soviet Union, and the failure of interventionist policies in most developing countries, virtually every industrialized nation has intervened heavily in industry since the war. Indeed, a recent OECD survey placed Japan only twentieth out of twenty-four industrialized countries when it came to state industrial subsidies.[7]

There may well be a case for arguing that a *dirigiste* industrial policy is relatively more effective and justified during the early stages of economic development, and such a policy is certainly more likely to work if carried out by a well-educated, cohesive bureaucracy with close business links and, above all, as long as the general policy is in line with market forces. But the very concept of state intervention in business nonetheless contains within it the inherent assumption that the choices of bureaucrats and politicians can be more efficient than the aggregate of thousands or even millions of decisions by those most directly concerned – industrialists and the consumers of their products. This is a very risky assumption – all the more so when in practice politicians are under continual pressure to make their decisions on political rather than commercial criteria.

State-directed industrial policies are not the key to economic prosperity. The fact that so many people assume them to be so is in part due to widely held misconceptions about the success of such strategies – the most recent of which is the conventional wisdom that industrial policies have played a part in Japan's post-war 'economic miracle'.

Interventionism has also been widely thought to have been a significant factor in Japan's rapid industrialization at the end of the last century. Yet studies have shown that most government-sponsored enterprises during the Meiji period were failures. Even the policy of providing model factories from which the private sector could learn is open to doubt. In the case of cotton spinning, the government imported unsuitable water-powered technology. It was the British steam-powered spindles brought in by a private concern which ultimately became the standard on which other plants modelled their operations.[8]

The role of government in industry during the United States' most overtly interventionist period, the New Deal in the 1930s, is also often held to have been a great success. Yet at the time, Federal government-sponsored reports on the industrial policies – which included price floors and enforced reductions in capacity – criticized the programme for being in the thrall of powerful industrial interests who used it to hinder expansion by smaller concerns.[9]

State-directed industrial policies are, in fact, almost invariably damaging. Most subsidies simply divert capital from economically to politically productive uses. For the harsh truth is that, without fundamental economic strength, interventionism represents at best ineffectual tinkering and at worst damaging meddling.

Notes

1 Cato Institute figure quoted in James Bovard, *The Fair Trade Fraud*, St Martin's Press, New York, 1991.

2 *Financial Times*, 11 October 1989.

3 R.E.Baldwin and P.R.Krugman, 'Industrial policy and international competition in widebodied aircraft,' in R.E.Baldwin (ed.), *Trade Policy Issues and Empirical Analysis*, University of Chicago Press for the NBER, Chicago, 1987

4 James Abegglen and George Stalk, *Kaisha, the Japanese Corporation*, Basic Books, New York, 1985.

5 Source: Economist Intelligence Unit.

6 Robert Ford and Wim Suyker, *Industrial Subsidies in the OECD Economies*, OECD, Paris, 1990.

7 Ibid.

8 See Frank Tipton, 'Government policy and economic development in Germany and Japan: a skeptical reevaluation', *Journal of Economic History*, March 1981.

9 See Michael Bernstein, The Great Depression, Cambridge, University Press, Cambridge, 1987.

9 Trade Barriers

It is the maxim of every prudent master of a family never to attempt to make at home what it will cost him more to make than to buy.

Adam Smith

State subsidies and direction of industry are, however, only one side of the interventionist coin. Trade restraints are the other side – and are, if anything, even more damaging. First, trade barriers reduce competition and so raise prices to consumers, distorting the economy and diverting resources from efficient to inefficient industries. An 1988 estimate in *What to Buy for Business* magazine put the cost of car import restraints in Britain at £2 billion, on the basis that ex-tax car prices in Britain were around 5 per cent higher than in Switzerland's free car market.

Similar restraints on imports of Japanese automobiles into the United States were estimated by the IMF to cost American car buyers $1,650 extra per car during the early 1980s – a total additional burden to US car buyers of $17 billion between 1981 and 1984.[1] EC anti-dumping duties on Japanese copiers pushed up prices by 20 per cent, adding $500 million a year to copier costs for European businesses.[2]

According to a British government-sponsored report in 1989, the Multi-Fibre Arrangement costs UK consumers close to £1 billion a year; while Britain's consumer watchdog body, the National Consumer Council, estimated in a study issued early in 1990 that anti-dumping duties added an average of £74 to the price of a computer printer and £20 to the price of a video recorder. The total annual cost to EC consumers of anti-dumping measures on electronic goods was put at £1,170 million – equivalent overall to slightly more than a 5 per cent price hike.[3]

The EC Commission has admitted that a variety of internal barriers between the supposedly mutually open national markets of EC countries alone is costing consumers no less than £83 billion a year. The US Institute for International Economics estimates that American trade barriers cost Americans the massive total of $80 billion a year.[4]

Brazil's 'informatica' law, which prevents the importation of many types of electronic goods, ranging from fax machines to personal computers, has resulted in Brazilian consumers paying three times the prices of their foreign counterparts for outmoded Brazilian-made machines. True, a $7 billion Brazilian electronics industry has been created in the process, but its technology is a generation behind and it is completely uncompetitive in global terms.

So, far from untrammelled competition leading to eventual monopolization of markets and exploitation of consumers, as the champions of protection often claim, barriers to trade are much more likely to result in consumers being gouged and ripped off.

Downstream costs

Trade barriers also cost industry dear, for many products subject to import restrictions are bought by downstream industrial users. Where such customers have to pay more for such products, they lose competitiveness and are themselves less likely to be able to export their own goods to other markets.

In the mid-1980s the price of cold-rolled sheet steel in the USA was nearly 40 per cent higher than in other markets.[5] United States steel processors generally pay prices for a variety of steel products that are 25 per cent higher than those in Japan and 20 per cent more than in West Germany. US steel users claim they would have saved at least $38 billion between 1981 and 1985 if they had been able to obtain steel at Japanese prices. As a result, instead of importing steel for processing into finished goods, America is buying in more manufactured products containing foreign steel. For every job preserved in the steel industry others are lost elsewhere in the economy.

The United States also protects machine tool manufacturers, raising prices and reducing the availability of sophisticated equipment for machine tool users. It does not take a great deal of imagination to discern that the competitiveness of a raft of American industries which use steel and machine tools is hardly enhanced by the protection given to their suppliers.

Successful lobbying for protection by the European semiconductor industry has also injured users of such devices. European semiconductor makers have for many years been protected by tariffs of up to 14 per cent, harming EC personal computer assemblers since the tariff on computers and printed circuit boards is under 5 per cent. It is often less costly, therefore, to import non-EC sub-assemblies or computers rather than paying more by bringing in microchips for inclusion in locally made products.

American semiconductor users have been similarly disadvantaged. Not long after the 1986 semiconductor accord between the American and Japanese governments, the industry's cycle moved from its feast to famine phase, shortages of microchips began to occur and prices of D-Rams in the USA increased by about 40 per cent – far higher than in Japan – provoking bitter complaints. According to Ken Flamm, a US trade expert at the Brookings Institute, 'Price floors for D-Rams have been a disaster in the US. Prices rose dramatically and there has been very little re-entry into the D-Ram market by US electronics companies.'[6]

As if that was not bad enough for American personal computer makers, the US International Trade Commission ruled in 1991 that Japanese manufacturers of flat computer display screens, used in laptop computers, should be subject to anti-dumping duties of up to 63 per cent. This was in spite of protests from IBM and Apple and the fact that there simply are no volume manufacturers of such displays in the USA. The result: Apple was forced to shift production of its higher-performance notebook computers to Ireland, while Compaq decided to make its latest portable computer in Scotland to avoid the duties.

Nor have the Japanese been immune from such damaging policies. When in 1988 the Japanese government halved duties on imported chocolate to 10 per cent, it nonetheless retained much higher tariffs on the ingredients for chocolate – sugar, dairy products and cocoa – to appease domestic vested interests. The effect has simply been to allow foreign companies to undercut Japanese chocolate makers, and M&M/Mars, Hershey, Jacobs-Suchard and Lindt are willingly reaping the profits.

The knock-on effects on downstream industries of raising the costs of their feedstocks in this way can be most clearly seen in the European electronics industry. Here, producers of silicon, the prime ingredient of semiconductors, are protected by anti-dumping duties. Semiconductor manufacturers are in turn shielded by tariffs and price maintenance agreements. The consumer electronics industry, a prime consumer of semiconductors, shelters behind import quotas and anti-dumping duties.

Each link in the production chain is protected, piling cost upon cost with the result that European-made televisions, video recorders and CD players are hopelessly uncompetitive in world markets. When, incidentally, silicon producers first petitioned for anti-dumping duties in 1990, the already protected semiconductor makers had the cheek to lobby against the duties on the grounds that they would raise costs for their industry!

In 1990 anti-dumping duties were imposed by the United States on Japanese mechanical transfer presses (MTPs), massive milling machines deigned to produce high volumes of identical parts which are crucial to the car industry. During the hearings, a Ford executive pointed out that Japanese MTPs worked up to three times as fast as American models, and that US companies would not produce the size of machine required by Ford. A former Chrysler vice-president told the hearings: 'If the US press manufacturers have been injured, it is the result of their own failure to commit the resources to develop the technology and expertise to compete.' Other US firms described the domestic MTP makers as 'inadequate in design', 'late in delivery' and 'generally not very interested in the business'. Nonetheless, the duties were imposed, and with them the American auto industry was handicapped.

A year earlier, the main US bearings manufacturer, Torrington, had petitioned for anti-dumping action against foreign bearings. A parade of representatives from companies which used bearings in their products begged for their supply of foreign bearings not to be cut off. One told of how they had 'to build Torrington's notorious unreliability into our production schedules'. A buyer from Caterpillar, the earth-moving equipment giant, said: 'We've repeatedly slipped our production schedule to work around Torrington's string of broken promises.' 3M's spokesman related how American companies had simply refused to produce the type of bearings they required. Yet hefty dumping duties were nonetheless imposed on imported bearings.[7]

Trade barriers on basic industrial feedstocks such as machine tools, presses, steel, semiconductors, bearings and chemicals, which are designed to protect certain industries, severely harm industries which use these products.

Trade barriers also create shortages and limit choice. Here again, US steel import restraints have severely hindered American steel processors. Several re-rolling companies in the United States – those that roll semi-finished slabs into strips – complain bitterly about shortfalls in their supply of raw materials. West Coast-based California Steel has reported that it had to turn away orders because of a lack of sufficient steel slabs.

When shortages of wire rod used to make steel wire became so severe

Trade Barriers

that the one American company producing the right grade of rod was rationing its customers and wire workers were being laid off, it took the US Commerce Department eight months to come to a decision to increase import quotas – and then it only allowed 820 of the 2,820 tons requested by the wire manufacturers.[8]

Diminutive wonders

Trade barriers pollute the environment. Each year Japanese motorists buy around a million microcars, scaled-down high-tech hatchbacks with engines below 550cc capacity and costing from as little as ¥600,000 (about £2,500). Apart from price and size, these microcars offer superb economy and produce little pollution, making them the ideal town cars. Moreover, intense competition has turned most of the models on offer into tiny technological masterpieces. For despite often having only three-cylinder engines, they are packed with features such as intercooled turbo-charging, multi-valve engines and twin overhead camshafts. Four-wheel drive, automatic transmission and power steering are also offered, as well as convenience features that make the most of limited space. The Suzuki Alto, for example, has large sliding doors and a swivelling driver's seat to allow you to step right out on to the pavement.

Sadly, very few of these diminutive wonders are on sale in the West due to import restrictions on the numbers of cars Japanese companies can sell, which result in Japanese manufacturers exporting more profitable and higher-priced larger cars. Nor has such protection encouraged European or American manufacturers to make comparable microcars of their own. When Raymond Levy, the boss of France's Renault, was asked if he would launch a really low-cost small car, he retorted: 'I see no room in our range for such a car. I don't think we could make any money by selling such a cheap model.'[9]

Yet lobbying by Renault, among others, has meant that western consumers are largely unable to acquire these space-saving and environment-friendly Japanese microcars, which would be a boon in traffic-choked cities and to those on low incomes. Trade restrictions, in this case, have harmed both the consumers and the environment without notably helping western industry.

This is a crucial point, for trade barriers rarely even ultimately help the protected industry. French and Italian motor manufacturers, even more protected than their British counterparts, have become disproportionately dependent on their home markets and have met with little success outside Europe. Not having fully to compete domestically with the Japanese, companies like Fiat, Renault and Peugeot find greater and greater difficulty in matching them in export markets where they have to meet the Japanese on equal terms.

Fiat and Renault's attempts in the 1980s to make headway in the United States met with dismal failure. The main reason for Peugeot's decision in 1991 to withdraw from the US market was the realization that, at a base price of $35,000, the company's new top-range 605 model would be more costly than the much more sophisticated Lexus from Toyota which had already been on sale for two years. As a result, by 1991 European cars accounted for only 5 per cent of US imports which they had once dominated. Volkswagen, which was selling 600,000 cars a year in the USA in the late 1960s, sold fewer than 100,000 in 1991.

The full seriousness of this problem may not yet be apparent. For the fastest-growing car markets are now in Asian countries like South Korea, where annual vehicle sales are forecast to rise to more than 3 million within the next decade. Protected European manufacturers will have little hope of succeeding in such markets against Japanese and local competition – in short, they will be locked into a high-cost, low-productivity European industrial ghetto.

Italian motorcycle manufacturers, also insulated from Japanese competition, are virtually unknown outside of their home market. It is no coincidence that the European car manufacturers most successful in selling outside of Europe are those of West Germany, which have enjoyed virtually no protection from Japanese products in their home markets; while the sole successful European motor-bike manufacturer is similarly unprotected BMW of West Germany.

Breathing space

One problem is that the reduced competitive pressures resulting from import restraints almost invariably merely compound the inefficiencies and weaknesses of protected industries, creating industrial oligopolies and cartelizing markets. Exposure to full international competition, on the other hand, frequently has the effect of sweeping away complacency.

Import restraints in the United States simply allowed Chrysler, General Motors and Ford to raise prices, rebuild profits and pay huge bonuses to their bosses without regaining market share or rebuilding exports. Protection has also done little to help the European copier industry. EC anti-dumping duties on Japanese photocopiers were used to boost the profits of European producers rather than their market share, which barely moved, rising from 29 per cent in 1986 to 31 per cent in 1990. The four main instigators of the anti-dumping action have actually seen their market share slump from 16 per cent to 10 per cent since the duties were imposed in 1985. Increasingly, moreover, the companies concerned have become mere distributors of Japanese products.

Maintaining a 14 per cent duty on semiconductor imports long after the United States, Canada and Japan abandoned their tariffs has done nothing to enhance the European industry's competitiveness, prompting a warning from the main industry research group in 1992 that European microchip makers would be wiped out if the tariff were removed and they had to compete on equal terms.[10]

Germany has made less use of the MFA to restrict textile imports, on the other hand, than most other industrial countries. While this has resulted in Germany being the biggest textile importer, the consequent competitive pressures have also helped the German clothing industry to become more efficient and to move upmarket, so also making Germany the leading textile exporter with a healthy trade surplus.[11]

Industrialists lobbying for trade restraints invariably say they only need protection for a few years to allow a 'breathing space' to restructure. But such people repeatedly come back for another fix at the end of the prescribed term – precisely because by postponing the need to adjust and make painful changes, trade barriers have left them even less able to compete.

Car, steel, textile and electronics companies have all solemnly assured politicians and the public that protection need only be short term. But with monotonous regularity they just come back with hands outstretched for more – the latest example being American machine tool makers who in 1991 requested the Bush administration again to extend five-year 'temporary' import quotas originally imposed in 1986. And as with state subsidies, those with the greatest lobbying power and the most friends in the corridors of power tend to command the greatest protection, so distorting the whole economy and penalizing successful sectors to give dubious assistance to deficient ones.

Trade barriers handicap industry by diverting resources from successful to inefficient producers. Land Rover, the British four-wheel-drive vehicle manufacturer, has suffered from market fragmentation resulting from protected state procurement in Europe. Goaded by their national champion car makers, which have argued that they need military orders to underpin their development of competitive four-wheel-drive models, the French, Italian and West German governments have bought locally produced vehicles for their military.

In the late 1970s, for example, Volkswagen persuaded its government to require the West German army to buy its vehicle rather than the Land Rovers which were the army's preferred choice. The consequent four-wheel drive from Volkswagen was never developed for the commercial market as promised, while such policies have resulted in small, fragmented national markets, making economies of scale difficult to achieve.

'The German housewife will just have to pay more for her bananas'

Sometimes efficient producers are disadvantaged through systems of preferential access whereby barrier-free imports are granted only to certain countries. Frequently, such policies are a hangover from colonial days when it was common for the imperial power to favour its colonies. The inoffensive banana provides a good example of how this practice unfairly distorts trade flows.

Britain has traditionally offered preferential access to bananas from the Caribbean – particularly the Windward Islands, which account for two-thirds of Britain's banana consumption – at the expense of more efficient South American producers whose costs are less than half those of the Caribbean islands. France and Spain offer similar preferential access to their former colonies. As a result, Windward Island and other Caribbean banana growers have had little incentive to improve efficiency or to diversify.

So the onset of the single European market after 1992, when cheaper bananas sold to other European countries would have also to be freely traded in Britain, France and Spain, provoked a flurry of lobbying by the islanders for a special European Community-wide deal. The prime minister of Dominica somewhat haughtily dismissed German complaints that they preferred to buy cheaper South American bananas with the words: 'My message to the Germans is that they are asking the impossible in wanting cheaper fruit – the German housewife will just have to pay more for her bananas.'[12]

Of course, one may well have sympathy for the Windward Islanders and feel that the average hausfrau could afford to pay a few pfennigs extra for her bananas. But the real losers are the South American countries, none of which enjoy high incomes, but which have been denied free access to many markets through the lobbying of the Caribbean countries, and which now have the prospect of sales to their traditional markets, like Germany, being limited too.

The islanders may, anyway, not even be the main beneficiaries of the system. According to the Canberra-based Centre of International Economics, only a fifth of the extra $1.44 billion that EC consumers spent on their bananas as a result of trade barriers actually benefited the exporting countries. The remainder went to wholesalers and importers.

Needless to say, the supporters of import restrictions on South American bananas habitually claim the moral high ground, declaring that protection was needed to assist the poor islanders who can produce little else but bananas. Yet frequently these same people are elsewhere found arguing for import restrictions on textiles at the expense of poor, developing countries which can produce little else but textiles.

Trade barriers kill people. In 1985 the French authorities deliberately delayed introducing a newly developed American blood test for AIDS because a rival French test had not yet been perfected. As a result, the French National Blood Transfusion Centre continued for several months to release untested blood for transfusions, contaminating some 7,000 people. The French government managed to pass the buck by charging three doctors with responsibility and tried to levy insurance companies for the enormous cost of compensation. But there can be little doubt that a niggling, state-inspired piece of protectionism bore the true responsibility for the tragedy.[13]

Trade barriers penalize the poor. Almost invariably, lower-cost goods are subject to stiffer import restrictions than premium products. The United States imposes hefty tariffs on imported mushrooms, but gourmets enjoy their truffles duty-free. Orange juice carries a 40 per cent tariff, but the café society can sip their Perrier water after paying only 0.8 per cent.

Lower-income groups spend a far higher proportion of their income on clothing and food, two of the most intensively protected industries in the USA and Europe. According to one US Congressman, trade barriers 'take away a whopping 32 per cent of the purchasing power of the family that is just at or above the poverty level.'[14]

Trade barriers help to discourage the use of safer condoms. US Customs has decreed that condoms which are electronically tested or include spermicide must pay import tariffs at a higher rate than lower-grade condoms. Presumably, US government policy is to encourage the use of less safe condoms.

'It sucks from the taxpayer'

Trade barriers encourage corruption and venality. When in 1985 the US government created a separate import quota for Canadian sugar-corn sweetener blends – used as a lower-cost alternative to heavily protected, and hence high-priced domestic sugar – American sugar growers objected that the quota (2 per cent of the US market) was still too high. So the growers got on to their friend Senator Jesse Helms, who persuaded the US Customs Service to ban all Canadian-blended imports. Helms denied receiving any benefits from his pro-sugar lobbying, but a journalist later revealed that the Cane Sugar Refiners gave Helms $2,000 for attending breakfast with them shortly after his successful efforts on their behalf.[15]

Protected industries are rarely low on the lists of political donors, particularly in the United States. Companies wanting protection reward sympathetic politicians with generous campaign contributions; and the politicians reward the companies with generous protection. Millions of dollars have flowed from the US steel, automobile, textile and agriculture industries to those politicians who best protect their interests.

The US merchant marine is one of America's most protected industries. It is looked after by the House Merchant Marine Subcommittee, of which former Congressman Thomas Ashley declared: 'it sucks from the taxpayer, it sucks from anything that isn't nailed down.'[16] Congressmen sitting on the subcommittee have received hundreds of thousands of dollars in campaign contributions from the merchant marine lobby. So generous have US shipping interests been that three of the last five of the subcommittee's chairmen have been indicted for criminal links to the maritime industry.

Trade barriers reward sloth. Hong Kong harbour plays host to a special type of boat – the 'quota boat'. These smart launches and yachts have been dubbed 'quota boats' because their owners have grown fat by selling quotas. Clothing manufacturers who have been lucky enough to acquire quotas to sell clothes in the United States and Europe often simply sell these on to companies which are short of quota.

Often these quotas are more valuable than the products themselves. For example, the cost of buying quota to ship cotton trousers to the USA is about $8, while the cost of producing the trousers is only $7. Sometimes it is the very European and American clothing manufacturers who have lobbied for import restraints who own the quota. They buy or make cheaply abroad and sell expensively at home.

Trade barriers cost jobs. The need to protect jobs is the argument routinely and most powerfully deployed in favour of protection – and the prospect of job losses usually galvanizes politicians into action. Consumers are often consoled with the argument that they are producers too – meaning that they also have jobs which could be lost to foreign competition without protection.

The implication is that, if one set of workers lose their jobs, no one will be able truly to consume. Consumers and workers are supposedly part of some mythical unity with a common interest. In a sense this is true: not in the sense that the government should force millions to pay higher prices to save a few hundred jobs, but rather because everyone – workers and consumers – benefits from an open competitive economy in which inefficiency is not shielded and capital is allowed to gravitate to where it can best be used.

The problem with protecting some jobs is that everyone does not receive equal protection – those with the greatest lobbying power get more, diverting resources from less cosseted industries and so damaging employment in other parts of the economy. This is why the costs of using protection to preserve jobs in threatened industries are generally extremely high. The anti-dumping duties imposed on Japanese copier manufacturers represent an annual expense of nearly £20,000 per worker at Xerox, the main complainant.[17] American consumers pay out $135,000 annually to maintain each job in the textile industry, where the average wage is only $12,000 a year.[18]

Each job preserved in the British car industry as a result of import quotas cost the equivalent of the wages of four British industrial workers, while the price in the USA of preserving a steel or car worker's job was estimated at $100,000 each by the World Bank.[19] More often than not it would cost far less to put workers in protected industries on permanent vacation on full pay than to maintain the protection.

So when it comes to jobs, an important question to ask of any trade barrier is not just how many jobs it will preserve in the protected industry, but also how many will be lost in other businesses which have to pay the costs – or how much more genuine employment could be created in efficient industries with the resources being diverted into inefficient ones.

The number of American jobs destroyed by sugar quotas since 1980 exceeds the total number of sugar farmers in the USA. According to the US Commerce Department, high-priced sugar has destroyed almost 9,000 jobs in the food industry since 1981. Ten sugar refineries and 7,000 refinery jobs have been lost, while confectionery manufacturers have closed factories and relocated overseas.

Some 240,000 Americans work in semiconductor production, but more than two million work in the industries which buy semiconductors. Their jobs have all been put at risk by measures taken to protect their suppliers. Up to 11,000 jobs were lost as a result of the Semiconductor Arrangement, which raised the price of Japanese semiconductors on the US market.[20]

World income would rise by $477 billion by 2002 if all barriers to trade were removed – a gain worth more than the entire income of China according to an OECD report in 1992.[21] Even the EC Commission produced a report in 1989 revealing that the removal of internal trade barriers between the EC's constituent nations, scheduled for 1992, would result in gains of more than £50 billion.

Intensified competition, the report went on, would also help to create up to 5 million new jobs, reducing consumer prices by as much as 6 per cent and increasing the Community's GDP by about 4.5 per cent. If the EC Commission, so often the champion of protection against non-Community competition, can see the huge advantages of free trade within the EC, why it is so blind to the wider benefits?

Notes

1 'The cost of trade restraints: the case of Japanese automobile exports to the United States', International Monetary Fund Staff Papers, vol.34, no. 1, March 1987.

2 Institut d'Etudes Politiques and Nomura Research Institute study, Quoted in *The Economist*, 18 April 1992

3 *International Trade and the Consumer: Consumer Electronics and the EC's Anti-Dumping Policy*, National Consumer Council, London, 1990.

4 *Washington Post*, 24 May 1989.

5 Source: OECD.

6 *Independent*, 1 August 1989.

7 Both of these cases are quoted in James Bovard, *The Fair Trade Fraud*, St Martin's Press, New York, 1991.

8 Ibid.

9 *Car*, January 1990.

10 *EC Semiconductor Tariffs and Related Issues*, Dataquest.

11 Source: GATT, *International Trade*, 1988/9.

12 Quoted in the *Financial Times*, 10 September 1991.

13 *Financial Times*, 28 November 1991.

14 Tom DeLay in Claude E.Barfield and John H.Makin (eds), *Trade Policy and US Competitiveness*, American Enterprise Institute, Washington, 1987.

15 Bovard, op. cit.

16 Quoted ibid.

17 Patrick Messerlin and Yoshiyuki Noguchi, 'EC industrial policy: worse than before', *Financial Times*, 10 February 1992.

18 William Cline of the Washington based Institute for International Economics, quoted in Alan Oxley, *The Challenge of Free Trade*, Harvester Wheatsheaf, London, 1990.

19 World Bank, *World Development Report*, 1987.

20 Center for the Study of American Business estimate.

21 *Trade Liberalization: What's at Stake*, OECD Development Centre, Paris, 1992.

10 Honourable Rice

It is often supposed that agricultural subsidies are different, and that, unlike other forms of protection, they preserve employment in the long run. They don't. They only do so at the expense of other sectors of the economy, reducing efficiency and incomes overall.

Sir Geoffrey Howe

Rice has for a long time maintained a disproportionate influence on Japanese life. Ever since wet-field rice cultivation was introduced from China around the second century AD, transforming much of Japan's agricultural landscape into small dyke-surrounded, water-filled plots of land fed by intricate artificial systems of tiny waterways, rice has been the staple of the Japanese diet. The high yields attainable from intensive rice paddy cultivation and double cropping have played a crucial part in allowing Japan, like much of the rest of east Asia, to support heavier concentrations of population than the drier or colder lands of western Asia and Europe.

So highly regarded is rice that the three main meals in Japan are still described in terms of *gohan* – literally, 'honourable rice'. Even today, around 40 per cent of Japan's agricultural land is devoted to rice.[1] Yet this inoffensive but essential food has, together with other agricultural produce, been for some time at the epicentre of perhaps the bitterest trade dispute between Japan and the USA.

For years the United States has been attempting, with only limited success, to gain the right to sell its food surfeit to Japan's masses in the teeth of fierce resistance from Japanese politicians who are disproportionately influenced by Japan's vociferous farmers' lobby. Underlying this conflict is the fundamental insecurity which the Japanese feel about their food supply, which stems both from the knowledge that their own agricultural yields are insufficient to feed the whole population, and from the memory of food shortages before, during and after the war.

Food security

The reason for Japan's low food output is the fact that only around 15 per cent of Japan's surface is viable for agriculture, the remainder being taken up by mountains, forests and towns. So the Japanese have to squeeze as much production as possible out of their farmland which is only one-hundredth that of the United States.

Agriculture is unlike most industries. In manufacturing, output can be cranked up simply by adding capacity in the form of factories and plant. The more you produce, the lower the cost tends to be. But if you increase production on a hectare of land, that production also becomes far more expensive because of extra inputs such as fertilizer.

So to maintain a reasonable degree of self-sufficiency from limited land by maximizing output, food prices have to be high in order to give farmers the incentive to produce more and to compensate for the increased cost of high yields. This has led both to import barriers to prevent low-cost foreign food from driving Japan's farmers out of business, and a network of controls, subsidies and price supports covering produce from wheat to oranges – but above all, rice.

Even so, Japan's relatively small cultivable area means that it still imports half of its food needs – up from only 15 per cent in 1967 – making Japan now the world's largest net importer of agricultural products. The leading exporter is, in fact, none other than Japan's greatest critic, the USA.

Unfortunately, the prospect of serious reform of Japan's farm system has been severely hampered by the sheer weight in numbers of Japanese farmers, which reinforces political support for the system. Japan's 4.5 million farmers represent in all about 15 per cent of the working population – a far higher proportion than in Britain or the USA where less than 3 per cent of the working population are on the land, and more even than France where around 8 per cent of the active population are involved in farming.

This force of numbers has given Japanese farmers a political clout greater than is the case in most western countries. Almost half of the 450 or so ruling Liberal Democrat (LDP) MPs have significant agricultural interests in their constituencies, and eleven out of forty-six prefectures have more than 30 per cent of their households classified as agricultural.

Nonetheless, pressure from the USA for easier access to Japan's food market has been a major factor in forcing some change in Japanese attitudes towards the food-control system, especially since it comes at a time when Japan has been under continual attack on other trade issues. The overall result of these factors has been a steady liberalization of the food market and the tentative beginnings of the dismantlement of the extensive regulatory system.

The turning point probably came in June 1988 when, after three rounds of cabinet-level negotiations, the USA and Japan ended one long-running dispute by signing an agreement on liberalizing imports of beef and oranges into Japan. But the rice system remains largely intact and Japan vigorously defended it throughout the Uruguay round of the GATT negotiations.

The Japanese are fond of alluding to President Nixon's decision in 1973 to cut off exports of soya beans to help reduce US meat prices in support of the policy of not being overdependent on imports. They assert that a country needs some security of supply in a product as crucial as food – especially as Japan is already dependent on imports for half of its needs.

Similar arguments have been used in support of the European Community's comparably restrictive farm policy, which has also been aggressively attacked by the United States. As in Japan, it is the political power of small farmers' lobbying groups, especially in Bavaria, France and southern Europe, which really underlies the system. The fact that many of these small farmers are only part-timers, often earning good wages in nearby factories, has not prevented gross absurdities such as huge subsidies to support the growing of tobacco in marginally suitable areas. The resultant crop is so low-grade that it can only be dumped at give-away prices to boost lung cancer levels in Third World countries.

Although there may be some justice in the argument that the rules of free trade should not apply to industries which are genuinely strategic, such as defence or agriculture, the Japanese system in particular seems to have achieved the worst of all worlds by costing consumers a great deal in high prices and hitting foreign producers in lost trade, while not really guaranteeing domestic food security in case of shortages. But despite the fact that much US criticism of Japan's farm policies is justified, the self-righteous tone of American rebukes should not disguise the fact that there is much to condemn in the United States' own agriculture system.

Cheeseburger and fries

Perhaps nothing so symbolizes the United States as the land of plenty as the ubiquitous cheeseburger and fries. It is ironic, therefore, that what has become virtually the national dish of a country which takes pride in its self-reliant, free enterprise culture is also among the most heavily subsidized and controlled food products in the world.

With the country's broad grasslands and lush pastures, you would not, perhaps, have thought that America's aggressively independent ranchers needed much state support. But the cost of the meat in America's burgers has been pushed up by import restrictions dating back to 1964, when Congress enacted the Meat Import Act which limited shipments of most types of meat.[2]

The cheese in the all-American burger also costs more than it needs to because the US government maintains a series of 'voluntary' import quotas covering cheese and other dairy products. American dairy products also benefit from price support in the form of government buying programmes which absorb surpluses to keep prices artificially high. As a result, by the late 1980s US government dairy subsidies amounted to no less than $835 per dairy cow.

Nor do those United States prairie farmers growing the wheat for the burger bun miss out on the handouts, benefiting from a policy called the 'deficiency-payment' system, whereby the US government makes up any difference between prevailing market prices and higher government target prices for grains – ironically including rice. Even the humble fries are not exempt – the United States maintained strict quotas on imports of Canadian potatoes until 1988, and non-tariff barriers still constrain imports of potatoes.

Restrictions, controls and subsidies do not end with burgers, however. No self-respecting American would consider breakfast complete without a glass of orange juice. But, as the world's largest consumers of orange juice sip their morning glassful, they are almost certainly blissfully unaware that their often huge and wealthy citrus producers are protected by a 40 per cent tariff on imported juice, a tariff which primarily discriminates against less well-off countries such as Brazil.

Requests from Peru, Bolivia, Ecuador and Colombia for the elimination of such tariffs on frozen orange juice to allow them to develop agricultural industries to replace the growing of coca leaves, the raw material for cocaine, were rejected after a campaign by the US citrus industry and its congressional supporters. Mexican melons and avocados are similarly largely excluded from the American market by quotas and non-tariff barriers. Overall, the USA imposes more than 500 different tariffs on foreign food, ranging from 20 per cent on yoghurt to 25 per cent on asparagus, and from 24.5 per cent on grape juice to 28.6 per cent on frozen chicken.

America's southern peanut growers do even better. Tariffs and a minuscule import quota give them almost total protection against cheaper peanuts from China and South America. When, in 1990, after a poor crop and a doubling of prices, peanut users and processors led by the peanut butter and confectionery industries asked for an increase in the import quota – a request backed by the US International Trade Commission, which recommended raising the quota from 1.7 million pounds to 300 million pounds – a storm of lobbying by American farmers resulted in President Bush only authorizing an increase to 100 million pounds. Even then, in a provision which must have had US peanut farmers chuckling with pleasure, the additional peanuts had to be imported by the end of the month – it generally takes more than 28 days for peanuts to be loaded and shipped from South America and China.

Overall, American farm import restrictions permit each American citizen to consume the equivalent of only one teaspoon of foreign ice-cream, two imported peanuts and one pound of foreign cheese a year.[3]

Fighting like a 'junkyard dog'

All of this may come as a surprise to those who associate the United States with trenchant criticism of both Japan's and Europe's well-known protectionist farm policies. Yet it was the United States itself which in 1950 instigated the moves which resulted in GATT rules not being applied to agriculture. At that time, the Americans contended that agriculture was a sector of economy which is peculiarly unsuited to being exposed to the full rigours of international market forces, not least because of the need to ensure food supplies – similar arguments to those now used by the Japanese, and indeed the European Community, to justify their farm trade barriers.

American farmers are, in fact, treated in many ways even more indulgently by their avowedly free-market government than their Japanese or European rivals. With a population around twice that of Japan, the United States spends nearly three times as much on its farmers at close to $35 billion a year. Each American farm household receives on average nine times as much state support as in Japan.

Even American honey producers benefit from a $100 million a year programme.

And however earnest the professions of American support for freeing up farm trade during the Uruguay round, the US agriculture secretary, Edward Madigan, declared that he would 'fight like a junkyard dog' to protect American farmers' interests during the talks.[4]

A touch of irony might be discerned in the fact that the United States so vigorously protects and subsidizes its beef and citrus farmers, while castigating the Japanese for following a similar policy. But more than a reputation for hypocrisy is at stake, for in one crucial respect the American system is far more damaging than that of Japan. Although they do not result in as high prices for domestic consumers as in Japan, US farm policies do create massive surpluses which are dumped on to world markets at subsidized prices, making it impossible for producers from poorer nations to compete.

Dumping

Take sugar – the United States first imposed tariffs on imported sugar in 1816, after plantation owners complained that growing sugar in the USA was 'warring with nature' because of the unsuitability of the climate. Import quotas were established as far back as 1934 and a price support programme for domestic producers was also introduced in 1977. When inroads on sugar usage were made by corn sweeteners in the mid-1980s it was the sugar import quota which was sharply reduced to compensate American producers, slashing the amount of sugar that Caribbean nations could ship to the USA by 74 per cent.

President Reagan even extended quotas to imports of sweetened products, such as cocoa, pancake mixes, wedding cake decorations and even chocolate covered ants, immediately creating enormous problems for importers of goods which often contained only minimal amounts of sugar, but which were nonetheless excluded as they had no sugar quota allocation. One Israeli company which sent 20,000 kosher pizzas with a tiny sugar content (0.005 per cent) to New York has its shipment seized, while Korean noodles with 0.02 per cent sugar content were also impounded as an unwarranted threat to American sugar growers.[5]

This American commitment to the free market has resulted in a large increase in expensive American sugar production during the late 1970s and 1980s, matched by a steep decline of around 80 per cent in sugar imports. Despite a request by GATT for the USA to terminate its sugar policy, its provisions remain in force. Indeed, while American negotiators were arguing at the GATT Uruguay round for an end to global farm trade barriers, the United States was actually slashing its sugar import quota for 1992 by a third.

The overall effect of the US sugar policy – and a similar EC programme – has been devastating for sugar-producing countries in the Third World. They are now largely excluded from Western markets, while subsidized exports of US and EC sugar destroy their chances of selling elsewhere. As a result, exports from the Philippines fell by 90 per cent from the early to the mid-1980s.

American dumping of wheat surpluses has also hit largely unsubsidized Australian farmers, many of whom are going broke because they cannot compete in export markets against subsidized American grain. EC beef subsidies have transformed the Community from a major importer to a leading exporter of beef, destroying in the process Argentina's chances to ease its debt burden, which would be manageable if it were able to export the amount of beef and other farm products that it used to. Uruguay, too, has stagnated as markets for its beef exports have shrunk.

Despite its manifest defects, at least the Japanese farm support system is less irresponsible than those of the EC or the USA, in that it does not dump agricultural surpluses and so wreck the economies of poor, single-commodity producers, or unsubsidized farmers around the globe. American and European export subsidies have done far more to distort world markets and impoverish poorer countries than Japan's ban on rice imports.

So efficient food producers have had to watch powerlessly over the years as agriculture has steadily been excluded from GATT provisions. The original GATT rules prohibited the use of import-restraining quotas – with the exception of agriculture. In 1955 the United States secured a waiver from GATT rules for parts of its farm production. In the early 1960s the subsidization of exports was banned by GATT – except for primary products such as food. In 1966 Switzerland negotiated its entry into GATT on the condition that its agriculture sector should be exempted from GATT rules. And when the EC's Common Agricultural Policy began to take off in the mid-1970s, the Community made it clear that GATT rules did not apply.

As a result, by the late 1970s the European Community was over-producing, dumping products, depressing prices and stealing markets, prompting the United States to establish a war chest to recapture markets from the EC. Both parties connived systematically to block serious discussion of farm trade in GATT until the mid-1980s. Producers of low-cost, high-quality food, meanwhile, watched frustrated and powerless as markets were rigged against them and the living standards of their people declined.

The worst of all worlds

If asked which country is the world's sixth largest wheat exporter you might guess Australia, France or maybe even Britain. The correct answer is, in fact, the desert kingdom of Saudi Arabia, whose farmers are encouraged by government payments of $500 a tonne – several times the market price – to grow wheat on unsuitable land, dangerously depleting scarce water resources. As a result, the country now annually produces four times the wheat it consumes, dumping the surplus on to world markets.

Saudi Arabia's farm policy is merely one of the most absurd examples of the type of agriculture support system operated by most countries, including those European nations which remain outside the EC, such as Switzerland, Norway and Austria.

In simple terms, these policies cost a massive $200 billion annually. But the ramifications go much further, producing a massive and unjust distortion of the international food market which groans under the burden of unsustainable surpluses, loading massive costs not just on to the taxpayers who fund the subsidies, but also on to the consumers who have to pay a further $150 billion for overpriced food.[6] Wildlife and the environment also suffer as a result of unnecessary overproduction; as do producers in countries whose produce is denied fair access to markets.

What makes the whole mess even less defensible is the fact that many efficient producers are from relatively poor countries. This is particularly the case with sugar producers in South America and the Caribbean, who are largely denied access to the developed world and pushed out of other markets by dumped American and EC sugar. Brazilian farmers, who produce wheat at $150 a tonne, are similarly not only denied the right to sell their produce in Europe, but also have to suffer unfair competition from French farmers whose costs are $230 a tone, but who can use EC export subsidies to dump wheat on the world market for a mere $85 a tonne.

And what of the farmers whose livelihoods are supposedly protected by this immense but unwieldy structure, designed to prevent efficient producers from selling to willing consumers? Have you ever heard a farmer who is not moaning? Perhaps with good reason, for the very policies which are designed to take some of the unpredictability out of farming have left most farmers with declining incomes, immobilized by the uncertainty caused by repeated government attempts to restructure the markets and reform irredeemable systems.

If anyone therefore requires evidence of the damage wrought by political and bureaucratic intervention in the workings of the market, agriculture provides perhaps the most potent example of how much harm an unholy mixture of state interference and trade barriers can do.

Farm support polices have resulted in the worst of all worlds for almost everyone concerned. Yet they have become so institutionalized that the supposed beneficiaries fear change, paralyzing policy makers against anything more than token reforms of the type proposed by the EC in the summer of 1992. A visitor from some other world would justifiably look at international farm support policies and wonder how supposedly rational beings could create such a bizarre, demented system which demonstrably wreaks so much damage in the name of supposedly benefiting so few.

Notes

1 Source: Agricultural Production Income Statistics, Japanese Ministry of Agriculture, Forestry and Fisheries.

2 Source: Gary Hufbauer, Diane Berliner and Kimberley Elliott, *Trade Protection in the US: 31 Case Studies*, Institute for International Economics, Washington, 1986.

3 Jim Bovard, quoted in the *Financial Times*, 11 February 1992.

4 Quoted in the *Financial Times*, 14 March 1991.

5 James Bovard, *The Fair Trade Fraud*, St Martin's Press, New York, 1991.

6 Source: OECD.

11 The Roots of Competitive Advantage

If you plan for a year, plant a seed.
If for ten years, plant a tree.
If for a hundred years, teach the people.
If you plant a seed once, you will reap one harvest.
If you plant a tree, you will reap ten harvests.
If you teach the people, you will reap a hundred harvests.

Kuan-tzu, Chinese philosopher, sixth century BC

If trade barriers and state-directed industrial policies are not the key to Japan's economic success, why has Japanese business gained mastery in so many significant industries? What, in short, are the real roots of Japan's competitive advantage?

The roots of national competitive advantage are complex and varied. Some are natural and indigenous. It is said, for example, that Swedish heavy truck companies have derived benefits from having a domestic logging industry which requires the transport of heavy loads over long distances in harsh conditions. France's quality-oriented food industry may well have profited by having to find markets for a surfeit of food; while Britain's has probably in part been pushed into the low-added value, commodity end of the market because it has traditionally operated in a country where it can sell everything it produces because Britain does not grow enough food for its own needs.

Abundant mineral wealth may have helped Australia to develop world-class mining companies, but such lavish natural resources have almost certainly also disadvantaged Australia's manufacturing capabilities by sucking capital resources into mining and tying its currency to volatile commodity markets.

Japan, on the other hand, may have plucked some of its natural

The Roots of Competitive Advantage

advantages from apparent handicaps. A lack of indigenous raw materials has led to an intense interest in advanced new materials such as ceramics and carbon fibres. A dependence on foreign energy has meant a concern with efficient energy utilization. Limited space has led to world-beating downsized products. Sophisticated and demanding domestic buyers have stimulated product quality and innovation.

But the real competitive qualities of a nation depend fundamentally on how productive it is; and a nation's productive abilities are crucially determined by the skills of its people.

Japan is fortunate in this respect. With just 2.6 per cent of the earth's total population, Japan nonetheless produces a tenth of the world's GNP. Some people assert that this achievement is due to the fact that the Japanese are fundamentally different, benefiting from a long Confucian tradition of harmony and order, resulting in a discipline and group ethos which has been invaluable to Japanese industry.

While a high degree of social cohesion undoubtedly characterizes Japanese society, a cohesion reinforced by the unifying task of rebuilding the nation from the ruins of the war, the image of a unified and consensual society has to be set against the often harsh and violent disputes and internecine strife which have characterized Japanese history as much as that of any other nation.

The inter-war years were particularly disastrous, with the military hard-liners pitched against constitutionalists, bitter 'rice riots' and frequent bloody assassinations, culminating in an army mutiny in 1936. After the war, Japan was for some time racked by severe labour problems. As late as 1960, an intensely violent strike broke out at the Miike coal mine. The same year saw vicious riots against treaties with the United States, while the 1960s and early 1970s were marred by ferocious street protests when masked and steel-helmeted students overturned cars, stoned police and set fire to Tokyo University.

In 1974 commuters smashed up Tokyo stations in frustration at a railwaymen's go-slow, while riots over Narita airport delayed its opening by seven years. Even now, Narita is heavily guarded and ringed with electrified fencing. Nor has the Diet, Japan's parliament, always been a shining example of the group ethos and consensus politics. Five hundred policemen had to guard the chamber in May 1954 to prevent fist fights between members, causing the Diet's stenographers to demand a pledge from the members that they would not walk over their tables or grab their notes during fights. Japan's education system, too, has been something of a battleground, with teachers' strikes and walkouts – inspired by the left-wing teachers' union – common in the 1950s. More recently, there has been heavy union opposition to the publication of exam results.

Even the prosperous Japan of 1990 witnessed police in Osaka battling for a week against thousands of day-labourers protesting about bribe-taking from gangsters who exploit temporary workers by controlling construction site labour. The firebomb-throwing protestors looted shops, cars and vending machines and were briefly joined by some office workers.

There is, therefore, no intrinsic, magical quality of Confucian cohesiveness about the Japanese. Japan has not simply moved harmoniously, smoothly and inevitably to its economic triumphs.

Assumed cultural differences are, moreover, no reason for believing that the West has little to learn from Japan. For Japan's real advantage stems rather from the basic attitudes and sound education of its people.

A good start

All the major comparative studies of international educational standards since the mid-1960s show Japanese pupils top of the class in science and maths.[1] Further comparisons have been made between Japanese and American youngsters which show Japanese children to be well ahead of their American counterparts at the age of six, the advantage steadily growing until they reach eighteen;[2] while American sociologists who have studied the Japanese high-school system estimate that it turns out graduates at the age of eighteen who are at about the same academic level as the average 22-year-old American college graduate.[3]

The importance of education has long been recognized by Japanese governments. The nineteenth-century Meiji reformers were well aware of the crucial role of education in modernizing Japan and strengthening its economy. They made primary education compulsory for all, regardless of class or sex, a mere seven years after the abolition of slavery in the United States. Since then, the provision of an exacting education system which is geared to the needs of industry has been a priority of successive Japanese governments.

Compulsory education in Japan begins when children are aged six, although about 85 per cent of pre-school children attend mainly privately funded voluntary kindergarten from the ages of three or four. In Britain and the United States, by comparison, only around 40 per cent of four-year-olds receive pre-school education. Moreover, Japanese kindergartens are not simply play schools; apart from helping to inculcate the capacity to work in groups, they include a formal academic curriculum covering the first stages of reading and arithmetic. Children are expected to be able to read and do simple sums by the time they leave. From there almost all Japanese children go on to state-funded junior high schools.

One important feature of Japan's educational system is that it provides schoolchildren with examination-based incentives for academic work which are far more powerful than those in many western countries. Although the strong examination orientation of the system does produce severe strains known as 'examination hell', it also encourages hard work and inculcates both discipline and concentration.

The first real test occurs at the age of fourteen, when Japanese children take entrance examinations to the senior high schools, many of which are private and which are ranked in a hierarchy of public esteem in each locality. Being at a prestigious senior high school confers both status and the benefits of good teaching, so places are keenly competed for. Once placed in these schools, Japanese teenagers are confronted with a fresh set of incentives in the form of university entrance examinations.

Another factor which differentiates Japanese education from that in most of the West is that it has a far stronger market element, owing to the presence of the mainly private kindergartens and completely private *juku*, supplementary crammer schools. Nearly half of Japanese children attend *juku* two or three evenings a week and for part of the holidays. Both the kindergartens and *juku* have to compete vigorously for parents' money.

In addition, nearly a third of senior high schools are private and even most of the state senior highs charge some fees, averaging £1,000 a year for tuition and books. In higher education, three-quarters of universities are private institutions, charging fees of between £2,000 and £5,000 a year, with grants only available to those going into teaching. The increasingly popular post-school vocational special training colleges for non-academic high-school leavers are also totally private.

Because so much of Japanese education has to be paid for, and because a high proportion of parents have significant choice of provision, education providers at all levels have to take care to cater for pupils' needs.

In addition, although Japanese schoolchildren may not be intrinsically smarter than those elsewhere, they undoubtedly have to work much harder. Overall, excluding *juku* sessions, Japanese schoolchildren work for 240 days of the year, compared to only 180 in England and the United States.[4]

Educating for industry

Japanese education is also considered to be an integral part of the economic system. Unlike parts of the West, where increasing emphasis has been placed on goals such as 'personal growth' and child-centred education, the Japanese system is unashamedly based on the overriding premise that the main priority of schooling must be to enable a living to be earned. This is enforced by a detailed core curriculum specified by the Ministry of Education, covering literature, English, history, geography, social studies and music, but with the emphasis clearly on language, maths and science. The outcome is that:

- Japanese twelve-year-olds spend nearly 70 per cent of their school time studying maths, science and language.[5]

- Fourteen-year-olds study science for 870 hours a year, as opposed to 720 hours in the USA, 648 hours in England and 553 hours in France.[6]

- All fifteen to eighteen-year-olds study maths and science as compulsory subjects – one visiting team of British school inspectors estimated that half of the pupils achieved at least A-level standard in maths by the age of eighteen.[7]

- Close to 40 per cent of university students study science, technology and mathematics – particular stress is placed on engineering, with about a fifth of undergraduates and a third of postgraduates specializing in this field.

- Engineering is, moreover, especially strong at the best universities such as Kyoto and Osaka, where engineers account for 40 per cent of all undergraduates.

- As a result, with just over twice the population of Britain, in 1983 Japan produced three times as many mechanical engineering graduates, five times as many graduates in chemical engineering and no fewer than nine times as many production engineers.

Many people are misled into thinking that the high quality of Japanese education must be very costly. Far from it. Japanese education is very dependent on traditional chalk and blackboard methods. Classes are large – you rarely see one of fewer than forty children, compared to between twenty and thirty in the United States and Europe. Modern teaching aids are rare and many schools are tatty, with rows of old desks and peeling paint. Teachers also only earn between £8,000 and

£23,000 a year – lower than in the USA and some European countries. Overall per pupil expenditure is about half that in the United States and approximately a quarter less than in the UK or West Germany.

One key underlying reason for the success of the Japanese system is a long-standing tradition of respect for education. The fact that so many Japanese parents are prepared to supplement state education provision with private kindergartens and *juku* as, well as being willing to pay fees to Japan's largely private universities, indicates the profound importance which they attach to learning.

This is strongly reinforced by the deeply ingrained attitudes which prevail in Japan. The Japanese live in a 2,000 mile long chain of mountainous volcanic islands, only a fifth of the land of which is habitable. It is also largely devoid of natural resources, prone to earthquakes and periodically racked by typhoons, so the Japanese feel intensely vulnerable. From an early age Japanese children have drummed into them that their country is poor and the only way to survive is to work hard.

Linked to the traditional insecurity of life in Japan, where hunger was common until shortly after the war, is a typically earnest desire to get on in life and to be successful. There has never been any opportunity to catch the British disease of living off past achievements. Indeed, the aspiration to be *Ichiban* (number one) is deeply etched on the Japanese consciousness in a way in which it is not in parts of the West, where such yearnings are sometimes frowned upon or even despised as grubby, and where anti-enterprise attitudes are still deeply entrenched among sections of the establishment.

Indeed, shortly after the Meiji revolution, a translation of Samuel Smiles' paean to individualism, *Self Help*, sold a million copies in Japan at a time when the population was only 30 million. A post-war modernized translation also became a best seller because it held a strong appeal to the Japanese, then struggling to claw their way out of the misery of defeat into a future when their small, resource-starved country would become one of the world's leading economies.

Such attitudes permeate almost all sections of a society in which the vast majority consider themselves to be middle class. Each year the number of new, small manufacturing start-up businesses is nearly equal to the existing total of factories. More significantly, close to three-quarters of all small and medium-sized manufacturing enterprises are run by former blue-collar employees.

A god of money

Nor do the Japanese suffer from any residual religious objections to money-making. There is no distinction in Shinto, Japan's indigenous religion, between gods and Mammon and no trace of the Christian belief in the sanctity of poverty. There is even a Shinto shrine to Ebisu, the god of money, in Osaka, the city of merchants, where businessmen come to pray for the deity's liberal favours. Ebisu was, in fact, formerly the god of fishing, but the advent of industrialization transformed the deity into a god of money. In January of each year a strange festival is enacted at the Ebisu shrine, attended by more than a million people, at which worshippers carry bamboo sticks hung with paper symbols of wealth such as wallets, accounting books, gold coins and banknotes which they throw into a giant net, clapping to attract the god's attention.

This outlook helps to explain why contacts between parents and schools are much closer in Japan than in the West, with regular, well-attended parent–teacher meetings, plus one-to-one meetings between individual parents and teachers once a term. Parents even sometimes sit in on classes. Such attitudes also explain why 94 per cent of Japanese children continue their education in upper secondary schools beyond the leaving age of fifteen – a far higher proportion than in most western countries.

A large number – 40 per cent – of Japanese youngsters also go on to colleges and universities, most of which charge high fees, while 750,000 fewer academic pupils attend privately run special training schools, the *sengushaki*, which provide a high level of technical training in one-year courses costing up to £4,000.

Many informed observers have remarked on the close link between Japan's educational system and the country's economic success. One of the great American authorities on Japan, the former American ambassador Professor Edwin Reischauer, noted:

It is probable that there is no country in which the people have a greater longing for education ... The importance given to education and the successes that have been gained in this field seem to be taken for granted in Japan, so much so that some Japanese do not realize what a great part they have played in the modernization of the country.

But perhaps Japan's business rivals feel the gap most keenly. In 1989 one industrialist told a British parliamentary committee that the Japanese education system produced production line workers whom he would be happy to see in his development laboratories in Britain.[8] And when

Nissan set up its plant in Sunderland in Britain's north-east, The company recruited some of the British motor industry's best production and engineering management, all of whom were 'amazed at the strength of their Japanese counterparts'.[9]

Conversely, when the American earthmoving and construction equipment giant Caterpillar embarked on a $2 billion factory modernization programme in the late 1980s, according to its manufacturing director one of the greatest problems he faced in implementing the programme was that whereas 'in Japan people running even small manufacturing systems are professional engineers', by contrast 'here in the US we sometimes start with people with very little education'.[10] That was what the New York Telephone Company found when it tested 57,000 job applicants in 1987 – 96.3 per cent lacked basic skills in maths, reading and reasoning.[11]

One case study of three cement plants in Japan, Thailand and Malaysia – all with similar levels of capital investment and training – found that the Japanese plant overcame its much higher wage costs by a productivity advantage of up to four to one. The reason: higher educational standards allowed Japanese workers to utilize complex machinery more effectively.[12]

The advantage bestowed on a nation by having a well-educated population is, moreover, growing. When industry was organized along centralized, hierarchical lines, with each worker doing a simple, repetitive assembly-line task, general education was not too important provided there was a college-educated élite to provide the brain of the corporate system. But global competition now means that companies are having to decentralize responsibility in order to respond rapidly to changing conditions.

Flexible manufacturing of a wide variety of goods tailored to specific needs is becoming far more important than rigid mass production. The technological changes which allow such flexible production require educated, skilled and adaptable workforces able to use more general-purpose machinery with less supervision. That is why Japan's educational system is becoming an ever more important source of competitive advantage.

Purpose and commitment

One notable by-product of Japanese attitudes and education is that Japanese industry does not need to spend very much on training. According to one estimate, training expenditure averaged a mere 0.07 per cent of companies' turnover – less than half the amount spent by British firms.[13] Moreover, virtually all training in Japan is done within industry, with virtually no government assistance.

This is not merely because recruits into Japanese industry are already well educated, although this alone constitutes a massive advantage. No fewer than 28 per cent of the 3,600 staff of Hitachi's Musashi semiconductor plant are university graduates,[14] for example, while overall nearly 90 per cent of top Japanese managers are university educated, compared to only around 24 per cent in Britain.[15] But just as important, the desire to get on leads to much training being carried out through correspondence courses which workers take in their spare time – and often at their own expense, as evidenced by the plethora of books on management technique and quality control in Tokyo bookshops. Post-high-school education in special training schools, a fast-growing source of technical training, is also mostly financed by the students or their parents.

Not that in-company training is ignored or not taken seriously. At consumer electronics giant Matsushita, about eight months are spent training all new employees, with a further average of four days' training per year. I visited the training centre of the electronics and telecommunications company NEC in Kawasaki, a grimy industrial suburb of Tokyo where the company trains 240 full time entrants for up to two years, as well as running one- to two-week skills upgrading courses for 1,000 workers and technicians annually. The facilities, the equipment, the advanced nature of the courses and the atmosphere of purpose and commitment were impressive and quite unlike anything I have ever seen in Britain or America.

Yet it would be wrong to think that the Japanese system produces mere uncultured drones. The French writer and Japan correspondent of *Le Monde*, Robert Guillain, who spent much of his life in Japan, observed:

One has to have lived in Japan fully to appreciate the way culture 'goes deep', penetrating all social levels right down to the humblest with a greater intensity than it does even in our most cultivated Western countries ... when one lives side by side with the Japanese, one finds on the whole that they posses not only a delicacy in feeling and action that is not often to be seen among our ordinary people, but also artistic, literary and intellectual taste and knowledge – in short, a cultivation, an openness of mind, and an interest in the outer world that is rarely to be found in the West among what are conventionally termed the common people.[16]

None of which is to say that the Japanese education system is without problems. There is frank and open criticism at all levels and a consensus about the need for reform. Among the concerns I heard on a visit to Japanese schools in 1991 was that mothers over-motivate their children, pushing them too hard; that the exam system is over-competitive; that there are too few computers in schools; that teaching is generally too systematic and based on learning by rote, stultifying individualism and creativity; and that teaching of languages is based far too much on grammar rather than the spoken word.

Certainly, at one high school I visited, few pupils in an English language class of sixteen-year-olds could string a sentence together. There is, moreover, too much reliance on educational background among employers, who tend to recruit simply on the basis of which university the applicant has been to.

Such concerns, which are expressed by everyone from parents to teachers and from university lecturers to education ministry officials, will almost certainly lead to significant changes in Japan's educational system. The headmistress of the British School in Tokyo, for example, told me that she received a senior education ministry official on what she had thought was a courtesy call, only to find herself being grilled for four hours on her methods to get ideas for reforms of Japanese education. Yet there is also very strong support for the fundamentals underlying the system. Even the critics are anxious not to throw the baby out with the bath water, so evolutionary reforms and development of the system are more likely than wholesale change.

Western observers of the Japanese system frequently echo the criticisms heard in Japan, often adding that the selective nature of the high-school system, together with the prevalence of private provision in the form of kindergartens, *juku*, private high schools, universities and colleges, creates unacceptable inequalities. The competitive and market elements in Japanese education have, however, been an important factor in ensuring quality – parents spending hard-earned money on their children's education are careful with their choices and more interested in the results.

The cost of *juku* and private kindergartens is, moreover, within the range of almost all Japanese families, who tend to be far more willing to make some private provision for their children than is the case in the West. In part this is due to their intense desire for their children to succeed, and in part it is because of the innate respect for learning which permeates Japanese society.

Moreover, standards across Japanese education, whether in the state or private sector, are far more even than in most of the West – partly due to the national curriculum. The result is that there is more real equal opportunity than in those predominantly state-run western systems where provision is uneven and the quality of schooling depends largely on what type of area you live in.

In addition, during visits to a number of Japanese schools I have never left with the impression of repression which is so often given in western media stories on Japanese education. Newspaper reports from British journalists accompanying one school visit which I was on ran headlines screaming of 'Kamikaze Kids' who were 'crammed from the pram' and so on, although the journalists in question blamed the stories to some extent on sub-editors back home who heightened the sensationalist element.

On another occasion, when the British secretary of state for education walked into a high-school classroom, the teacher simply continued with her lesson and the pupils refused to look round and answer his questions, prompting press comments about Japanese schoolchildren with their noses to the grindstone. What was not mentioned was that, while tough classroom discipline prevented those kids from interrupting their studies – even for a visiting politician, after the lesson was over they crowded around the secretary of state, answering his questions, laughing and shouting just like schoolchildren anywhere.

Whatever rebukes westerners can offer to Japan's schools, above all the fact has to be faced that virtually all children leaving the Japanese educational system have a solid grounding in the basic academic skills, with the result that Japan does not have the problem endemic to the West of large numbers of illiterate and innumerate adolescents.

Finally, despite the commonly held belief that the strains of Japanese schooling lead to high suicide levels, suicide rates among Japanese children are, in fact, rather lower than in most western countries. Nor does the pressure of life in Japan produce a significantly higher overall suicide rate than other developed countries. The figures for Japan are 194 per million of the population, lower than the 227 per million in France and 207 in West Germany – although higher than the 182 per million in Sweden, 123 in the USA and 89 in England.[17]

Government for growth

The Liberal Democratic Party, which has ruled Japan since 1955, is not a political party in the western sense. Rather, it is a loose coalition of mini-parties grouped around individual leaders who maintain their power by mobilizing political funds and dispensing patronage in the form of government offices and benefits to members' constitutuencies. Control of the party passes back and forth between the leaders of the largest political cliques, with success being measured by the number of official posts meted out to faction members and the pork-barrel largess heaped on their constituencies. Overall, the system is one of which an eighteenth-century English politician would have been proud.

When asked by a journalist what expectations he had of Takeshita's prime ministership, for example, a local businessman in the prime minister's constituency just held out his cupped hands and grinned broadly. Fund-raising for electioneering purposes is also an important part of the Japanese political system. But this well-oiled system of money politics also verges on straightforward corruption. In 1989, much to the embarrassment of the Japanese, the attention of the world was drawn to this unsavoury aspect of Japanese politics by the Recruit bribery scandal, which led to the resignation of prime minister Noboru Takeshita. But Takeshita may just have been unlucky, for at least eleven of the twenty-one post-war Japanese prime ministers have been investigated for corruption at some stage in their careers.

Notwithstanding this somewhat unpromising background, post-war Japanese governments have presided over an unparalleled economic success story. Education has played a crucial part in this, but so has the fact that, more than most of their western counterparts, Japanese governments have ensured a stable economic environment conducive to economic growth. Their policies have included the following:

- Relatively low state spending to allow more resources to be channelled into industry – in the 1960s, for example, the Japanese government spent only a fifth of GNP, compared to nearly a third in the USA and two-fifths in most of Western Europe. Although by 1988 Japan's state spending had risen to nearly a third of GNP, this was still comfortably the lowest of the twenty-four OECD countries, as was the proportion of the workforce in the public sector.[18]

- Taxation has also been relatively modest. Japan's base rate of taxation is extremely low at 10 per cent, compared to 15–30 per cent for most western countries. In addition, with some exceptions, the Japanese pay no capital gains tax. Although local taxation is typically around 10 per cent, which is higher than in many western countries, as is company tax, the overall ratio of all taxes to GNP is low at around 20 per cent.

- Japanese governments have generally balanced their budgets and eschewed public-sector deficits – the exceptions being during economic shocks such as the recession of the late 1970s induced by the oil crisis, which left Japan with a large long-term government debt.

- When the Japanese government does spend, it lavishes its resources – to a far greater extent than most countries – on public works and infrastructure improvement projects rather than on consumption.

- There has been very little spending on subsidizing state-owned industries – with the significant exception of Japan National Railways, privatized in 1989, which was losing $7 billion a year at one point and had accumulated $100 billion in losses.

- Defence spending, at about 1 per cent of GNP, is about a quarter of Western European levels and around a sixth of American expenditure. Japan has been able to get away with such low levels largely because since the war it has been shielded by the American military umbrella in the Pacific.

- Japanese spending on health, pensions and social security is also comparatively modest. Social expenditure as a proportion of GDP has long lagged behind that of Western industrial rivals. Even though spending in this area has risen faster than GNP growth in recent years, it remains significantly lower than in the West at under two-thirds of the OECD average.

A nation of savers

Relatively low state social spending has been mitigated in Japan by several factors. Among these is the fact that Japan has low unemployment, a high proportion of young people and a tradition of family provision – in 1985, 15 per cent of households still had three generations living together, and approximately 70 per cent of older Japanese share their homes with their offspring. These factors help to explain why, despite relatively low spending on health and social services, Japan nonetheless had achieved the lowest infant mortality rate in the world by the mid-1970s, and recently surpassed Sweden's life expectancy to become the longest-lived nation.

The Japanese propensity to save to cover for retirement and health emergencies also helps. Overall, the Japanese save close to a fifth of their income – about three times the level in the USA and twice the British level. Cause and effect are obviously related, for low levels of state provision necessitate savings, while high private savings in turn permit lower levels of health and social spending.

But a tradition of thrift and the need to provide for old age or ill health has been strongly reinforced by government incentives for savers. Indeed, boosting savings levels has been a major plank of government policy which dates back to the late nineteenth century. Since the war, savings in the Post Office Savings Bureau have been encouraged through tax exempt accounts of up to £20,000. As tax officials are not given access to post office records, people can have several tax-exempt savings accounts simply by giving false names, with the result that the post office has come to have more accounts than the total Japanese population. The Bureau's 23,000 branches are now the most popular place for savings, and its approximately $1,000 billion in deposits make it the world's largest savings institution.

Credit restrictions have reinforced the savings policy – although many western countries have also operated credit controls and Japanese restrictions were largely lifted in the 1980s. More important, the strong Japanese savings ethic has also been bolstered by the almost total absence of the tax credits for interest payments on loans or for purchases of homes or company cars which are so common in the West.

So Japanese policy has been the mirror image of most western systems, exempting savings from tax to encourage thrift, but giving no tax benefits to consumption. By contrast, many western governments penalize savers with high taxes, while subsidizing purchases with tax breaks. This encourages domestic consumption, sucking in imports and pushing up inflation and interest rates. Combined with large government budget deficits, these policies have led to excess demand for capital for consumption, starving industry of investment funds, while exacerbating their plight with overvalued currencies induced by high interest rates – a recipe for industrial failure.

In contrast, since the war Japanese governments have pursued a consistent series of policies geared towards one primary, overriding objective – economic growth. Moderate taxation and low government spending, together with generally balanced budgets, have minimized the state's demands on capital and productive industry. The discouragement of excessive domestic consumption allied to support for savings has helped to provide a pool of finance which has boosted productive investment in the economy, as well as helping to restrain inflation, keeping interest rates low and the currency at a sensible value.

Japan's high savings levels have been a crucial element in its economic success. Savings have provided the funds which have allowed a nation with only just over 2 per cent of the world's population to account for 20 per cent of its investment – more than the United States and about the same level as the European Community, despite the populations of both the USA and EC being more than twice that of Japan. As a result, the Japanese economy has been strongly geared to production rather than consumption, permitting rapid, sustainable, non-inflationary growth.

Making its way quietly

History has allowed post-war Japanese governments to give their industry one final important advantage. For the loss of empire and international commitments has allowed Japan to place business firmly ahead of politics. So, in 1953, when Mussadeq tried to nationalize the Anglo-Iranian Oil Company, it was the Japanese who took advantage, buying oil cheaply from the Iranians. Nor was the war in Vietnam enough to interrupt trade between Japan and Vietnam – both North and South; the American bombing of Haiphong only slightly slowed shipments of Japanese goods to the North. During the 1973/4 oil crisis, Japan quickly adopted a pro-Arab stance, was reclassified as a 'friendly country' by the Arabs and soon received all the oil it wanted.

Closer to home, Japan's eagerness to maintain trading links with China has sometimes taken on a ridiculous aspect. In the 1960s, at the height of the Cultural Revolution, one condition of trade was that a quasi-official Japanese delegation should annually sign a communiqué condemning in highly coloured language the 'rise of Japanese militarism' and 'American imperialism' in a ritual analogous to the old kowtow ceremony.

Such attitudes should cause no surprise. The Japanese, devoid of natural resources, feel that economic survival comes before all else. Further, unburdened by empire and with its military might broken after the war, Japan anyway had no course but to make its way quietly in the world and concentrate its energies on economic recovery. So unlike Britain, France or the United States, Japan has been fortunate enough to run in the race of international competition carrying as little weight as possible and with few distractions to divert the country from the task of making steel, ships, cars and TVs better than anyone else.

Japan could neither bask in the type of complacency that afflicted its conquerors, nor afford to be inspired by the romantic delusions of grandeur that led some of them to attempt to build a 'New Jerusalem' in the form of a welfare state long before they could afford it.[19] Instead, while others dabbled, dreamed and erected the costly scaffolding of new Utopias, Japan's strictly managerial post-war governments primarily contributed to the country's economic success by concentrating almost single-mindedly on the mundane and unromantic objective of building a first-class economy.

Growth first

Recent criticisms of Japan have centred on the claim that close links between government and industry make Japan a 'producer-dominated' society, where the interests of state and business merge and bureaucrats collude with industrialists to form cartels at the expense of consumers and living standards in general.[20]

The problem with this thesis is not just that it ignores the degree to which western governments have also given in to special interests, such as industries lobbying for protection or subsidies at the expense of consumers. It also confuses two quite different things: being in the thrall of special interest groups, be they industries, trade unions or any other bodies, is one thing; running a government in such a way that economic growth is given priority is quite another.

For what really differentiates Japanese post-war government from its western rivals is the consistent way in which Japanese policy has been geared to sustainable economic growth. This was reinforced by a realization after the war of Japan's desperate position, which helped to free Japanese government from some of the constraints under which many western countries laboured.

So the Japanese system has been less the frequently portrayed close, conspiratorial public–private sector embrace, than government which has understood that industry and commerce, rather than politicians and bureaucrats, are the true engine of progress and wealth creation. By generally putting economic growth first, Japan's governments have helped their industry; and industry in turn has created a great deal of wealth for the Japanese people.

Some commentators point to the existence of cartels and price fixing in some Japanese industries to justify the thesis that government in Japan favours industry over consumers. But cartels are not unique to Japan. In 1990 the French government found 123 construction companies guilty of fixing prices and conspiring to carve up major public contracts. British cartels since the mid-1970s have involved glass manufacturers, concrete producers, roofing supplies companies, road material suppliers and steel bar manufacturers. Often, cartels in the West flourish under the protective blanket afforded by trade barriers such as anti-dumping duties, as has happened in the European Community on several occasions.

In some instances the Community itself sanctions cartels, such as the one set up to cover the steel industry in the late 1970s. The type of managed trade agreements increasingly favoured by the US government are also little more than officially condoned price-fixing arrangements. In fact, in most areas the Japanese domestic market is intensely competitive and, despite occasional bureaucratic moves to consolidate industries by merging competitors and sanctioning cartels – policies not unique to Japan – they have very rarely followed the European practice of creating single, monopolistic national champions in major industries.

Ants in tiny flats

Another commonly heard criticism is that the Japanese have paid a heavy price for their material success. There is much talk of pollution and people living in 'rabbit hutches'. Recently, the would-be populist French prime minister Edith Cresson commented in an American TV interview that the Japanese live like 'ants in those tiny flats'. She went on to declare: 'we cannot live like that, we want to live like human beings as we have always lived'.

Perhaps Mrs Cresson, who was raised by an English governess in a smart Parisian suburb, went to a private boarding school and married a wealthy Peugeot executive, was thinking of her own past and present generously sized residences in the grander *arrondissements* of Paris. But those Japanese who watched television reports of rioting in France's high-rise ghettos, and read accounts of the French social security system in chronic deficit and 3 million people unemployed, might have been excused a wry smile at her comments.

The fact that many Japanese live in small flats has less to do with their economic system than with the fact that Japan is only marginally larger than the British Isles, but has more than twice the population. Japan's 4,000 islands are also predominantly mountainous, so its 122 million people are largely crowded into the one-fifth of the country which is not.

Nonetheless, the average dwelling space for each Japanese – at 870 square feet – is not in fact much smaller than the average Frenchman's 920 square feet. Moreover, visitors who travel outside the central belt of Japan's main island, Honshu, which stretches from Tokyo to Osaka and houses 70 per cent of Japan's population, are often surprised at how lushly wooded much of Japan is and how relaxed and roomy many of the smaller towns are.

And although the breakneck economic growth of the late 1950s and 1960s brought tremendous environmental problems, causing children to collapse gasping for air during exercise sessions, and inducing cats fed on mercury-laden fish to jump into the sea, heavy spending on anti-pollution programmes since the early 1970s has significantly improved the situation. In fact, nowadays the Japanese have the toughest emission standards in the world and pollution in Japanese cities is no worse than in their western equivalents.

Nor has not living in the style to which Mrs Cresson has become accustomed prevented the Japanese from becoming the longest-lived nation in the world. According to the *British Medical Journal*, a Japanese boy born in 1990 can expect to live for 75.2 years and a girl until she is 80.9 – three years longer than their French equivalents.[21] Moreover, a United Nations agency ranking of 160 nations on the basis of a human development index which measures three basic indicators of human well-being (life expectancy, adult literacy and basic purchasing power) put Japan in first place – some way ahead of France.[22]

Notes

1 See *The Funding and Management of Education*, Institute of Economic Affairs Education Unit, London, 1987; and *Science Achievement in Seventeen Countries*, International Association for the Evaluation of Educational Achievement, Pergamon, Oxford, 1989.

2 J.W.Stigler and H.W.Stevenson, *Journal of Educational Psychology*, 1982; and H.J.Walberg, *Mathematics Productivity in Japan and Illinois*, 1985.

3 T.P.Rohlen, *Japan's High Schools*, University of California Press, 1983.

4 Richard Lynn, *Educational Achievement in Japan: Lessons for the West*, Macmillan/Social

Affairs Unit, London, 1988. This study shows that of the major western nations West Germany comes closest to Japan with 230 days of schooling a year.

5 Her Majesty's Inspectorate for Education, *Report on Japanese Education*, 1991.

6 Ibid.

7 Ibid.

8 *Relations Between the Community and Japan*, House of Lords Select Committee on the European Communities, 13th Report, June 1989.

9 Peter Wickens, *The Road to Nissan*, Macmillan, London, 1987.

10 *Financial Times*, 6 June 1990.

11 *New York Times*, 17 August 1990.

12 Kazuo Koike and Takenori Inoki (eds), *Skill Formation in Japan and South-East Asia*, University of Tokyo Press, 1991.

13 Source: UK Manpower Services Commission figures for 1985.

14 Ronald P. Dore and Mari Sako, *How the Japanese Have Learned to Work*, Routledge, London, 1989.

15 Gavin Laird, General Secretary of the Amalgamated Engineering Union, *Anglo-Japanese Economic Institute Special Report*, 1988.

16 Robert Guillain, *The Japanese Challenge*, Hamish Hamilton, London, 1970.

17 Source: World Health Organization figures for 1985.

18 Source: OECD.

19 See Correlli Barnett, *The Audit of War*, Macmillan, London, 1986, for a superb analysis of the failure of post-war British policy.

20 See Karel van Wolferen, *The Enigma of Japanese Power*, Macmillan, London, 1989.

21 Reported in the *Independent*, 7 August 1989.

22 United Nations Development Programme, *Human Development Report 1991*, Oxford University Press, Oxford.

12 The Bicycle Economy

The glory and the nemesis of Japanese business, the life's blood of our industrial engine, is good old-fashioned competition.

Akio Morita, joint-founder of Sony[1]

Not many people remember Tohatsu now. Yet in the early 1950s, with a 22 per cent market share, this company led the Japanese motorcycle industry, then rapidly growing at 40 per cent a year. Tohatsu's major rival at that time was a company called Honda, although Honda's high debt and Tohatsu's clear profitability placed Honda a clear second. Yet five short years later, Honda was to emerge the undisputed market leader with a 44 per cent market share, while Tohatsu's sales had plummeted to less than 4 per cent. In 1964, its funds exhausted and with bills unpaid, Tohatsu filed for bankruptcy. It was not the only casualty of the Japanese motorcycle market; of the fifty motorcycle manufacturers of the early 1950s, a mere four survived by 1970.

Honda triumphed by concentrating on expanding its market share, borrowing heavily to invest in production and pushing sales up by close to 66 per cent a year. As sales grew, increasing profits and volume allowed the company to reduce production costs and prices, so further boosting sales. Complacent Tohatsu, on the other hand, chose the conservative course of only trying to maintain market share – a fatal mistake in a rapidly growing market.

Collusion, or competition?

Western writers have often claimed that collusion, rather than relentless competition, is what typifies Japan's industry. Some have argued that the Japanese 'model' supersedes that based on open competition and free trade. One well-known writer on Japan, for example, asserts that Japanese firms take very few risks. 'They are ensconced', he says, 'in a protective environment that not only shields them from foreign competitors but also fosters forms of mutual protection. It is this basis that permits them to move simultaneously into foreign markets with rock-bottom prices.'[2] A former US trade negotiator further contends in his widely read book that in Japan 'reduction of risk by the government was the key to the whole game'.[3]

Disregard this illusion that the Japanese market is cozily carved up among Japanese big business in league with MITI bureaucrats. For what characterizes Japan's successful industries above all is the intensely competitive nature of their markets, epitomized by the enormous number of entrants into any new field which opens up. There were thirty-six Japanese camera manufacturers in 1950 and forty companies producing electronic calculators in 1960. The relentless, Darwinian competitive process of the Japanese market has honed these down to seven and four respectively – and those survivors have been sharpened by the pressure of incessant competition and hardened in the world's most difficult market.

The facsimile machine industry witnessed three different market leaders in three years; and there are still twenty-five significant audio equipment producers in Japan, along with nine car makers, fourteen photocopier manufacturers, thirty-four semiconductor makers, twenty sewing machine producers, eleven truck builders, six mainframe computer makers and no fewer than 112 machine tool producers.

Further evidence of the burning pace of Japan's domestic market lies in the high level of bankruptcies. Between 1980 and 1986 bankruptcies of companies each with debts of more than ¥10m (about £4.5 million) averaged more than 15,000 a year – a higher figure than for the United States, even though Japan's corporate population is 60 per cent smaller than America's. The Japanese call this the 'bicycle economy'. To stay on, the rider has to pedal forward; if he slows down, he topples and falls.

The latest manifestation of this competitive process has been in computers, where Japanese manufacturers are vying to pack even more features into smaller portable models for an ever lower price, resulting in the new generation of notebook computers – truly portable machines weighing under 3 kilograms and the size of an A4 sheet of paper.

Toshiba were first into the fray with their Dynabook model launched in 1989 for under £800; but by 1992 most of the rest of Japan's electronics industry had piled in, as well as several companies not normally associated with computers or electronics. As these companies leapfrog each other with new products and innovations, prices are tumbling and sales accelerating – only 200,000 notebooks were sold in 1989, but by 1992 the market was moving toward well over 1 million. Once again, the competitive pressures which led Japanese industry to produce world-beating radios, TVs and cars are at work.

Low price, high market share

The experience of Japan's companies in this intensely competitive environment has led them to a series of fundamental conclusions: first, market share is vital; second, the principal weapon with which to gain and hold market share is price; third, to ensure low costs, investment in production capacity must at least keep pace with – and preferably exceed – the market's growth; fourth, new products must be constantly introduced to continue the cycle of investment, cost reduction and market share gain; and fifth, exporting is one way to lower costs by increasing production runs and so boosting economies of scale.

The reactions of western businesses to the low-priced, quality products which are the result of such policies have at times been almost paranoid. Charges of 'predatory pricing', 'targeting markets until competitors have been bankrupted', 'kamikaze tactics' and, needless to say, 'dumping' are common.

Commentators, too, often fall into the trap of attributing Japanese industry's high-volume, low-cost products to unfair tactics. Even those pundits who accept the competitive nature of the most successful sectors of Japan's economy often argue that Japanese competition on the international scene is 'predatory' and needs to be restrained. The idea that competition from American and European companies is, by contrast, somehow benign is a strange one. It just happens that at the present time the Japanese are usually rather better competitors than their western rivals.

One writer recently cited the fact that Japan's seven video recorder manufacturers pushed up output between 1979 and 1986 from just over 2 million units to 33.8 million machines – five-sixths of which were exported – as an example of over-investment and 'dumping' which drove US producers out of the market, also severely threatening Europe's Philips and Grundig who were then producing only 700,000 units annually.[4]

This begs a number of questions. If the Japanese exported five-sixths of their production, how could they feasibly use profits from selling the remaining one-sixth – even in a supposedly protected home market – to subsidize the 'dumping' of such a high volume of exports? And why did Grundig and Philips – the latter a very substantial and well-financed company – produce only 700,000 recorders a year? Surely the truth is that the Japanese industry did what the Americans and Europeans were simply not prepared to do, namely they invested, geared up and took the risk of raising production, so lowering prices to the great advantage of consumers – although clearly not to the liking of their slow-footed western competitors.

Xerox strategist Lyndon Haddon succinctly illustrates the difference between Japanese and western corporations thus: 'The Europeans would be very happy with a three times mark up. Americans would try to figure out a way to make it four times. And the Japanese would cut the price in half and sell four times as much'.[5]

A potent symbol

In many Sony offices, a popular slogan is 'BMW', which stands for 'Beat Matsushita Whatever', epitomizing the intensely competitive environment which has moulded Japanese industries' attitudes in a number of important ways. First, because any basic advantages such as low labour costs or cheap capital are shared by rivals, Japanese companies have not been able to rely on such primary factors, but have rather been forced to seek competitive advantage by upgrading manufacturing technology, product variety and quality to outdo competitors.

Japanese car makers, for example, offer consumers more up-to-date models by changing their ranges on four-year cycles, compared to the eight-year-plus changeovers common with western manufacturers. By the time Ford's top-selling Escort model, launched in 1980, was replaced in 1990, Toyota's similarly sized Corolla and Honda's Civic had been through no fewer than three model changes.

Moreover, Japanese companies have been far more willing to satisfy market demands than many western producers. Take sports cars. Just as most European manufacturers were pulling out of a market they considered too small to be profitable, the Japanese were getting in. Early Japanese sports models already offered more car for less money – like the Honda N360 which caused a sensation during the 1967 Paris and London automobile shows, provoking what one English magazine called 'an anxious rage' in the hearts of European manufacturers.

Later, in the 1980s, Toyota's mid-engined MR2 gave enthusiasts a sophisticated, low-cost sports car of the kind that the western volume manufacturers had not made for years, while Mazda's low-cost MX-5 small sports car was a runaway success when it was launched in 1988. Consequently, not only did the Japanese succeed in selling far more sports cars and coupés than the Europeans had ever done, but by producing desirable cars they also managed to improve their perceived status. They are now even beginning to produce micro-sports cars, such as the Honda Beat, measuring only 130 by 55 inches, with an engine of just 660cc and costing a mere £6,000 in Japan. Needless to say, the other five microcar producers, led by Suzuki and Mazda, are all now feverishly preparing competitors.

Perhaps the four-wheel-drive market, that most potent symbol of male machismo, offers the best example of how the Japanese have often been hungrier than their western competitors. Land Rover, Jeep, Ford, General Motors and Chrysler dominated world 4×4 markets in the early 1970s. But American products subsequently became over-large, uneconomical and too geared to domestic needs to be competitive in export markets.

Land Rover's models, by contrast, were in great worldwide demand in the mid-1970s. But rather than sharply step up production to reduce costs and satisfy their customers, the company only marginally increased volumes with the result that its vehicles were available only after a twelve-month wait – or for a huge premium.

This, of course, provided precisely the opening which the Japanese wanted. Delighted, they swooped in on the neglected customers with a new class of mid-range 4×4 using standard car and truck components to lower costs. These vehicles satisfied those Americans who did not want huge, thirsty 4×4s; Europeans who did not care to wait for high-priced British vehicles; and buyers in developing countries who could not afford either, with the result that 'Land Cruiser' has largely replaced 'Jeep' or 'Land Rover' as the generic name for 4×4s in many parts of the world.

More than that, the Japanese discovered new markets for four-wheel drive which western manufacturers never thought existed. Subaru led the way by adding four-wheel drive to ordinary family cars, producing a vehicle which is as much at home in the supermarket car park as churning through axle-deep mud, while Daihatsu and Suzuki successfully mass-marketed very small, low-cost, utility four-wheel drives.

And whereas by 1980 virtually every Japanese car manufacturer was in the 4 × 4 market, the only serious new western entrant was Daimler Benz of West Germany, which went into production with a very highly engineered 4 × 4 called the Gelendawagen in 1978, but produced it in such tiny volumes that it was far too costly for most buyers. As a result, by 1990 Japanese producers accounted for three-quarters of the 250,000 4 × 4s sold annually in Europe.

Meanwhile, it had taken Land Rover until the mid-1980s finally to double capacity for its top-end Range Rover model to about 25,000 units a year; and it was not until 1987 that it began selling its luxury 4 × 4 in the American market – seventeen years after the vehicle's launch. Land Rover also barely altered the basic Land Rover utility model from its 1948 launch until 1985; and when, in 1989, Land Rover finally came up with a lower-cost, intermediate 4 × 4 vehicle to compete with the Japanese, the company again made the error of introducing it at production volumes which were far too low, causing waiting lists and delaying export launches. The Japanese have suffered from no such inhibitions, eagerly seizing market opportunities left to them by sleepier western companies.

Attention to detail

Associated with this responsiveness to the requirements of customers is an almost obsessive attention to detail. Concealed among the paddy fields near Shibetsu, on Japan's northern island of Hokkaido, there is a Toyota proving ground which they call 'Little Europe'. Covering more than 1,000 acres and costing well over £100 million, it contains exact replicas of every type of road on which Toyota cars are driven, including American-style freeways, autobahns and poorly paved minor roads – all painstakingly reproduced by photographing, measuring and analysing the surface materials of the originals.

It was here that Toyota managed to make its 4-litre V8 Lexus luxury saloon handle so uncannily like a European thoroughbred car. When noises were tracked down during the six-year, $500 million development programme, rather than merely stifling them with sound-deadening materials, Toyota designed them out.

To ensure that the quality of the resulting product is of an even higher standard than Mercedes, Jaguar or BMW, white-gloved inspectors feel every Lexus car all over for the smallest imperfection as it rolls off the assembly track at the Tahara factory, near Nagoya. Every Lexus 32-

valve V8 engine is also run on a test bench while a robot microphone scans the unit, locating and analysing every source of noise to ensure each car is as perfect as possible.

In developing the car, Toyota design teams even spent three months in the affluent Laguna Beach area of southern California studying the market and their customers' needs. Honda went one better. Its R & D engineers attended Hells Angels' bike rallies and found that American riders were adding fairings and saddle bags to their machines and using them as long-distance tourers rather than as street 'superbikes'. So Honda's engineers redesigned their powerful Gold Wing model into a luxury touring machine to suit the market.[6] This exhaustive regard for detail, increasingly seen in the design of Japanese products, is one of Japanese industry's greatest but least quantifiable skills.

According to Vaughan Beals, chairman of Harley-Davidson, the last remaining American motorcycle manufacturer which was almost bankrupted by Japanese competition in the mid-1980s: 'We were being wiped out by the Japanese because they were better managers. It wasn't robotics, or culture, or morning callisthenics and company songs – it was professional managers who understood their business and paid attention to detail.'[7]

Diversify and grow

Another effect of the withering competition of the Japanese market is the tendency for Japanese companies to diversify in order to find new markets and so gain competitive advantage. NEC, for example, has managed to move into product areas related to its original telecommunications base, such as computers, fax machines and consumer electronics. Canon is another Japanese company whose ability to broaden into new product areas has been unmatched by any western company. Still the world's leading manufacturer of quality 35mm SLR cameras, in just two decades Canon has also advanced into calculators, photocopiers, electronic typewriters, personal computers, fax machines and computer printers.

Contrast the progress of Canon and NEC with their western equivalents. In the 1960s and 1970s the West boasted a large number of diversified electronics and electrical engineering companies such as General Electric in the United States and Siemens in Germany. At that time these firms dwarfed their Japanese rivals. But most of them have long since been overtaken by Japanese competitors, while none has managed to venture successfully into the range of product areas which Canon and NEC have penetrated.

Even Japan's steel companies have got in on the act. Steadily falling steel output has prompted Nippon Steel, the world's largest steel maker, to move into computer software and, more recently, notebook computers. Kawasaki Steel and Kobe Steel are both now established semiconductor producers, while NKK has developed advanced computer-aided design technology.

Vertical diversification has also been a feature of large Japanese electronics companies, which gain competitive advantage by producing many of their most sophisticated components in-house, ensuring rapid access to new developments. Seiko, for example, only managed to turn the electronic, digital watch into a saleable proposition by developing and manufacturing key parts itself. The company's prototype in 1958 was a huge clock, the size of a freight locomotive, using large numbers of bulky vacuum tubes. Two years later, they had produced a crystal-based electronic watch compact enough to be held in the palm of the hand.

But in order to be a success the device had to be small enough to be used as a wristwatch. This involved three separate technical breakthroughs – engineering a tiny motor, developing a highly integrated circuit and producing a small crystal device. By 1969 Seiko had developed the motor and the crystal and proudly announced its new electronic wristwatch to the world for a price of around $2,000. A year later, the company's top management made the decision to go into full-scale production. But there was still one final problem to be solved – how to obtain small enough integrated circuits for successful mass production. Unable to buy them from outside, Seiko again took the decision to produce the chips themselves, forming a research team to study integrated circuit technology.

Finally in 1971, thirteen years after the locomotive-sized crystal clock had been produced, Seiko succeeded in mass-producing small, low-cost liquid crystal wristwatches. At that time, Japanese watch manufacturing was only one third of Swiss production, but a decade later the Swiss had been decisively overtaken.

This type of vertical integration, involving producing components in-house, is very much a feature of Japan's high-tech industries. For although it is often better to leave component production to competing specialist firms which can achieve the economies of scale not always available with in-house manufacture, producing certain types of leading-edge components in-house is crucial in a rapidly moving field like electronics.

Sony, for example, could never have become the undisputed leader in the camcorder market with its TR-55 in 1989 – a product which, at just 7 inches long, marked a significant size breakthrough – without the ability to produce key components in-house. Toshiba's success with its downsized T1000 Dyna Book notebook computer was also achieved in part due to the company's technology which allowed it to 'super-integrate' semi-customized chips, so that only one chip was required to control both the keyboard and the input.

Matsushita also produces a very high proportion of its components in-house, but ensures that competitive pressure is maintained by never guaranteeing that it will buy parts from its subsidiaries, while achieving economies of scale by allowing in-house components units to sell outside the company.

Keiretsu and *Zaibatsu*

Many of Japan's leading companies are also members of large families of companies, such as the Mitsubishi group. Foreign observers have seen these huge Japanese conglomerates as a sinister new manifestation of the pre-war *zaibatsu* industrial groups which then dominated Japan's economy. Often closely linked to powerful *sogoshosha* trading houses, these corporate families are considered by some to be the epitome of the Japanese conspiracy to dominate world markets.

But while it is certainly true that old-style industrial groups like Mitsubishi and Sumitomo still wield great power within Japan, many companies within the traditional groups are mainly in slow-moving or declining industries. This is partly due to the fact that, historically, the groups were major players in the older raw material processing and heavy industries. It is also worth considering whether it actually helps the Japanese economy when group members bail each other out, as often happens, leaving rafts of weak, medium-sized manufacturers in industries such as chemicals, where Japan is a poor competitor.

Moreover, many companies which epitomize the growth and success of Japan's post-war economy are not group members at all. Hitachi, Sharp, Matsushita and Sony in electronics; Fuji, Canon and Ricoh in cameras, photocopiers and office automation; Minebea in components; Seiko in watches and consumer products; Kubota in farm equipment; and Toyota, Honda, Hino and Suzuki in vehicles are all highly independent companies with relatively recent origins which have succeeded on their own terms in the fastest-growing and highest-technology sectors of the market.

Soichiro Honda was, perhaps, the classic example of industrial success outside of the charmed circle. Born in 1905, the son of a village blacksmith, Honda bought 500 war surplus engines after the war which he attached to bicycles to make a basic form of motorbike. The bikes were such a success that he soon moved into large-scale manufacture and began exporting in 1957. By the late 1960s Honda not only dominated the Japanese market, but had driven the British manufacturers out of world markets and was exporting a million motorbikes a year.

From there, Honda has moved into cars, microvans, generators and lawn mowers. Far from being squeezed out of Japan's economy by huge combines, controlled by sinister businessmen in league with grasping politicians and shadowy bureaucrats, Honda's success epitomizes the competitive and entrepreneurial nature of Japan's post-war economic achievement.

Another associated criticism of Japanese industrial practices relates to the *keiretsu* or 'enterprise group' system such as Toyota's kyohokai, a grouping of 300 car component manufacturers most of which do almost all of their business with the automobile giant. Toyota owns stakes in many of the kyohokai suppliers and buys the bulk of its parts from them; similar groups are run by other major companies.

American automobile manufacturers in particular deploy the *keiretsu* in their special pleading for trade restraints against the Japanese, arguing that the *keiretsu* system is fundamentally anti-competitive and gives Japanese car makers unfair advantages. This is a strange argument because, if Japanese car producers were simply limiting their purchases of components to a handful of favoured suppliers, they would, in effect, be restricting their own options and so making themselves less rather than more competitive – surely a cause for rejoicing among their American competitors.

The truth is, however, a little more complex than that. *Keiretsu* have been developed as a compromise between the competitive benefits, low costs and management time-saving advantages of totally contracting out component manufacture; and the close supervision and quality control which can be maintained by in-house manufacture. The system also fits in well with Toyota's tight, 'just-in-time' parts delivery schedules.

As with the electronics companies, Toyota limits the system to certain types of component, making most of the more sophisticated parts and assemblies itself. Enterprise group companies are used for middle-range parts such as crankshafts, castings and engine components, while untied producers supply plastic mouldings and other low-tech parts.

John McMillan, an economist pioneering the study of incentives in industry who has researched the *keiretsu* intensively, confirms that the enterprise group system has little to do with Japanese culture or collusive behaviour, as is often alleged. Rather, he says, clear economic logic underlies the long-term links between procuring and supplying firms. Pointing out that American industry is now slowly moving in the same direction, he concludes that with the *keiretsu* 'Japanese industry can be understood as having attained, at the end point of an evolutionary process, a complex system of incentives, to which firms respond rationally.'

Typically, Japanese automotive component suppliers work with the car manufacturers to develop parts for new models from the earliest stages, sharing costs and ensuring that they are suited to existing machinery. Western car makers only involve parts suppliers after model planning is completed; parts are rarely designed to suit production machinery and the car makers shoulder all of the costs. Individual vendors usually then bid for the work, and contracts often go to the lowest bidder. Japanese car makers, by contrast, set price 'goals' which they expect to be adhered to, but other factors are deemed more important.

Unlike their western counterparts, the Japanese also send engineers to monitor and refine the component's manufacturing process, resulting in lower inspection costs at the assembly plant and fewer defects. Finally, suppliers follow lean production techniques and deliver on a just-in-time basis up to sixteen times a day, allowing manufacturers to stock only small inventories.

The *keiretsu* system facilitates the more complex organizational tasks which make such a system possible; and although most European and American car makers now also aspire to similar goals and are working hard on just-in-time delivery, they still hold significantly higher component stocks than their Japanese counterparts.

So although these networks of tied suppliers are often cited as a 'structural impediment' by western manufacturers who claim that they prevent the sale of foreign parts to Japanese car makers, they do contain industrial logic.

Partly or wholly owned suppliers are also not unique to Japanese industry. The Italian car maker Fiat, for example, holds a majority stake in Magneti Marelli, one of Europe's largest automotive component suppliers – although Fiat does not utilize its relationships with such suppliers as effectively as its Japanese rivals.

More to the point, most American and European car manufacturers still favour in-house production – or manufacturing by wholly owned subsidiaries – for the bulk of their parts. General Motors sources 75 per cent of its parts internally – a far higher proportion than its Japanese competitors. GM, for example, buys a very large part of its electronic parts from wholly owned AC Delco, while its Saginaw subsidiary, which manufactures steering systems, makes 80 per cent of its sales to GM. Ford also makes its own car radios.

This in-house strategy may lack the flexibility or residual competitive discipline of the *keiretsu* system, but it is no less an obstacle for Japanese and other components suppliers trying to sell parts to GM or Ford.

Variety, design and innovation

Although the competitive strength of Japanese companies has, since the late 1950s, been based on high-volume production of quality mass consumer goods, flexible manufacturing systems are rapidly altering production economics. As a result, many Japanese manufacturers are now eagerly grasping the opportunity of gaining competitive advantage by using new manufacturing technology to offer expanded model variety at a low cost, increasingly making product innovation and state-of-the-art features the basis of their competitive capabilities.

Canon began the process with its cameras as far back as 1960. Originally operated by gearwheel mechanisms, the product was redesigned into a flexible assembly of electronic devices. A major upgrade in the form of the electronic eye was introduced in 1960, following which range finders, focal-plane shutters, single lens reflex systems and flashes were all steadily fitted to ordinary, low-priced cameras, culminating in 1980 when Canon developed an automatic focusing camera which was an immediate hit.

Recently, Nissan has produced a series of original speciality vehicles in volumes as low as 50,000. Japan's second largest car company does this to service niche markets and can do so because its advanced production enables it to produce profitably at such low volumes. It also allows Nissan designers more freedom to express themselves in models which could never be best sellers.

As a result, Japanese products are increasingly becoming the design leaders in their fields. Japanese volume cars, for example, have taken on an attractive, non-derivative design coherence of their own, far from the garish, mid-Atlantic look of the Japanese cars of the 1970s, with their acres of mock-stitched plastic interiors.

There has been a tendency to see the stark simplicity and beauty of some of the better examples of Japanese design as being the product of some kind of deeply inbred Zen minimalism. But the fact that Japanese products have by no means always been paragons of good design, and have sold rather on price than quality, should indicate that these cultural factors are at best a minor influence.

Although it may in part be true that the Japanese design sense is conditioned by the country's problem of limited space, what really lies behind the recent massive improvement is the great effort that Japanese companies are now putting into design as they upgrade their products and move into the more sophisticated areas of the market. More and more, Japanese consumer product companies see design as a major strategic weapon, and their design departments are increasingly being given equal status to other departments. In many western companies, by contrast, design is still often an afterthought, rather than something that is engineered into the product.

According to Art Blakeslee, an American designer who worked for Chrysler before joining Peugeot and now heads Citroën's styling studio, Japanese design students also get broader training than their western counterparts. 'Many of their designers doing courses are already qualified engineers,' Blakeslee claims, 'and then they may go on to work as salesmen at car dealerships. By the time they begin work as designers, they know so much more about the total car-producing process. Too many European-trained designers know how to draw pretty pictures – but that's about it.'[8]

In most Japanese corporations, moreover, all functions from design and development through to production and marketing are now involved right through the product cycle, allowing continuous feedback, a process facilitated by the frequent rotation of staff between disciplines. At computer maker Fujitsu, for example, half of the central laboratory researchers move to other parts of the company every ten years.

Design also has a wider function than simply making a product look good. According to Takeomi Nagafuchi, general manager in charge of quality control at the camera and office technology giant Ricoh: '70 per cent of quality control is determined at the product design stage.'[9] Japanese manufacturers design quality and ease of production into their products to ensure quality on the production line.

Far from costing extra, this built-in quality actually helps to reduce

Japanese industry's costs. In a comparative study of American and Japanese air conditioner manufacturers, Harvard Business School professor David Garvin found that the highest-quality American manufacturer spent three times as much money on warranty claims as the average Japanese manufacturer – and the lowest-quality American supplier spent almost nine times as much. The extra money which the Japanese spent on designing higher quality into their production came to only half what the Americans spent on repairing defective units.[10]

Long-termism

Each year, Japanese industry spends nearly £7,000 in fixed capital investment per employee – twice as much as in France or Germany and nearly three times as much as in Britain. The ability of Japanese industry to invest such huge sums in improvements to their factories and production equipment, with the aim of gaining long-term market share, has been contrasted with the pursuit of short-term profits which is said to typify many western corporations.

It is frequently asserted that the Japanese companies' use of debt rather than equity finance facilitates such 'long-termism'. Since equity stock accounts for only 30 per cent of the average Japanese company's capital needs, the argument runs, they are therefore under less pressure to show a profit and a return to shareholders each year, and are also less in danger of takeover by predators.

The banks which account for the ownership or debt which make up most of Japanese industry's capital requirements are, the argument goes on, more prone to take risks and more interested in the company's long-range growth. This is in contrast to the situation in the United States and Britain in particular, where stockholders – especially financial institutions and pension funds – account for around half of the average large corporation's capital and are always ready to sell out to the highest bidder.

As with most widely held pieces of received wisdom, there is some truth and a fair amount of exaggeration in this view. There is certainly evidence to support the belief that the Japanese banks, with their close relations with industry, and the Japanese financial system in general, have played a major part in Japan's economic success. It is also undeniable that Japanese companies have used debt aggressively in order to finance their breakneck growth. According to one study, in the late 1970s and early 1980s the average Japanese company could sustain a growth rate nearly 25 per cent higher than its American counterpart because of its greater use of debt finance.[11]

There is also some justice in the assertion that the tendency for Japanese companies to raise money less through tradable equity than through debt finance has helped to secure them from the unwanted attentions of hostile bidders – especially as even those Japanese companies which have sold equity have often guarded their positions by selling chunks of their shares to friendly corporations, which often reciprocate to form interlocking 'cross-holdings'.

Why, then, have western companies not gone down the same route and borrowed to finance growth rather than selling equity? There are several reasons. First, selling freely tradable equity, with full voting rights, on the open market is usually a cheaper way to raise capital than limiting equity sales to a small number of other companies, or issuing stock with restricted voting rights to safeguard against takeover. Industrialists who raise finance through share offerings must realize that they are steadily relinquishing total control over their companies, but obviously feel that it is worth trading some freedom of manoeuvre in return for the low costs of raising such equity capital.

Second, one of the benefits of equity finance is that, while it does not allow for as fast growth as loan finance, it is also far less risky – dividends to shareholders can be cut during bad times, but the interest on loans has to be paid, as well as which the debt is redeemable when the term expires. So while Japanese companies' higher exposure to loans helps them to sustain rapid growth during good times, it also creates problems during downturns, as evidenced by Japan's very high bankruptcy rate. Third, one of the major reasons why share flotations have been so popular among the western business community is that going public is one of the fastest routes to personal wealth. Directors and managers who own part of the company make huge gains – and those profits are all the greater if they offer attractive shares with as few limitations as possible. Directors of companies where these choices have been made can hardly complain if, as a result of freely selling chunks of their business, it becomes a takeover target.

The cost of money

These are among the reasons why debt finance or restricted equity options have been eschewed by many – although by no means all – western companies. But a further argument deployed by those who feel that Japanese industry benefits from unfair advantages is that it has gained from artificially low interest rates on its debt – in other words, the cost of capital is lower in Japan.

It is certainly true that the monetary policy pursued for most of the post-war period by successive Japanese governments has been geared to keeping both inflation and interest rates at low levels, a policy reinforced by the limits placed on domestic consumption and incentives for savings. It has been open, of course, for western governments to pursue similar policies, but for the most part they have been subject to different political imperatives which have led to greater priority being given to increasing domestic consumption to keep voters happy. In many cases governments have, for ideological reasons, also penalized savers through high taxation, leading to a shortage of available capital and hence higher interest rates.

In short, Japan's relatively low interest rates and high availability of capital for industry derive from legitimate economic policy decisions – policies which western governments would do well to emulate. Nor can the choice made by many Japanese corporations to use debt finance or to sell restricted shares really be said to equate to the unfair advantages or illicit obstacles to takeovers so often claimed by westerners. Moreover, while the predominance of debt finance and other factors have made corporate takeovers less common in Japan than in Britain or the United States, takeovers are now becoming far more usual in Japan and the number is accelerating.

Anyway, hindering takeovers, by legitimate means or otherwise, is not a uniquely Japanese trait. Many western corporations have also protected themselves from takeovers by issuing non-voting shares, or relying heavily on debt financing. In Italy, only seven out of over 200 leading listed companies have the majority of their shares in public hands.[12] No hostile takeover has yet succeeded in the Netherlands owing to a network of restrictions, including limited voting rights for shareholders, priority shares and special powers enjoyed by sitting management.

The secretive Swiss corporate culture is also known for its restrictions, particularly on foreign shareholdings. Yet it is interesting that a vigorous debate is resulting in increasing pressure for change, owing to what a report by the leading Swiss bank Julius Baer described as a vicious circle of slack demand for Swiss shares, resulting in low prices which provoke takeover bids calling for yet more defensive measures. Lower share prices mean higher financing costs which inhibit growth, resulting again in low stock market valuations.[13]

State intervention to block hostile overseas bids is also far from uncommon in the West. In the late 1960s the British government blocked a Swedish takeover of the leading UK bearings producer, and in 1986 it prevented General Motors from buying Land Rover and Leyland Trucks. The British government also holds 'golden shares' in several companies precisely for the purpose of blocking unwelcome – which effectively means foreign – bids. When in 1988 Ford looked likely to take over troubled Italian sports saloon manufacturer Alfa Romeo, the Italian government stepped in and ensured that their national champion car maker, Fiat, pipped the American multinational to clinch the deal. And in 1984 the West German government was partly responsible for preventing the British electronics company GEC from taking over the ailing German company AEG Telefunken.

Nor has the United States been innocent of such tactics. When, in 1987, Fujitsu wanted to take over semiconductor pioneer Fairchild Semiconductor, it was prevented from doing so by the Pentagon, which claimed that the California-based chipmaker was of vital strategic importance – even though it had been owned by a French company since 1979.

There is one further point. A well-managed company which optimizes its business opportunities should be a very difficult target for predators, who, after all, are going to find it tough to service the finance raised to purchase the company if they cannot enhance that company's performance.

Indeed, despite the bad press often accorded to acquisitive companies like the Anglo-American giant Hanson Industries, the fact is that they often do industry as a whole a great service by restructuring badly managed companies and getting the best out of them. And if they in the process make money by offloading some businesses which they bought at a discount, does not at least some of the responsibility lie with the old management that allowed itself to get into that position? The very threat of buy-outs and takeovers should, therefore, be an excellent source of motivation for management to become more efficient.

So for all of their disadvantages, hostile takeovers remain an important link in the chain of managerial accountability, and some of the prime targets for hostile bids have been companies whose own management and performance have left something to be desired. To argue the same case from another angle, the Dutch electronics giant Philips has been sheltered from the consequences of its poor performance and hostile takeovers by a variety of elaborate devices, largely immunizing the company from short-term pressures and interference from its shareholders, whom the company has been able to treat with lordly disdain. Nonetheless, by almost every measure, the company, which has an £18 billion a year turnover, has performed far worse than its main Japanese rivals, with sales per employee at only one-seventh those of Matsushita and a pre-tax profit margin of just over 2 per cent, compared to the Japanese company's 10 per cent. These shortcomings slashed operating profits and led to an urgent boardroom reshuffle in the spring of 1990. Might not the stolid Dutch company have performed better if its management had been placed under more pressure?

The inflexibility caused by the relative lack of takeovers has also been a two-edged sword in Japan and has resulted in severe disadvantages for some Japanese industries. It would make good economic sense, for example, if several of the fertilizer companies within the Mitsubishi group were to merge. But despite difficult trading conditions in that sector, they have been unable to do so.

Money working harder

Finally, it is far from true that western industry has invariably been short of capital. On the contrary, many large western corporations have had huge sums at their disposal – between 1982 and 1990 General Motors spent a massive $70 billion, but has still lost ground to Japanese competitors. When, for example, the American car-making giant decided to put $3 billion into a new, state-of-the-art plant for its import-busting Saturn subcompact, the company found that much of the technology it had hoped to use was unworkable and the car took far longer than anticipated to develop.

Honda, Nissan, Toyota and Mazda now take less than a year to move from a basic clay model to a working prototype, and only another two years before the first production model rolls off the line. The Saturn, by contrast, was only finally launched after eight long years of development. And the Japanese car producers are more flexible. While the Big Three American car makers have the luxury of sixty-two plants, most of which cannot build more than 250,000 cars a year and only one of which can build more than two models on the same line, Honda requires only two factories to churn out more than a million cars – and it can assemble up to eight models on the same line.[14]

All of which illustrates that pumping huge amounts of money into capital investment is not, of itself, enough to guarantee success. The Japanese simply manage to make their capital work harder. For it is not low-cost capital, but capital expenditure plus effective organization and management which has made much of Japan's industry so awesomely efficient.

Notes

1 Akio Morita, *Made in Japan*, Collins, London 1987.

2 Karel van Wolferen, *The Enigma of Japanese Power*, Macmillan, London, 1989.

3 Clyde Prestowitz, *Trading Places: How We Allowed Japan to Take the Lead*, Basic Books, New York, 1988.

4 See van Wolferen, op. cit.

5 Quoted in Gary Jacobson and John Hillkirk, *Xerox: American Samurai*, Macmillan, New York, 1986.

6 *The Economist*, 15 April 1989.

7 Quoted in *Fortune*, 25 September 1989.

8 Quoted in *Car*, April 1991.

9 Jacobson and Hillkirk, op. cit.

10 Quoted in Robert Christopher, *Second to None: American Companies in Japan*, Tuttle, Tokyo, 1987.

11 James Abegglen and George Stalk, *Kaisha, the Japanese Corporation*, Basic Books, New York, 1985.

12 *Financial Times*, February 1990.

13 *Financial Times*, 14 November 1991.

14 *Car*, March 1990.

13 No New Fish

Although Japanese success in recent years has been based on adaptation of Western, mainly American, technology, and on the capacity to commercialize it more rapidly than its competitors, it would be wrong to conclude from this that the Japanese are mere imitators ... it may be only those who try continually to reinvent the wheel that will lose out in the innovative race.

Professor Harvey Brooks of Harvard University, in reply to a question by the US House of Representatives Committee on Science, Research and Technology as to whether the USA was losing the technological race[1]

Sun Tzu, the fifth-century BC Chinese military philosopher and author of *The Art of War*, urged army commanders: 'Regard your soldiers as your children, and they will follow you into the deepest valleys; look on them as your own beloved sons, and they will stand by you even unto death.'

Twenty-five centuries later, Akio Morita of Sony, one of the grand old men of Japanese industry, summed up what he called the 'shared fate' attitude prevalent in Japanese industry: 'What we in industry learned in dealing with people', he wrote, 'is that people do not work just for money and that if you are trying to motivate, money is not the most effective tool. To motivate people, you must bring them into the family and treat them like respected members of it. Granted, in our one-race nation this might be easier to do than elsewhere, but it is still possible if you have an educated population.'[2]

From strife to enterprise unions

Motivating employees involves establishing relative equality between different levels of workers. Plant managers in Japan wear basically the same uniform as newly hired workers and all use the same canteen and washing facilities. The method of wage payment and bonus schemes are also similar. There is, admittedly, another side. Despite the identical basic workwear worn in many Japanese factories, rank is nonetheless indicated by different cap markings, and it is not uncommon for Japanese managers to have their own reserved car parking spaces, while even in single status canteens the managers usually sit together. Generally, however, Japanese companies manage to inculcate a sense of togetherness which is frequently lacking in Western industry.

There has been a temptation for westerners to view Japan's good labour relations as a peculiarly Japanese phenomenon, implanted by Confucianism and the traditional group ethos. Yet after the war, when the occupation forces released many left-wingers and union leaders from gaol in an attempt to foster democratic ideas, thousands of unions sprang up. Early in 1947, 300,000 workers gathered in a sea of red flags and placards in front of the Imperial Palace in Tokyo to declare a general strike which was only called off after being outlawed by the American military.

Japanese industry remained beset by labour problems for many years, and for some time it looked likely that Japan would become less an economic superpower than a lame duck. In 1950, for example, assailed by high inflation and a market downturn, Toyota suffered from severe labour strife and had to be bailed out by the banks. Sony and Nissan are other well-known Japanese names to have experienced industrial unrest in the 1950s.

One answer to the problem was the establishment of in-house enterprise unions, organized along company, rather than industry, lines. These had a number of advantages, including the fact that the union structure posed no demarcation barriers to the movement of workers from one job to another. In addition, the enterprise union system means that Japanese corporations deal with a single negotiating unit.

Crucial to the success of the whole structure is the mobility between enterprise union personnel and company management. One survey showed that three-quarters of 313 major companies had at least one executive director who had been high up in the company's union, while more than 50 per cent of full time officials in the Nissan company union are also foremen.[3] Kenichi Yamamoto, president of Mazda, was actually the leader of the company union. As a result, Japanese industry in general, although not free from labour problems, has for long had an enviably low strike record and minimal absenteeism. The annual Japanese wage round, the *Shunto*, is now a largely ceremonial affair.

But ensuring amicable labour relations is only part of the Japanese industrial system. Original ideas, inventions and discoveries emanating from those actually carrying out assembly work can lead to dramatic improvements in the operation of the company. Workers in Japan are seen not merely as providers of labour, but rather as people who, through their training and education, can give additional value beyond their hourly wage. As a result Japanese employees are typically closely involved in company suggestion schemes which often play only a token role in western companies.

The role of motivated and engaged employees is particularly crucial in quality circles (QCs) – self-managed, small groups of workers who initiate improvements within their own work area. Usually consisting of five to ten people with a group leader, the emphasis is on individual worker responsibility for the quality of the goods and on dealing with production and safety problems. Often the improvements are small, but incrementally and over large volumes they add up to a great deal. A Canon photocopier plant QC consisting of women who drive in 8,000 screws a day, for example, suggested boosting efficiency by rearranging the assembly line so screws went in vertically, not horizontally.[4]

But the key point is that there was nothing inevitable about the Japanese system. Nor is it primarily a cultural legacy or due to some semi-mystical group loyalty inherent in the Japanese race. Rather, Japanese employers foster commitment by engaging workers' loyalty as well as giving them a sense of belonging and pride in what they do. The system largely grew up after the war, following a period of severe labour problems, when, galvanized by the shock of defeat, Japanese management began to accept that loyalty had to be worked at and earned, while employees came to the sophisticated realization that their fate and that of their companies was much the same.

Even the more peculiarly Japanese practice of promotion only by seniority was largely a post-war development, designed to retain skilled workers; it was far from universally adopted and is steadily being abandoned in response to social change. More emphasis is now being placed on the need to encourage individualism and creativity, with the result that promotion by merit is increasing. Nissan, for example, has recently moved away from the seniority system, which was seen to be partly responsible for the car company's poor record of innovation and inferior performance relative to Toyota in the 1980s. The lifetime employment system, also to a significant degree a post-war phenomenon restricted to a limited number of companies, is likewise under pressure from job-hopping young employees less willing than their fathers to devote whole careers to a single organization.

Nothing new

In July 1950, a little known American statistician called Dr W. Edwards Demming was invited as a guest of the allied occupation forces in Japan to speak at the Industry Club of Japan on the use of statistics in quality control. At that time Japanese products were not noted for their superiority and it seemed unlikely that Dr Demming, whose views were largely ignored in his home country, would make much difference.

Now each year Japanese industry honours Dr Demming by competing fiercely for the annual Demming Award, which goes to the company considered to have made the greatest improvement in quality. Virtually all major Japanese companies have long since implemented Dr Demming's method of using statistical analysis to monitor quality control and Japanese products are renowned the world over for their excellence.

Toyota's now famous just-in-time parts delivery system, which minimizes stock levels and associated costs, was adapted from the ideas of Dr Goldratt, an Israeli consultant. Other Japanese management practices, such as going for high-volume production and adding sophisticated features to mass market products, have similarly been foreshadowed by advanced western thinkers such as General Motor's pre-war chief, Alfred Sloan.

Yet the misconception that Japan's management success, like its labour relations, is based on a unique, non-transferable cultural background is still common. Even that most Japanese of industrial institutions, the company song, was foreshadowed before the war by several American corporations. IBM, for example, had a company song book which included such Japanese-style choruses as:

> EVER ONWARD – EVER ONWARD!
> That's the spirit that has brought us fame!
> We're big, but bigger we will be.
> We can't fail for all can see
> That to serve humanity has been our aim!
> Our products are known in every zone.

> Our reputation sparkles like a gem!
> We've fought our way through – and new
> Fields we're sure to conquer too
> For the EVER ONWARD IBM.

In fact, most of the characteristics of Japanese management style were formed after the Second World War, largely as a result of picking the best business practices and theories from the United States or Europe. As a foreign visitor to a Japanese business was once told: 'There was no new fish, but the method of cooking was better.'

The ideas of Dr Demming and Dr Goldratt, together with the western technology so often utilized by Japanese industry, were, of course, available to all. What made the difference was the ability to assimilate, exploit and improve on those ideas which has made the Japanese the winners that they are.

This capacity to adapt and assimilate technology is frequently dismissed as 'copying' or 'aping' western ideas. Yet the process is, to a large extent, part of the normal progression of industrial rise and fall. Successfully developing economies tend to begin by simply copying imported technology, before going on to improve it, then to innovate before the cycle ends with increasing complacency and consequent economic decline.

As late as the sixteenth century, for example, when Chinese technology was still superior to that of Europe in many areas, the Dutch learned porcelain production techniques from China. The British, in turn, borrowed these techniques from the Dutch. During a later phase of industrial development, the British themselves became more innovative, but were beginning to lose the skills and attitudes necessary for successful production.

At the Great Exhibition of 1851 British industrialists strolling around the Crystal Palace in London were horrified at the quality of the latest American guns, and claimed that the pernicious former colonials were unfairly using British ideas to produce weapons with greater precision than the British themselves. Later British complaints related to American exploitation of British inventions such as artificial fibres, radar, penicillin, jet engines, carbon fibre and many more.

When the French sociologist Alexis de Tocqueville visited the United States in the last century, he found the Americans too preoccupied with making money to be capable of innovative and original thought. During the early period of American industrial development, American Nobel prize winners were scarce, US universities were not noted for their original research and the United States was frequently dubbed a 'copycat' economy. Today it is Japan that wins few Nobel prizes and, likewise, is often derided for getting a 'free ride' from the research of others. But Japan is simply showing the same flair for creative adaptation that the United States did in an earlier era.

Catching up

Although it is a characteristic of successfully advancing economies to borrow technology from more developed nations, it is true that the Japanese are peculiarly well suited to this process. This is due not just to education and an economy geared to production, but also to a priceless cultural advantage – a sense of inquiry, an open-minded willingness to examine the ideas of others and the lack of a stifling tradition of technical conformity.

The Japanese trait of assimilating foreign ideas has a long pedigree and owes much to Japan's role as a late developer. Throughout their history the Japanese have found themselves needing to catch up, and they have used great skill and painstaking effort in mastering and refining imported technology.

In the sixth century, when Japan first came into contact with T'ang China, then the most sophisticated nation on earth, Japan was still a primitive, tribal society, lacking even a writing system. The Japanese became voracious pupils, however, and received a large measure of their culture from China, establishing an enduring attitude towards self-improvement and learning from outsiders. The imperial cities of Nara and Heian, for example, were laid out in the eighth century as copies of the great Chinese capital Chang'an (modern Xian).

It was not long before the Japanese caught up with their mentors, however. From the sixth to the ninth centuries, in one of the periodic spurts of development which are such a feature of the country's history, the Japanese surged forward. By the end of the ninth century the population of Heian, later to become Kyoto, was about 500,000, making it one of the largest cities anywhere. Japanese bronze-casting technology was unrivalled and by the twelfth century the steel of Japanese swords had become the finest in the world.

Subsequently, under the Ming dynasty (1368–1644), China became increasingly isolated and began to stagnate under emperors who saw their country as culturally superior and economically self-sufficient, with nothing to learn from other countries. The process continued under subsequent dynasties until China became a huge, torpid, inward-looking empire, oblivious to the scientific advances by then taking place in Europe.

By contrast, although Japan's geographical isolation was responsible for its relative backwardness before it learned so much from China, the country lacked any great indigenous tradition of scientific progress, and had no empire to induce smug complacency or self-satisfaction. So when ideas from overseas arrived, they tended to be welcomed and assimilated.

The Japanese have even gone so far as to worship the conveyers of new ideas, like the English pilot Will Adams, shipwrecked in Japan in the early seventeenth century, who is still revered as a Shinto deity for bringing advanced shipbuilding techniques. An early twentieth-century German printing machine was even worshipped in a Shinto shrine in the port city of Kobe.

This openness is a key factor in Japan's more recent successful assimilation of western technology. When, for example, the old shogun military regime fell and a new reforming government under Emperor Meiji came to power in 1868, Japanese scholars were sent out to America and Europe to search out the best of western practices to bring back to Japan for adaptation; and for most of the subsequent century, Japanese industry largely relied on western technology and ideas.

Of course, imitation can sometimes go too far. There have been numerous controversial cases of Japanese companies illegally pirating western products. The same is true of Taiwanese and South Korean companies. But it is worth noting that the biggest ever case of industrial copying came not from a Japanese or even Taiwanese firm, but rather from good old all-American Eastman Kodak, which lost a lawsuit in 1985 for infringing Polaroid instant photography patents, resulting in a patent damages settlement of nearly $1 billion.

The three creativities

For the most part, however, Japanese industry has learned from the West by legitimately purchasing product licences and then improving and commercializing the technology. This helps to explains why, although Japan might have had only three Nobel prize winners – fewer than half the total won by scientists at AT&T's Bell Labs alone, and way beneath Great Britain's sixty-three – it nonetheless has the world's strongest manufacturing industry. For example Matsushita, now the largest consumer electronics manufacturer who employs 135,000 people worldwide, has purchased no fewer than 49,000 patents.

Indeed, Japan has for some time been by far the biggest purchaser of foreign intellectual property. In 1985 it spent four times as much on overseas licences, royalties, patents, trademarks and copyrights as the US and five times more than Britain – both the United States and Britain still sell more patents and technology licences than they buy. It is no coincidence that Japan's most vigorous industrial rival – Germany – is also the second largest purchaser of intellectual property.

Anyway, according to Akio Morita, president of consumer electronics giant Sony, industry requires not just inventiveness, but three types of creativity. The first, basic creativity, is necessary to make discoveries, but this alone is not sufficient for a strong industry. The second type of creativity involves using the new technology in an appropriate way – product planning and production. The third type of creativity is in marketing your products – without which the most advanced and best manufactured items will fail. 'In basic technology', Morita says, 'it is true that Japan has relied on a number of foreign sources. But turning that technology into products is where Japan is number one in the world.'[5]

The transistor radio is a good example. It was an American company, Regency, which made the first transistor radio with help from Texas Instruments, but Regency pulled out of the market. Sony, however, felt that the proliferation of radio stations had created a market for small, portable radios which would allow each person to tune into the station he or she wanted. Using this sales concept Sony persevered, and despite being second on to the market with its product, Sony's marketing creativity brought it success – and who has now heard of Regency?

According to a former Porsche engineer, who now works for Nissan, there were plenty of good ideas at the German company, 'but the management just wouldn't give the go-ahead'. At Nissan, in contrast, forward thinking is just as much encouraged: the difference is that the ideas go into production.[6]

Japanese car makers have been particularly adept at commercializing sophisticated technology, most of which was originally developed in the West. Japanese car makers, for example, led with the introduction of low-cost multi-valve car engines which offer the more efficient delivery of greater power. By 1990, most Japanese car makers were installing such engines throughout their ranges, at a time when European manufacturers were only offering them on premium-priced models and the American automobile producers were still at the drawing board stage. The Japanese are also well in advance with the introduction of four-wheel steering, which allows easier parking and better handling.

In the 1920s and 1930s, during an earlier era of economic development, it was American car producers who were the masters of the art of making technology affordable – electric starters, automatic wind-shield wipers, crank-type window lifts, syncromesh gears, automatic transmission, power steering, car radios and heaters were all pioneered by American companies. In the domestic appliance market, too, it was American corporations which first produced mass-market vacuum cleaners, washing machines, refrigerators, toasters, coffee makers, radios and electric typewriters.

An outdated concept

So if Japan's industry has 'copied' from the West, it is only following a well-worn route. Imitation and the acquisition of imported techniques is an unavoidable first stage in the process of economic development, and one for which Japan's history made it particularly well suited. But the notion of Japanese industry as merely imitative, whether just as a copier or an improver of imported technology, is anyway fast becoming outdated. For although Japanese spending on primary research has been modest in the past, as long ago as 1978 Japanese companies had already almost caught up with their main western rivals. Now, Japanese industry is embarking on an accelerating thrust into R&D and more innovative research, which is inevitable as it moves on to the next stage of its development.

As Japan's economy shifts to higher levels of production and income, so the point is being reached at which autonomous research and development becomes a necessity. Moreover, as the Japanese have already overtaken the West in many areas, buying in licences is becoming a less viable game. A detailed analysis of US patent applications from 1975 to 1987, for example, showed that the number of Japanese patents had more than doubled and exceeded the total issued to the British, French and West Germans combined.[7]

Further evidence of the Japanese advance came in a report in 1987 from the US National Academy of Engineering, which concluded that Japan was superior in twenty-five out of thirty-four critical technologies.[8] Moreover, OECD figures for 1985 show that Japan spent the second highest proportion of GDP on research and development out of nineteen industrialized countries – up from fourth place in 1981.

The Japanese already lead in important areas such as superconductors – materials which conduct electricity with minimal resistance, offering the potential for lower-cost power transmission, ultra-fast electric motors and vastly more powerful computers as superconducting chips permit more processing power without overheating.

The scale and nature of Japanese industry's superconductor effort sets it apart from other countries. At NEC, for example, superconductivity is the biggest single project at the company's fundamental research laboratories. Already, a 5.2 km-long underground magnetic levitation train, called 'Maglevel', which uses a superconducting linear motor, has been built in Osaka. Superconducting magnets and electric coils are positioned on the train and propel it over a metal bar running down the centre of the track. Japan's main rival in this field is West Germany, but whereas the German experimental floating train has only managed a levitation height of 8 millimetres, the Japanese experimental train has been raised as high as 10 centimeters, allowing it to accelerate safely to speeds of nearly 300 miles an hour.

In January 1991, moreover, shortly after a US commission on superconductivity had recommended a five-year programme to develop a powerful superconductor-based electromagnet, American experts were stunned to learn that Sumitomo had already built a prototype of the proposed device.

Another area in which the Japanese are leading in innovative effort is microrobots, tiny robots powered by minute motors made from silicon, which one day are likely to be developed for medical use, entering the bloodstream to examine the digestive system or repair artificial organs, as well as being used in industry to mend intricate parts of sophisticated equipment. Far-fetched though it may sound, researchers at Tokyo University have already developed motors the size of specks of dust.[9]

But the new Japanese research effort is not limited to headline-grabbing high-tech products. One reason for the success of Japan's construction contracting industry in international markets is that the Japanese spend about 1 per cent of their sales on research – far more than their American counterparts. The Big Five Japanese contractors employ an average of 400 researchers each, in well-equipped labs doing research into areas such as earthquake resistant concrete. One result is a machine that bores 30ft-wide holes for tunnels by turning the soil into slurry and piping it to the surface, while sensors relay data to a computerized control room on the surface.[10]

Full circle

Will the Japanese license their new technology to the West, or will they, as some commentators fear, hog it to reinforce their dominance? So far it looks as though these fears are unfounded. Between 1970 and 1985 sales of Japanese technology overseas rose sharply from $373 million to $898 million, indicating both increasing R&D levels and a willingness to trade their technology.

Whether the West will benefit from Japan's new technology will, of course, depend in part on the willingness of western industry to take advantage of what is on offer. When the American Electronics Association wrote to 17,000 of its members advertising a subscription newsletter on Japanese electronics, it received only twenty-one orders and had to close it down.[11]

At least some western companies are now belatedly beginning to realize the research potential in Japan. Motorola, one of America's technologically most advanced companies, already uses Japanese technology where it outperforms its own, swapping some of its microprocessor knowledge in return for Toshiba's memory chip designs. AT&T, one of the pioneers of the semiconductor industry, also signed deals early in 1990 involving the manufacture and marketing of a type of memory chip called Static RAMs, designed by Mitsubishi Electric, as well as NEC-designed gate array chips which are used for customized applications.

So the wheel is beginning to turn full circle. In the 1950s Matsushita was largely dependent on Philips' technology and was a major licensee of the Dutch company. But in 1960 Matsushita built its own large R&D centre and by the mid-1970s the Japanese company's income from licence fees exceeded its pay-outs. Japan's steel industry also now earns six times more in royalties and fees for its technology than it pays out.

But one of the most significant recent Japanese technology sales occurred when Hitachi agreed to sell semiconductor-manufacturing technology to the South Korean group Goldstar, in the first technology transfer of its kind between a Japanese semiconductor maker and South Korea. According to MITI figures for 1987, there were no fewer than 816 cases of Japanese technology transfers to South Korea in that year, making the Koreans among the most eager customers for Japanese technology.

There may, however, have been just the faintest feeling of *déjà vu* when in 1989 Hitachi sued the semiconductor arm of South Korean conglomerate Samsung for illegally using its semiconductor-manufacturing processes. It is, perhaps, not too far-fetched to imagine disgruntled Japanese businessmen in the not too distant future muttering into their Suntory Special Reserve 'Scotch' about the pernicious, upstart South Korean 'copycats'.

Age of fruition

The Japanese are haunted by the vision of being overtaken by their rapidly advancing east Asian neighbours, particularly Taiwan and South Korea, whose economies have been closely linked to Japan's over the past decades in a virtuous association that is at the same time co-operative and competitive. For Japan is no more likely to remain for ever top of the economic pile than was Britain or the United States. Decline is unavoidable – and already certain structural problems are becoming apparent.

Since the war, Japan has had on average a significantly younger population than most of its main competitors. But with a life expectancy of 81 years for women and 76 for men, the proportion of Japan's over-65s is likely to more than double to nearly a quarter of the population by the year 2020, switching Japan from having the lowest to the highest proportion of elderly among the leading industrial nations.

The Japanese term for their growing elderly is *jitsunen*, which means 'age of fruition', and therein lies a problem. For the 'silver generation', as they are also called, will inevitably wish to gather in their harvest in the form of pensions; and as the elderly begin to spend what they have accumulated, savings rates will also fall. In fact, Japan's savings rate has been slipping since the mid-1970s as social security and pension schemes have become more generous, making saving for old age less necessary – both Italy and Taiwan now boast higher savings ratios than Japan.

As well as that, Japan can expect an increase in welfare costs which will result in social security and medical spending rising from 14 per cent of GNP in 1985 to as much as 29 per cent by 2010.[12] The four Japanese of working age who will by then be supporting each pensioner will have to contribute more in tax to pay for the elderly, forcing up wages to compensate, all of which will damage the competitiveness of Japan's industry. By then, Japan's main export might, in fact, be the silver ones themselves. A government agency called the Leisure Development Centre has produced feasibility studies with foreign and domestic companies on the possibility of shipping Japan's

No New Fish

elderly abroad into specially developed retirement communities.

This ageing of the population is also beginning to cause contradictory problems for industry: on the one hand there is a surplus of senior managers without enough posts for them to fill, while on the other hand the reduction in size of the working population will lead to increasing recruitment difficulties. Already, a severe labour shortage is apparent. A Labour Ministry survey of 15,000 companies found that 60 per cent had been forced to modify business plans or practices for lack of suitable workers.

Meanwhile, the percentage of engineering students going into manufacturing industry plunged from nearly half in 1987 to just over a third in 1988 as more students were lured into the glamorous and highly paid worlds of finance and real estate. So concerned has MITI become about the brain drain from industry to the booming service sector that it has formed a group called the Feel Good Manufacturing Committee to deal with the problem.

And as MITI wrestles with a situation with which other industrialized countries are more than familiar, middle-aged Japanese executives in late-night bars habitually gripe about the decline of the work ethic among the *shin jin rui* – the soft, young Japanese – prompting a Toshiba executive to remark: 'The spirit of the corporate warriors is dying.'[13] He may have a point, for ever since the mid-1970s opinion polls have confirmed that a majority of Japanese think that home life, health and happiness are more important than material success and wealth.

With Japan's economic success, the country's growing affluence, the overseas holidays and the flashy gifts, have also come new problems. In fact, the very prosperity provided by Japan's material achievements contains within it some of the seeds of its future relative decline. For the old, austere values and unity of purpose which have for the most part characterized Japan since the war are breaking down, and with them some of the traditional cohesion is also fading.

The second half of the 1980s has seen the emergence of a newly wealthy and ostentatious élite, which has unsettled Japan's social stability by provoking increasing resentment at the disparities of wealth and lifestyle which have emerged. While conspicuous displays of wealth used to be frowned upon in most circles, it has now become increasingly common to flaunt affluence.

People who have seen more money being made in property in a year than they can earn in a lifetime begin to ask what they are working for. At the root of the problem is high land prices, caused by Japan's chronic land shortage, but exacerbated by the tax system. The result has been that the middle-class backbone of industrial and bureaucratic Japan is increasingly being priced out of the market.

Resentment at all of this is now creeping into Japan's normally fairly deferential political system. The LDP's ability both to create and to reflect the post-war national consensus has recently been strained by the newly wealthy, who have eroded the Japanese self-image of being middle class. Political and financial scandals in the late 1980s involving the resignation of Prime Minister Takeshita, followed by revelations that his successor, Uno, had indulged himself with pretty ladies ranging from an under-age seventeen-year-old to a mature matron of sixty-three, crystallized public resentment concerning the huge amounts of money sloshing around in the murky world where business and politics meet.

It seemed that the politics of envy had gone to work in Japan as ordinary people became aware of the widening gulf between themselves and the rich and powerful segments of society. As a result, in 1989 the LDP lost its Upper House majority for the first time since 1955.

Other problems might emerge from Japan's financial system. The massive stock market fall of 1990, when nearly one-half was knocked off share values, followed by continuing declines over the following two years, showed that the Japanese market was just as prone to instability as its western counterparts.

The popularity of warrant bonds as a source of corporate finance may also cause difficulties. These bonds include an option to buy equity at fixed prices in the bond-issuing company, the attraction being that if stock prices rise, the bondholder can pick up equity on the cheap, leaving the issuing company free of the obligation to redeem the bond. But the stock market fall has made it unlikely that warrant holders will exercise their options to buy equity, instead demanding repayment which may lead to liquidity problems for Japanese industry in the mid-1990s.

A widening gap

So has Japan already peaked? Will these factors now lead to a period of decline? Certainly, Japanese industry will steadily lose some of the structural advantages which it has enjoyed since the war and will have to compensate by improving its productivity at a very rapid rate if it is to finance the added burdens and maintain its edge. But whatever comfort it may afford disgruntled western industrialists to think that the collapse in Japanese asset prices and the slowdown in Japanese growth in late 1991 and 1992 presages the beginning of the end, and that Japan may soon get its come-uppance, their rejoicing may yet have some time to wait.

For harbingers of Japanese decline have proved to be premature in the past. Many predicted that student riots in the late 1960s heralded an early end to the economic miracle. The so-called Nixon Shock of 1971, when the American president devalued the dollar and announced a 10 per cent import duty, sent Tokyo stocks spinning downwards. The two oil crises of the 1970s also hit Japan, with its almost total dependence on imported energy, particularly hard. Yet not only did the Japanese economy weather these shocks, but the fundamental strength and resilience of Japan's industry allowed the country to emerge from each more powerful than before.

Again, in the late 1980s the most striking feature of Japan's economic performance was that, despite the massive appreciation of the yen, which in two years doubled in value against the dollar, Japan's manufacturing sector confounded the pessimists by advancing strongly, improving productivity through automation, upgrading into more sophisticated product areas and globalizing production. As a result, in less than five years up to the middle of 1991, Japan enjoyed economic growth equivalent to France's total GNP.

One of the front-runners in the new investment wave has been Japan's vehicle industry – now the world's biggest – illustrating that, far from relinquishing their lead, Japan's corporations will increasingly stamp their dominance in areas like vehicles and electronics, where they are currently already strong. Huge capital investment, together with efficient and flexible industrial organization, will more and more allow the Japanese to make product innovation and differentiation their competitive hallmark in the 1990s.

Visitors to the Tokyo Motor Show late in 1991 were amazed at the variety and technology on display from Japanese manufacturers whose models managed to make even the sleekest European offerings look dowdy and dated by comparison. The Japanese car industry is already five years ahead of its western rivals – and the gap is widening. Japanese producers employ 'lean' production, which uses less effort, less space and less time to develop and manufacture models, allowing greater flexibility as well as lower costs.

As a result, whereas most western volume car manufacturers' product lives are still as long as eight years, with production runs of up to 2 million vehicles needed for profitability, Toyota's lead time for a brand new model is now three and a half years, with profitable production runs as low as 500,000.

The true measure of the widening gap only really began to dawn on stunned western car manufacturers when a $5 million, five-year Massachusetts Institute of Technology study based on a survey of ninety plants in seventeen countries was released.[14] Among the report's revelations were the following:

- Toyota's project development teams, at a maximum of 500 people, are only half as big as Ford's or Volkswagen's.

- The average Japanese luxury car plant requires one-half the effort of its American equivalent and one-quarter the effort of the average European plant.

- Toyota plants have virtually no rework areas. By contrast, most western car plants devote 20 per cent of plant area and 25 per cent of their total hours to fixing mistakes.

- At Mercedes' Sindelfingen plant in south-western Germany, the huge rectification area accounts for a third of the total assembly effort – in other words, the German plant is expending more effort to fix assembly-line problems than the Japanese take to create an almost perfect car the first time.

- Toyota can churn out a Corolla in only thirteen hours, while a VW Golf takes twenty hours. The more complex Lexus luxury model takes eighteen hours to build – an equivalent Mercedes takes more than twice as long.

- Only one European plant can match average Japanese quality levels – and that takes no less than four times the effort of the Japanese plant to assemble a comparable product.

In short, it takes Europeans double the engineering effort to develop a car; the Japanese will finish the development job in under two-thirds the time; and it takes Europeans twice as long as the Japanese to assemble the resulting car.

But it is not just production technology where the Japanese have notched up a huge lead: they are also now way ahead in many areas of automotive technology, such as multi-valve engines, the use of ceramics in engines and four-wheel steering. So as the 1990s wear on, western vehicle makers who not so long ago sneered at low-tech Japanese tin-boxes may find themselves taking a back seat as the Japanese exploit their technological lead and manufacturing flexibility in order to shower the market with models designed to appeal to every segment of the market – including the executive and luxury sectors currently dominated by European manufacturers.

In electronics, too, while European producers still struggle to match the Japanese at building relatively basic products like video recorders and CD players, companies like Matsushita, Sony and Seiko are already two steps ahead with wristwatch data-banks, sensor watches which can determine atmospheric conditions, filmless cameras which digitally record images, flat TV screens you hang on your wall, translation telephones, tiny but fully functional personal computers and high-definition TV.

Ultimately, the factors which probably differentiate much of Japan's industry from the West's are these: an open-minded willingness to adopt the best technology and practices for a given situation; an eagerness to enter new fields and markets as a means of surviving in the face of unrelenting competition; the high quality and educational attainment at all levels of Japanese industry; and a preparedness to take pains to make employees feel part of their organization. Above all, there is the seemingly infinite capacity of Japan's managers to take trouble and to ensure that the customer is their chief priority.

Of course, one day Japan will surely decline in its turn. But the sources of Japanese competitive advantage are still immensely strong. In the meantime, western vehicle, electronics or computer manufacturers which are relying on an imminent loss of Japanese competitiveness to come to their rescue may end up very disappointed indeed.

Notes

1 House Sub-Committee on Investigations and Oversight and the Sub-Committee on Science, Research and Technology of the Committee on Science and Technology, *Japanese Technological Advances and Possible US Responses using Research Joint Ventures*, 29–30 June 1983; quoted in James Abegglen and George Stalk, *Kaisha, the Japanese Corporation*, Basic Books, New York 1985.

2 Akio Morita, *Made in Japan*, Collins, London, 1987.

3 Peter Wickens, *The Road to Nissan*, Macmillan, London, 1987.

4 Gary Jacobson and John Hillkirk, *Xerox: American Samurai*, Macmillan, New York, 1986.

5 Akio Morita and Shintaro Ishihara, *The Japan That Can Say 'No'*, Tokyo, 1989.

6 *Car*, October 1991.

7 *The Japan Technology 50 Report*, Venture Capital Economics, London, 1989.

8 *Strengthening US Engineering Through International Cooperation: Some Recommendations for Action*, National Academy of Engineering, National Academy Press, Washington DC, 1987; quoted in Clyde Prestowitz, *Trading Places*, Basic Books, New York, 1988.

9 *Japan Times*, 30 May 1991.

10 *Fortune*, 25 September 1989.

11 *The Economist*, 20 May 1989.

12 Source: Japanese Ministry of Health and Welfare and Ministry of Finance.

13 Masahide Tsuji, quoted in the *Financial Times*, 20 February 1991.

14 James P. Womack, Daniel T. Jones and Daniel Roos, *The Machine that Changed the World*, Macmillan, New York, 1990.

14 More of the Same?

Europe has rested on its laurels and slept for decades after having dominated the world. This is all too human and understandable. We have seen the same phenomenon in recent years in the United States. And nothing guarantees that Japan could be saved from the same destiny, when she attains one day the same quality of life as the Westerners.

This European sleep has been disturbed by the intrusion of the 'damned Japanese' and the Japanese industrial challenge has not entirely been taken up by the Europeans. Will they succeed? The answer is no, if they continue to think that Japanese enterprises are competitive 'because they benefit from government aids, close their market against foreign products, copy Western technologies, exploit their workers and subcontractors etc.'

Professor Masaru Yoshimori[1]

The world trading system is in crisis, its plight caused by short-term responses to deep-seated economic and industrial problems, exacerbated by self-serving assertions by industrialists and politicians that the Japanese have succeeded by unfair means and must be responded to in kind.

What makes this crisis so dangerous is that it has crept up furtively, almost unobserved. There has been no sudden big bang of protectionism such as occurred in the early 1930s when the United States enacted massive tariff increases on imported products under the Smoot–Hawley legislation, provoking retaliatory action from other countries, aggravating the Depression and bringing on a slump during which industrial production in the USA fell by nearly half, 9,000 banks closed their doors and a quarter of the labour force was unemployed. Nor are European and American stores suddenly being emptied of Japanese goods.

Rather, it is protectionism by stealth through a series of largely unreported and unnoticed measures. These are steadily influencing trade flows, distorting the world economy, damaging its capacity to produce wealth for both developing and industrialized nations, dividing the world into competing blocs and intensifying political tensions.

The fair trade rip-off

The main justification for trade barriers against Japanese goods is that Japan itself is an 'unfair' trader. Yet the phrase 'unfair trading practice' has, in effect, become a comforting substitute for 'producing a better product for a lower price'. If a foreign competitor makes a cheaper product, it is 'predatory' or 'dumping'. If you do it, it is 'the efficient exploitation of economies of scale'. When politicians and business people talk of unfair trade, more often than not what they really mean is that the bargains individual citizens choose to make to buy imported goods do not suit them. Underlying these bleats about unfair trade is an unholy mixture of greed, hypocrisy and the need for good, old-fashioned scapegoats.

American steelmakers pleading for import quotas have whined with dreary regularity throughout the past three decades that foreign steel was unfairly subsidized. Yet time and again US anti-dumping and subsidies investigations have found only minuscule subsidy levels – often lower than in the USA itself, where state subsidies have included a $265 million loan to four US steel companies in the late 1970s (never paid back); a $30 million grant for the two largest American steelmakers to develop new technology; $3.7 billion in benefits as a result of the government assuming steel industry pension liabilities; and other assorted grants worth $130 million. Congress was also good enough to enact a special tax provision for the steel industry in 1986, which resulted in direct payouts of $540 million for steel companies.

The American steel industry's real problem is that it has not invested enough, and when it has invested, it has too often spent money on obsolete technology, like the giant Bethlehem Steel which installed $200 million worth of open-hearth technology at Sparrows Point in 1956, just as improved basic oxygen furnace techniques were becoming available.

America's motorbike craze in the mid-1970s should have been good news for Harley-Davidson, the last American motorcycle maker, whose products were an institution, their raw power a macho-symbol to legions of fanatically devoted owners. But despite trebling production to 75,000 by the late 1970s, quality had deteriorated so much that more than half the cycles came off the line missing parts. The boast that Harley's roar made other bikes sound like effete sewing machines rang increasingly hollow as bikers found that those despised Japanese machines offered smoother power and greater reliability for less money than the all-American product.

That, of course, was 'unfair'. So in 1982 Harley-Davidson filed a petition asking for a restriction on motorcycle imports. The government duly obliged, recommending a large hike in import duties and a tariff-rate quota – aimed primarily at the Japanese – by which imports above a certain level were subject to high tariffs. These applied to all motorcycles with a capacity of 700cc and over, despite the fact that Harley-Davidson sold few motorcycles smaller than 1000cc.

When in 1981 Japan was forced by American pressure to restrict car exports, US manufacturers cited 'unfair' Japanese advantages in support of the restrictions. At that time it took twice as many hours for Detroit to produce a mid-sized car as it took a Japanese manufacturer. Cars from the big three US producers also regularly propped up league tables for defects and consumer satisfaction.

European and American politicians perennially exaggerate the threat from foreigners in order to justify increasing their power over their own citizens. Industrialists do the same to justify their pleading for subsidies and protection. But the truth is that almost invariably it is the uncompetitiveness of western industry, rather than unfair trade, which has led to trade deficits and job losses. General Motors is not cutting jobs because it cannot sell cars in Japan. It has never made much serious attempt to do so. Rather, GM workers are being laid off because the company cannot sell enough of its cars in the United States.

Yet while the lumbering American automobile giant is drastically pruning its North American operations in response to a tumbling market share, Japanese manufacturers are still managing to expand sales and their US production, which already accounts for a quarter of American car output and is scheduled to reach close to three million cars and trucks by 1994.

Perhaps the Japanese are just doing something right which GM are not. After all, something must be badly wrong with a corporation which has to pay a board member $700 million to leave and keep quiet about the company's failings, as the automobile giant did with Ross Perot in 1985.

One reason why American corporations are so often being beaten by their Japanese rivals may have less to do with 'unfair' trade than with the fact that top US chief executives have increased their own pay by more than 400 per cent in real terms over the past two decades. They now receive an average of $2.8 million a year – far more than their Japanese counterparts. Another clue to American car buyers' 'unfair' preference for Japanese cars may be that the 1990 *Consumer Reports* survey of car quality found that, of the thirty-three worst rated models, all but one were produced by the big three manufacturers.

Meanwhile in Europe, where Ford has been one of the most aggressive pleaders for restrictions on Japanese imports and transplant investment, the company should consider whether its own declining position has less to do with unfair competition than with the fact that its small car engine range is only just being renewed after a quarter of a century.

'Fair' trade is one of the great intellectual frauds of the twentieth century. If European and American politicians were really concerned with fair trade, they would at least abolish import restrictions which affect countries with open markets. Yet when in 1988 a US Senator proposed an amendment to exempt from textile import quotas those countries that are less protectionist than the United States, he was overwhelmingly defeated.

Hong Kong is probably the world's most open market and its industrial subsidies are nil. Yet textiles, electronics, toys and other products of the colony are among the most protected against in Europe and America. Even where countries have subsidized exporters or protected home markets, the nations erecting retaliatory barriers have almost invariably been just as guilty themselves. And where this is not the case, do you really create a 'level playing field' by clogging your own half with ruts and bumps?

Have, anyway, countries like Brazil and India really gained 'unfair' advantages by closing their markets and aiding exporters? Or have they simply distorted their economies and impoverished consumers by pandering to the loudest lobbyists – or those who can best afford to fund political re-election campaigns? India and Brazil are, after all, hardly paragons of economic success, while Japan's most protected and subsidized industries have done least well in international markets.

It is no coincidence that Japan, which is so often vilified as an 'unfair' trader, is also the most competitive in many key industries. Yet the reality is also that western companies and products can and do succeed in Japan – if they are competitive. Germany's car sales to Japan are, for example, worth more than its car imports from Japan; while the United States exports more to the Japanese that to France, Italy and

Germany combined – even though these three European countries together form a larger economic unit than Japan.

Dunlop accounts for 50 per cent of Japanese golf ball sales; 30 per cent of electric shavers sold in Japan are made by Braun; Nordica and Salomon dominate the Japanese ski boot market; 70 per cent of all stainless steel razor blades bought by the Japanese are produced in Connecticut by the Schick Division of Warner-Lambert; Applied Materials of San Jose, California, make 40 per cent of their $500 million annual sales of sophisticated semiconductor manufacturing equipment to Japan; and at one point half of the disposable nappies used by Japanese mothers were imported by Procter & Gamble.

Then there are the numerous joint ventures, local manufacturing operations and licensing deals which also help to enrich western corporations. McDonald's, Coca Cola, Kentucky Fried Chicken, Nestlé and IBM are almost as big names in Japan as in the United States or Europe. Unilever's Timotei shampoo was the number one seller, and the company's Lipton tea is the top black tea brand.

Of course, the Japanese market is difficult. It is intensely competitive and requires commitment, together with an understanding of its special requirements. But the number of western companies that have shown the long-term dedication and patience necessary for success in Japan calls into question the view that the Japan market is impenetrable.

Furthermore, far from being the epitome of a successfully implemented 'industrial policy' of targeted subsidies and trade barriers, Japan's economic rise is, on the contrary, in many ways the result of more consistently applied market-oriented policies than those practised in much of the West.

An open mind

Not all westerners, however, blame their industrial problems on Japan. For example, one congressional report on trade problems states: 'It has become increasingly clear to us, and to many businessmen dealing with Japan, that our trade problems result less and less from Japanese import barriers, and more and more from domestic American structural problems of competitiveness and quality. There are clearly lessons to be learned from Japan.'[2]

Those lessons are numerous – and the first has to be that an open-minded willingness to learn from others is the precondition for successful reform. When, in the middle of the last century, a series of small

American, British, French and Russian naval squadrons bombarded Japan into ending two centuries of isolation, the brutal western challenge galvanized the ancient and fossilized Japanese society into a cathartic orgy of self-reform.

Life was made more difficult for the Japanese by a series of treaties which prevented Japan from raising significant tariffs against imports from more economically advanced nations. There could be no refuge behind trade barriers. Rather, western technology and civilization had to be studied in an attempt to gain a place for Japan among the wealthy and powerful nations of the world.

As a result, the old privileges were swept away and a series of major political, social, industrial and educational reforms were implemented. *Samurai* privileges were given up and the old warrior class was put on an equal status with ordinary citizens. The navy was reformed on British lines and a French-style army and criminal code was introduced, together with a constitution based on German practice and universities along American lines.

Industry looked to Europe and America for ideas, technology and equipment – Japanese sake producers even invited over Frenchmen to show them how to make wine. But above all, in 1872 a national education system was established with compulsory primary schooling for all, regardless of class or sex, largely using unemployed *samurai* as teachers. Since the war, the Japanese have steadily reformed and upgraded their educational system so that although it is not free from criticism, it has nonetheless become one of the country's most important competitive advantages.

Other policies central to Japan's economic achievement include a monetary policy designed to maximize the productive side of the economy by restraining government spending and giving incentives for savings. This has helped to create a pool of capital for industry while bearing down strongly on inflation and interest rates.

Furthermore, although there are significant areas of the Japanese economy which remain protected from internal and external competition, Japanese governments have generally encouraged competition to a far greater extent than in most Western countries – it is no coincidence that those sectors most exposed to competition have also been the most successful.

So although Japanese society may have its faults, its achievements are sufficient to render unreasonable the dismissive sneering which so often characterizes western analyses of Japan. A more constructive approach would be carefully to examine the real underlying reasons for

Japan's many successes. In a changing world, the West must drop the arrogant assumption that it has nothing to learn from others, and must be prepared, where possible, to adopt the best parts of the Japanese system – not with a view to slavish imitation, but with a balanced and open-minded respect for their achievements.

Some lessons

There are those who still assert that Japanese business methods rely on unique, non-transferable attributes which cannot be adapted to western conditions. Of course, the Japanese do have particular cultural traits. Yet Japan itself has succeeded to a significant degree by modifying and improving on the best western practices. Japanese companies, moreover, have often managed successfully to transplant many so-called Japanese methods to their plants in Europe and America.

Soon after Sony opened its Californian plant in 1972, the world was hit by an oil crisis. But rather than lay off employees as American companies were doing, Sony president Akio Morita refused, making further funds available from Japan to support the US company. Educational and training programmes were developed to keep the workforce busy, helping to increase employees' sense of involvement with the company. The Sony plant now employs 1,500 people, has never been unionized and enjoys excellent management/workforce relations.

Greenfield factories with brand new workforces are, of course, one thing, but Japanese companies have also met with considerable success when taking over troubled companies in declining sectors. When Sumitomo Rubber Industries bought Dunlop's European tyre operations in 1985, its acquisition included the Fort Dunlop plant, one of British manufacturing's truly historic sites set in a part of England's Midlands then most hit by decades of decay in the vehicle industry. Most of the factory buildings dated back to 1916, on top of which the old workforce was inherited virtually *en bloc* and the company had to deal with a bevy of traditional craft unions.

Yet by the end of the decade, production at the site was up by a half using only two-thirds of the workforce, while an annual £20 million loss had been transformed into a respectable profit. This was not achieved by heavy-handed management directives from Sumitomo's HQ in Kobe, for Japanese management is now limited to only three board members and a small technical and production team.

Apart from sweeping away a divisive hierarchy of seven canteens, the turnaround was accomplished by investment of about £10 million a year in the site as well as the adoption of radically new methods of communication, including monthly team briefings, question and answer sessions when shop floor workers can question boardroom management, common uniforms for all employees and an extensive quality training programme involving 1,000 staff a year, including management, sales and office staff.

But perhaps the most astonishing transformation through the use of Japanese techniques has been wrought at the old General Motors plant in Fremont, California. In the past, the Fremont factory was a byword for all the traditional motor industry ills – strikes, 20 per cent absenteeism, poor quality and low productivity – with the result that in 1981 GM closed the plant and laid off the employees. Two years later, the world's largest automobile maker joined forces with Toyota, Japan's biggest car manufacturer, to reopen the plant for the production of Toyota's Corolla model, which is sold by GM as the Prizm. Now the factory boasts some of the highest quality in GM, and Fremont has been metamorphosed into a success story.

The main change has not been the workforce – about 90 per cent of the new workers were rehired from the old plant. Nor was it the union – a new deal was signed with the United Auto Workers. And there has not been much in the way of new production equipment either. What has changed is the approach of the new management group and its emphasis on teamwork.

Slow suicide

Many European and American companies are now beginning to learn from these methods. Yet many still choose easier options, such as taking refuge in the high-margin, low-volume upper reaches of their markets in order to escape Japanese competition. This policy is grounded in a fallacious assumption that high-volume, mass-market products are necessarily low margin and low added value. It is also based on the dangerous notion that Japanese manufacturers will not bother to chase you upmarket.

There are, no doubt, areas where a low-volume, high-margin strategy makes very good sense. But it has certainly failed in a great many western industries. When, for example, the British motorcycle manufacturers Triumph, Enfield, Norton and BSA fled upmarket from Honda and Yamaha, they soon found themselves cornered at the top of the market and were finally crushed by Honda's lower costs and huge volumes.

Sometimes called 'segment retreat' by economists, this type of behaviour is usually little better than a slow form of suicide. But today General Motors and other large western manufacturers appear to be repeating the mistakes of the motorcycle industries by withdrawing from the small car market to concentrate resources on larger cars in the hope of insulating themselves from low-priced imports. If they and Europe's luxury car manufacturers, Mercedes, Porsche, BMW, Audi, Saab and Jaguar, believe that they can successfully distance themselves from Japanese competition, they have left themselves open to some unpleasant shocks. For the Japanese are already relentlessly following them upwards.

The first attack came in the upper reaches of the sports car market, where throughout the 1980s cars from Nissan, Toyota and Mazda edged closer to Porsche in quality and performance. In 1989 Nissan's 300ZX finally bettered Porsche, offering a 3-litre, 24-valve V6 engine with twin-intercooled turbochargers, air conditioning, ABS brakes and an array of other upmarket goodies for less than the cost of a four-cylinder and fairly basically equipped Porsche 944 Turbo SE.

But worse was to come. In 1991 Honda also tackled Porsche head on with its pavement-ripping Acura NS-X which comfortably undercut and outperformed its Porsche equivalent. This may help to explain why Porsche's American sales, which had peaked in 1986 at more than 30,000 annually, plunged to a mere 4,388 units in 1991. Japan's most competitive manufacturers have also moved strongly into the executive and luxury end of the car market where their presence was virtually non-existent up to the mid-1980s. Honda was first with its Acura marque, while Nissan began selling its Infiniti luxury models late in 1989, at the same time as Toyota shocked Europe's luxury automakers with the quality, performance and price of its new Lexus marque.

Needless to say, the Japanese manufacturers are following their familiar routine of producing their products in relatively high volumes, thereby cutting costs and expanding the market, enabling them significantly to undercut their competitors. In its first full year, Toyota's Lexus outsold Mercedes and BMW combined in the all-important American market, forcing Mercedes to cut into its fat margins by offering unprecedented $9.000 dollar rebates and prompting BMW's chairman to dark mutterings about Japanese 'dumping'.

But the car industry is just the latest to suffer from segment retreat. When the Japanese expanded the market for computer-controlled lathes in the early 1980s by producing standardized products in volume,

European and American producers responded by focusing their efforts on more complex products which they sold to large firms. As a result, the Japanese share of world production of these lathes soared from 10 per cent in 1975 to more than 50 per cent by 1984. Where the Japanese saw a market capable of rapid growth, western suppliers had hardly recognized its existence

Deeper changes

To match the Japanese, western manufacturers have to tackle them head on in volume markets. But to do that, changes have to go further and deeper than those already adopted by the more far-sighted American and European companies. For to give their companies a real chance in the type of industries in which the Japanese excel, western governments must solve fundamental structural problems of persistent domestic over-consumption, budget imbalances, protected and cartelized markets and poor education.

Any government which either squeezes industrial investment by over-taxing savings and taking too large a share of the nation's resources, or over-stimulates domestic consumption, or legislates in a way which positively encourages labour militancy, or promotes anti-business attitudes is bound to end up with a manufacturing sector which is shrinking relative to its competitors. Reforms must involve tough policies of trimming excessive state spending, cutting out tax breaks for consumption, providing incentives for savings, encouraging competition and taking on strong vested interests in industry.

Moreover, any country which neglects the fundamental truth that the prime object of education should be to equip its people with the ability to earn a living is unlikely to enjoy a successful and competitive industry. For, above all, a thorough examination of Japan's educational system would greatly profit the West.

It would, of course, be foolish to expect any western country to adopt the Japanese system wholesale; nor would it be desirable to do so. But there are elements in Japan's relatively low-cost, high-quality school system which could be extremely beneficial. These include the emphasis on pre-school education; the element of parental choice; the stress placed on learning the basics of language, mathematics and science; the number of pupils staying on beyond the age of sixteen and going on into higher education; the use of regular testing as a means of assessing performance; and the inherent vocational bias of the system.

In the United States in particular, the century-old high-school system, which in its day was a world-beating social innovation, providing the unrivalled mass education which was a major factor in America's economic success, is now hopelessly outdated. School years are far too short, competition among students and exam discipline have been played down, truancy levels are too high, schooling is too divorced from the needs of industry, the average quality of teachers has fallen, and the problem of making provision for ethnic minorities while maintaining high standards has not been tackled. Moreover, despite areas of excellence, American education is patchy and uneven at all levels.

This, rather than 'unfair' Japanese practices, is the greatest millstone around the neck of American industry. And initiatives such as the proposed chain of 1,000 technologically oriented Whittle schools across America are likely to do more for American competitiveness than all of the 'structural impediments' initiatives, managed trade agreements, anti-dumping duties and tub-thumping special pleading from Detroit and Silicon Valley.

A historical perspective

There are, in fact, parallels between the United States' recent economic problems and the early days of Britain's decline in the last century. Writing just over a century ago, the great British free-trade advocate Richard Cobden was a great admirer of America, which at that time concentrated on its own internal development rather than on foreign adventures, and maintained an excellent educational system. This was why Cobden correctly predicted the rise of the United States, writing that 'it is to the industry, the economy, and peaceful policy of America that our statesmen and politicians ... ought to direct their anxious study; for it is by these ... that the power and greatness of England are in danger of being superseded'.[3]

By contrast, Cobden blamed a scarcity of capital for British industry on the high government spending needed to finance a 'passion for meddling with the affairs of foreigners'. For at that time, Britain was absorbed by the maintenance of the balance of power in continental Europe, the threat of Russian expansionism in Asia and the need to defend the Empire.

'In all my travels three reflections constantly occur to me,' Cobden wrote: 'how much unnecessary solicitude and alarm England devotes to the affairs of foreign countries; with how little knowledge we enter upon the task of regulating the concerns of other people; and how much better we might employ our energies in improving matters at home.' As a result, Cobden concluded, Britain was 'suffering the slow but severe punishment inflicted at her own hands – she is crushed beneath a debt so enormous that nothing but her own mighty strength could have raised the burden that is oppressing her.'

If that sounds familiar, the argument that the United States now needs a period of inward-looking reflection and reform is not necessarily to criticize American post-war foreign policy. Whatever its faults and errors, many believe it to have guaranteed the freedom of the West during extremely difficult times. Yet there is also a legitimate view that the United States has sometimes become too obsessed with foreign matters, bearing more than its fair share of the military burden, being too prone to accommodate lobbying by the armed forces and weapons producers, while neglecting increasingly pressing domestic concerns.

Unfortunately, so far little has been done to tackle these basic domestic problems. Rather, foreign affairs and complaints about 'unfair' competition from Japan have diverted attention from the need for reforms at home. The result is that more comfortable policies of yet more intervention in the economy and subsidies for favoured industries have been the preferred palliatives for industrial ills.

A quick fix

Calls for 'national industrial strategies' resound along the corridors of governments in most 'western countries, but nowhere now more loudly than in Washington, where a growing band of influential Americans are arguing that bureaucrats know better than the markets. There has always been an academic fringe in the USA willing to assert the benefits of a 'trade and industry policy', while politicians such as Senator Kennedy have long argued that 'the basis for the restoration of the US economy is the development of an industrial policy'.[4] But over the past few years they have been joined by more influential figures, such as former secretaries of state Henry Kissinger and Cyrus Vance.

Behind this trend towards what has been called 'Technology America Inc.' is, of course, 'the Japanese threat'. For the prospect of losing global technological superiority is leaving American industry feeling extremely beleaguered. According to Bill Krause, chairman of the American Electronics Association which represents over 3,500 US electronics companies: 'We are facing economic warfare.'

More of the same?

The currently fashionable form of state intervention is government-backed consortia of companies. Proposals to build collaborative research groups to work in areas such as superconductivity have already won widespread support, but leading the movement is the semiconductor industry. A number of US computer and chip makers, including AT& T, DEC, Hewlett-Packard, Intel, IBM and Motorola, have come together in a six-year, $1.5 billion advanced semiconductor research initiative called Sematech, which receives half of its $200 million plus annual funding from the US Defense Department. This constitutes just part of a $1.6 billion aid package to the semiconductor industry channelled through the Defense Science Board.

Another example of this trend towards pre-competitive research groups is the Advanced Battery Consortium, formed by GM, Chrysler and Ford with support from the US Department of Energy to develop advanced battery technology for electric vehicles. The Bush administration has also actively considered a proposal by nineteen US computer and electronics companies, including IBM, AT&T, Apple, Texas Instruments and Hewlett-Packard, to relax anti-trust laws to allow the formation of a private sector consortium to develop high-definition television (HDTV) products in competition with Japan.

The Defense Advanced Research Projects Agency (Darpa), the Pentagon's industrial agency, offered part of its $1 billion-plus budget to help the HDTV group. Further, while it has been suggested that European TV makers operating in the United States, such as Philips and Thomson, should be allowed to join in the proposed consortium, the Japanese television makers, whose operations in America are far more extensive, have been excluded.

The Europeans have also been following the same path. Siemens and Philips, the two leading European semiconductor producers, joined together in Mega Project in 1984, a scheme partly funded by the Dutch and German governments with the aim of propelling their national champion semiconductor manufacturers ahead of the Japanese in the race to produce 1 Megabit D-Ram memory chips. Despite the fact that the Japanese comfortably won that race, forcing Siemens to license Toshiba technology, the consortium went on to attempt to develop the next generation 4 MB D-Rams, but once again were beaten by several Japanese producers.

Nonetheless, Mega Project clearly demonstrates the drift of European thinking on how to compete with the Japanese. For Mega Project has spawned the Joint European Semiconductor Silicon (Jessi), which got into gear in 1990 and runs for five years. Its original aim was for Philips and Siemens further to develop microchip technologies in a £1 billion programme, much of it financed by Bonn and The Hague. But this has since been upgraded to embrace other European semiconductor makers, and funding has been boosted to £1.4 billion over eight years.

HDTV is also seen in Europe as a 'strategic' industry worthy of state support. Although at first it looked as though the European industry would accept as the world standard the Japanese system, which was well in advance of anything in the West, at a meeting of industrial and political leaders in 1985 a decision was taken to fight off potential domination by Japanese technology. As a result, the Eureka 95 programme was set up by the European Community with a budget of £150 million to develop European HDTV technology. Overall, the EC plans to pump more than £4 billion into collaborative research in the four years up to 1994 – in addition to cash from national governments.

The allure of state-backed consortia and other interventionist policies is that they appear to offer neat and easy quick-fix prescriptions for western industrial problems. Yet the approach is hardly a new one and its history is littered with costly failures. Concorde, the loss-making supersonic airliner programme, was the product of an Anglo-French government-led consortium. The main beneficiaries are the few hundred wealthy people who each day save around three hours' flying time crossing the Atlantic.

Another best forgotten episode was the European, state-sponsored Unidata computer consortium, which linked Philips, Siemens and Bull in the early 1970s. At about the same time, the British government encouraged the electronics firms GEC, Plessey and STC to collaborate with the state-owned telephone network operator to produce a new 'world-beating' digital public exchange. The resulting System X has so far chalked up only one overseas sales success – in the Virgin Islands.

Britain's Alvey Programme, implemented in 1983 with £200 million in government finance, established collaborative R&D projects linking industry with the universities in areas such as very large-scale semiconductor integration and intelligent systems software. Yet according to a government-funded report, although the project was liked by the academics involved, it failed to result in saleable products or to enhance competitiveness in information technology because it did not address the fundamental structural problems of the industry, such as its inability to commercialize products and manufacture efficiently.[5]

Nor even have Japanese government-inspired consortia, on which many of the European and American efforts are consciously modelled, invariably been crowned with success. The ten-year programme to

More of the same?

develop 'fifth generation' computers and software, set up in 1981 with $500 million in funding, largely failed to come up with any results.

The similar American MCC consortium, organized in 1983 in response to the Japanese effort at the instigation of William Norris, Chairman of computer maker Control Data, has likewise been short on results, even though it comprised some of America's most powerful companies, including DEC, 3M and Boeing. MCC certainly seems to have done little for Control Data, which has since plunged into severe financial difficulties.

The R&D myth

Driving the movement towards state-funded research consortia in Europe and America is the feeling that the West must increase its industrial research effort to match steadily advancing Japanese technology. But the real lesson from the Japanese is that it is not always necessary to carry out a great deal of research, especially if the economy of the country in question is not at a stage of development where it can best exploit the fruits of such research.

Pouring government funds into advanced projects which are out of line with the underlying, fundamental productive capabilities of the country is likely simply to distort the economy as a whole, draining the best scientists and engineers away from other industries.

Being first with a product or in the lead in the early days of an industry is not an advantage if you do not have the production, engineering and marketing skills to capitalize on that lead. The British built the first jet airliner, the Comet, and invented penicillin, but soon lost the lead to the Americans. Britain, too, at one time led the way in commercializing computers – English Electric's models were the first to be aimed at businesses in the early 1950s; while Ferranti built the world's fastest computer in the early 1960s, the Atlas, before going on to pioneer customized semiconductors, but is now largely out of both markets. Britain also led the world during the 1950s in harnessing the power of the atom for generating electricity, but rapidly lost the edge.

As a result, laments about the failure to exploit indigenous technology have been a constant motif of discussions of Britain's post-war industrial performance – a feature now increasingly echoed in the United States. This inevitably led to a series of government initiatives to help British companies to capitalize on British inventions. Stung by the rapid lead established by American industry in jet engines and penicillin, for

More of the same?

example, the post-war Labour government established the National Research and Development Council (NRDC) whose attempts to persuade companies to commercialize computer memories and hovercraft in the 1950s and 1960s met with little success.

The necessary capital, marketing and engineering resources simply were not there. But the unwillingness or inability to invest and the lack of production and marketing skills were often exacerbated by the weaknesses inherent in government intervention in industry. When, for example, research into hovertrain technology in the 1970s clashed with British Rail's high-speed train project, the state-owned railway company had the edge in lobbying power and ensured the cancellation of its rival. Eventually, the high-speed train proved a failure and was never fully developed, leaving Britain lagging badly in mass-transit technology.

Later attempts by the NRDC to aid the development of British-pioneered medical scanners were also counterproductive, while the organization's failure to see the potential of monoclonal antibodies led to the discovery being exploited by an American company, which stumbled across it in a issue of *Nature*.

More recently, European Community efforts to sponsor HDTV development have been frustrated by an inability to agree on exact standards and a failure successfully to commercialize the technology. As a result, after six years of generous funding the European television industry is still several years away from commercial HDTV production; by contrast, early in 1992 Sharp had already announced a set for just over £4,000.

The inherent ineffectiveness of state research funding has been graphically illustrated in a study of EC R&D programmes which catalogues the internal wheeling, dealing, politicking, lobbying and buttering-up of EC officials required to secure funding. The study advises hopefuls to pick at least one partner for joint projects from Portugal, Greece or Spain, regardless of underlying suitability, to salve consciences about the Community's poorer members; and to steer clear of Japanese partners, which might excite officials' prejudices. It also details the daunting logistics of endless meetings and negotiations before funding is authorized; and if the application is successful, the study advises setting aside at least a third of the budget to cover the cost of attending yet more meetings and submitting progress reports.[6]

Another important point often missed by the R&D lobby is that despite the increasing Japanese research effort, many western companies still spend more than their Japanese rivals on research, but nonetheless fail to beat them in the marketplace. Consider the following:

More of the same?

- In 1989 Siemens of Germany had the biggest R&D budget of any electronics company bar IBM, yet it has failed effectively to break into consumer electronics or information technology markets, while its semiconductor arm badly trails Japanese rivals.

- Philips of the Netherlands spends more on research than Canon and Toshiba combined, yet has difficulty matching the product ranges of either of those companies.

- No fewer than six European electronics companies spent a higher proportion of their turnover on R&D than NEC or Sony, yet none has enjoyed anything like the success of these Japanese companies.

Throwing money at research and development will not solve the problem of underlying uncompetitiveness. And those politicians and pundits who constantly urge western industry and governments to spend more on R&D should bear in mind the fact that, until relatively recently, Japanese industry spent little on research.

For it is often better for companies which do not represent the leading edge of their industries to buy in technology and concentrate their energies on strengthening production and marketing methods. Otherwise, any fruits of expensive research programmes are likely to be exploited by others.

Yet according to the information director of the UK Patent Office, which keeps records of technology, a self-satisfied unwillingness to accept that others might have a better way of doing things – the 'Not Made Here' syndrome – leads European companies to waste £20 billion a year 're-inventing' what has been done before.[7] Hitachi, by contrast, has no less than 150 employees whose sole task is to scour the world's patent offices for ideas, exemplifying the more open-minded attitudes which prevail in Japanese companies.

A Limited Triumph

The British motorcycle industry would not appear to be a very likely candidate for leading a fightback against the Japanese. After all, motorbikes were the first product with which companies like Honda really shook the West in the late 1950s and early 1960s, paving the way for a stream of Japanese industrial conquests. British motorbike manufacturers, on the other hand, exemplified much of what was worst about British industry. Great British names like BSA, Norton and Matchless were blighted by poor productivity, bad labour relations, failed rescue

More of the same?

bids and continual political interference, until the last of the breed, Triumph, finally succumbed and closed its gates in 1983.

Yet behind the walls of a nondescript looking factory near the small town of Hinckley, deep in the English Midlands, not far from where the old, problem-plagued Triumph factory has now given way to a housing estate whose roads sport names like Boneville Crescent, Triumph motorcycles are being revived with some considerable success.

There is nothing technologically innovative about the new range of high-powered Triumph bikes for which buyers in Britain and Germany are now queuing. For just as in an earlier era Japanese manufacturers rose by copying and improving upon European bikes, the new British motorcycles return the compliment by mimicking the layout of big Kawasakis, with in-line three- and four-cylinder engines that emit the muted whine and sewing machine smoothness which has come to characterize Japanese machines, rather than the hoarse Triumph roar of old.

According to John Bloor, the building magnate who is responsible for the revival: 'Our philosophy is that it's technically interesting to be first, but commercially more profitable to be second.' Bloor goes on to point out that 'You can design the best bike in the world, but if you can't productionize it and build it competitively, it's no good'.[8] So instead of investing millions in risky, state-of the art bike design, Bloor has simply used the best available Japanese technology, investing his cash in a hangar full of computer-controlled machines and testing equipment, as well as in a cost-effective, easy-to-assemble modular design for his range, allowing a mere 100 employees to build 10,000 bikes a year.

John Bloor's Triumph is more likely to succeed than a host of government-backed, research-intensive projects because he has recognized the basic need to get production and marketing right and appreciates the limitations imposed on him by the economic environment in which he has to work.

Whatever the advantages or otherwise of state-funded research programmes and a hands-on government industrial policy, the fact is that such strategies cannot succeed unless the fundamental productive basis of the economy is sound – and that essentially depends on having a properly educated and motivated workforce. Without this precondition for economic success, debates over industrial policies are no more than a diversion.

Likewise, arguments over whether American and British financial markets have resulted in too many hostile bids and takeovers, leading to 'short-termism' and an aversion to risk taking, are a side issue to the real problem, namely that large parts of productive industry in the West have been starved of capital as a result of high taxation on savings, subsidies for consumption and, in the case of the United States, huge budget deficits.

Until these basic weaknesses have been addressed, discussions about industrial policy will remain no more than a distraction from underlying problems, with protectionism an addictive sedative on which western industry will become increasingly and dangerously dependent, maintaining a fleeting delusion of prosperity, while in reality postponing reform and hastening inevitable economic decline.

Notes

1 Quoted in Ali M.El-Agraa *Japan's Trade Frictions*, Macmillan, London, 1988.

2 *Report on Trade with Japan of the Subcommittee on Trade of the Committee on Ways and Means*, US House of Representatives, 1980.

3 From speech on the 'Russian War' in Manchester, 1857; in Richard Cobden, *Speeches on Questions of Public Policy*, Vol. II, Macmillan, London, 1870; and *The Political Writings of Richard Cobden*, Cassell, London, 1886.

4 Cited by Bruce Bartlett, 'Industrial policy: Crisis for liberal economists', *Fortune*, 14 November 1983.

5 DTI, SERC, PREST and SPRU, *Evaluation of the Alvey Programme for Advanced Information Technology* HMSO, London, 1991.

6 Martin Collins *A Complete Guide to the EC's Research Funds*, Kogan Page, London, 1992.

7 Quoted in The *Financial Times*, 29 August 1991.

8 Quoted in *Car*, October 1991.

15 Stumbling Blocs

A wise man blames himself – a fool blames others.
Confucius

Any comfortable illusions that the defeat of communism means that the world is moving inexorably in the direction of liberal economies and open markets should be dispelled by an analysis by David Henderson, head of economics at the OECD, who in July 1991 pointed out that the global economy was by then further away from full integration than it had been in July 1914. According to Mr Henderson, only Japan, New Zealand and Turkey of the OECD's twenty-four member states ended the 1980s with trade regimes that were more liberal and open than at the beginning.

Some commentators excuse burgeoning trade barriers on the grounds that at least they encourage the siting of Japanese factories in protected markets. The imposition of penalties for 'dumping' on a whole raft of Japanese-made electronics goods in the mid and late 1980s, for example, provoked a fresh wave of inward investment to circumvent the levies. Following an anti-dumping case in 1987, Japanese computer printer manufacturers set up fourteen new European factories in 1988 alone.

Such transplant production certainly helps to impart Japanese ideas and methods. It also increases competition, thus to some extent mitigating the damaging effects of trade barriers. But overseas investment which is artificially induced by the need to hurdle trade barriers, as has so often been the case in Europe and America, cannot match the overall benefits of businessmen and consumers freely making their own choices of where to invest and what to buy, free from constraints imposed from above.

The establishment of Japanese plants, for example, rarely has the result of bringing prices down to the levels which would apply in truly open markets – not least because Japanese manufacturers are more than happy to take advantage of the high prices prevailing in protected markets.

Moreover, investments which are primarily designed to serve the domestic market, rather than being integrated into a genuinely global production organization, do little to prevent the steady erosion of the world trading system. This process has been exacerbated by impediments increasingly being placed in the way of Japanese-owned plants, forcing them artificially to buy an unreasonably high proportion of their parts locally, with the result that they are even less part of a real world economic system than might be the case.

Screwdriver plants

These restrictions on Japanese manufacturing operations in the West arise from the unwelcome competition such plants offer to local manufacturers. The problem faced by such producers is that despite some political hostility to Japanese inward investment – particularly in France and Italy where Japanese factories are characterized as 'Trojan Horses' – Japanese firms have been able to turn the jobs argument against the protectionist lobby by using the creation of employment – often in depressed areas – in support of their plants.

Local producers have hit back by ensuring that their governments have imposed stiff local content requirements on Japanese-owned plants. Japanese manufacturers have typically been told that between 60 and 80 per cent of the value of their products must be local to qualify as domestically-produced – a far higher level than the 50 per cent local content usually required of non-Japanese producers.

But this did little to stem the flow of Japanese investments. So the threatened domestic interests went further, arguing that even with 60–70 per cent local content, Japanese assembly plants were still just 'screwdriver' operations – that is, factories which supposedly imported so many of their parts that the workers were left only with the task of 'screwdrivering' them in. The argument is that the 'local content' of a product could include everything from labour costs to the soap in the washrooms, allowing a plant technically to achieve a high local content while in fact importing most of its parts.

In Europe, the EC Commission's response was to give itself the power to extend anti-dumping duties to imported components used in Japanese-owned production facilities in the Community. And the new local content rules were drawn up in such a way that even a Japanese-run factory whose products included only a small proportion of imported components could nonetheless be subject to anti-dumping duties.

Meanwhile in the United States, a University of Michigan study which found that 38 per cent of a transplant Honda's components were made in Japan[1] prompted threats of congressional action, as well as a controversial ruling that cars from Honda's Canadian plant should no longer enter the US duty-free because the engines came from Japan.

On the face of it, making Japanese-owned factories use more locally made parts sounds admirable. But apart from the unfairness of restricting Japanese-run factories in a way in which Western ones are not – American-owned Xerox copier factories in Europe, for example, can buy in as many non-EC parts as they want without penalty – there are other difficulties. For these so-called 'anti-circumvention' measures greatly diminish the competition which Japanese plants might have injected into the European market.

Such penal local content requirements, for example, have made Japanese plants in Europe 10 to 20 per cent more expensive than their plants in Asia.[2] The distortions introduced by such measures are epitomized by the Japanese computer-printer maker which had to 'design out' American semiconductors from its circuit boards to raise its EC-component content and so avoid dumping duties on its European-assembled printers.

This question of circuit boards graphically illustrates the illogicality and contradictions inherent in trying to enforce rigid country-of-origin rules in complex industries which require inputs from all over the world. It also demonstrates how, when you start down the road of setting up niggling import barriers in an increasingly global marketplace, the impact is seldom restricted to the intended target. But above all, it exemplifies the way in which such rules are forcing manufacturers to make choices based on political rather than economic considerations, dividing the world trading system more and more into separate trade blocs.

Virtuous interaction

A good example of this effect is provided by MITI figures which show that 40 per cent of the output of Japanese plants in the newly industrialized and rapidly developing countries of east and south-east Asia is exported – half of it to Japan itself. By contrast, only around 5 per cent of the production of Japanese factories in the United States and Europe is sold abroad.[3]

Why? Because while Japan's plants in Asia are to a significant extent part of a genuinely efficient, integrated production system, in the West they tend to be stand-alone units, geared primarily to circumventing trade barriers and supplying local markets.

The electronics giant Matsushita, for example, has forty-one plants in Asia and already sources a quarter of its Asian colour television set production from Malaysia. Japan itself imports a million colour televisions and video-recorders from the region each year, along with more than 10 million calculators and an increasing quantity of other medium-technology products.

Because, moreover, Japanese investment in Asia is genuinely economically integrated to a far greater extent than that in the West, it has played a significant role in enabling the countries of the region steadily to supplement or replace Japan as major suppliers first of low-technology goods such as black and white televisions, radios, toys and textiles; then of medium-technology products such as steel and ships; and more recently of fairly sophisticated goods like colour TVs, video recorders, CD players, personal computers and certain types of semiconductors.

This virtuous interaction has resulted in a genuine, international division of labour in Asia, allowing less-developed countries access to capital, enabling them to do what they can best do and so to evolve their economies. As a result, according to the International Monetary Fund, trade between Japan and the region increased far faster during the 1980s than trade with the West and has now surpassed Japanese trade with either Europe or the United States. Before long, Japan's overall trade with the Pacific Basin nations will be greater than her total trade with the rest of the world – and a further step will have been taken towards the division of the world into competing regional trading blocs.

Of course, Japan's trade relations with the newly industrialized countries such as South Korea and Taiwan, as well as the other increasingly developed nations of the region like Thailand, Malaysia, Indonesia and the Philippines, are not without friction. But the point is that barriers between these fast-growing economies and Japan are steadily being dismantled, whereas between the West and Japan they are multiplying.

Fear of domination

Arousing fear of Japanese domination has been an important element in the lobbying effort against their plants – particularly in the United States. Japanese investment in the West should, however, be placed in perspective. For headline-grabbing stories about new Japanese plants disguise the fact that Japan's investments are still a very long way from reaching a dominating position in the West.

By the beginning of 1990, for example, Japan's stake in the United States still totalled just over half of British-owned investments in America and not much more than those of the Netherlands. Overall, foreign groups only own about 5 per cent of US assets and Japan accounts for less than a fifth of this. Japanese investment in Europe is also still just a quarter of US direct investment.

Americans in particular should also bear in mind that their own industry has invested far more in overseas markets than foreigners have invested in the United States. If IBM can make three-quarters of its profits outside of the USA and General Motors can subsidize its loss-making US operation with earnings from Europe, why should Japanese companies not in turn make money in America?

But there is a further, related point. For a significant part of America's overseas investment is accounted for by industries which have moved manufacturing offshore to supply the US market. Over the past thirty years, American car and electronics manufacturers have rushed to shift production of cars, semiconductors and televisions to countries with low labour costs. Ford, for example, makes one of its best-selling cars, the Topaz, in Mexico. Television-maker Zenith has likewise moved most of its production across the Rio Grande.

Japanese companies, by contrast, have invested in more efficient production to reduce the impact of higher American labour costs and so have been able to establish reasonably competitive production facilities in the US itself. If Japanese companies are able efficiently to use American labour to build cars for the domestic market, that should be a cause for rejoicing, not complaint. Moreover, the American automobile industry can hardly complain about the Japanese presence when about 25 per cent of US transplant production comes out of joint ventures between Japanese manufacturers and the Big Three US producers, much of the production from which is sold under domestic brands.

Besides, the growth in Japan's overseas investment is no more than a normal stage in the development of its economy, closely paralleling the expansion of British and American investment in earlier eras. In the late nineteenth and early twentieth centuries it was European, and particularly British, money which went to the Americas and Africa. After the war, the major flows were of US investment into Europe and Asia. Now, in turn, Japanese money is coming to the West.

Unfortunately, beneficial though such investments are, the effect that Japanese plants could have in moderating the impact of trade barriers is greatly reduced by the hindrances and limits placed on their investments, with the result that they can play little real part in preventing the steady drift towards detached trading blocs – especially as the entreaties of western industrialists against Japanese plants are steadily reaching a new crescendo.

'Constructive co-operation'

According to the editor of *Car* magazine, conversations with the chiefs of French car-makers Renault and Peugeot are nowadays peppered with self-serving references to 'the poor little Japanese worker' and 'Japan's invasion plans'.[4] European car chiefs also habitually justify their own lobbying for protection by referring to 'hidden' measures restricting the sales of Western cars in Japan.

Most people hearing these remarks take them at face value and as a result are more willing to accept limits on Japanese imports or plants. Yet as the editor of *Car* points out, the Japanese market has for some time been one of the most open in the world. Sadly, lobbying by powerful industrial interests in Europe and America increasingly involves such innuendo to justify special pleading for subsidies and protection, reinforcing the tendency to see trade as a zero-sum game, a narrow view of competitive advantage which tends to degenerate into 'us versus them'.

Partly as a result of such tactics, the new European Community-wide EC–Japan car agreement concluded in 1991 is stricter than the national import quotas which it replaces, cutting the share of the overall EC market for Japanese imports from 10 per cent to just over 8 per cent. In addition, despite claims that transplant production from Japanese-owned factories in Europe will have 'free circulation' in the EC market, the deal is more than a little ambiguous on this issue.

For one thing, the accord, blandly entitled 'Elements of Consensus', contains references to the 'expectation' that output from Japanese-owned factories will not exceed 1.2 million by 1999. Originally unpublished appendices to the agreement, moreover, contain a further declaration

Eighty years ago, Japan was compelled to open her door to Europe and America. Japan's small-scale industries could not stand the competition of Western goods which were produced with superior machinery. Consequently they all ceased to exist. That is history. By discarding industries which did not suit her, and by concentrating on those best suited to her, she has now attained that stage where some of her industries are superior to those of the old industrial countries.[7]

It would also be wrong to conclude that the protection of infant industries ensures their success. Many more developing countries have failed to build successful industries behind trade barriers than have succeeded. Growing protectionism, moreover, did little to rescue Britain from steady economic decline in the first half of the twentieth century; nor were trade barriers effective in restoring American competitiveness during the 1980s.

So generalizations about rising economies tending towards protectionism and successful ones supporting free trade tell only part of the story. Moreover, notwithstanding the firmly held convictions of many Americans that theirs is an open economy, there has also been a consistent disposition towards trade barriers in the United States even during periods of undisputed economic pre-eminence.

Levering open markets

Another defence of trade barriers is the seemingly reasonable argument that the threat of action can be an important weapon in levering open foreign markets. The problem with this reasoning is that too often it has degenerated into specious claims that a particular foreign market is closed to justify the erection of tit-for-tat trade barriers.

Even where reciprocal action can be justified by the existence of foreign trade barriers, it rarely has the desired effect of prizing open markets. The outcome is more often escalation and increasing trade barriers. In 1963 the United States punished the European Community for a 45 per cent tariff on American frozen chicken by slapping a 25 per cent tariff on truck exports which primarily hit Volkswagen. Apart from the morality of penalizing companies which are unconnected with the offending trade barrier, the 'chicken war' failed to open EC markets, while the American truck tariff persists to this day, resulting in a $30 billion tax on US consumers since 1963.[8]

Reciprocal retaliatory action in effect holds domestic consumers hostage to the policies of foreign governments. The essence of the case is that your government is obliged to reduce the freedom of domestic consumers because a foreign government has decided to limit the opportunity of a producer in your country. This places the interests of that producer above those of millions of consumers. The fact that foreigners maintain trade barriers and that international trade conditions are not ideal is surely no justification for your own government to assume political control over trade and so make those conditions worse.

The debate has, moreover, recently been further debased by claims that reciprocal trade should involve not merely countries maintaining open markets, but also those importing a like amount of goods from one another. Ford's European chairman, for example, during one of his regular bouts of special pleading, argued that the EC should insist on 'reciprocity' with Japan, by which he meant not that their market should be equally open, but that Japan should import as many cars from EC countries as it exports.[9]

As there are no formal or informal restrictions on imports of European cars to Japan, this is, of course already possible – though unlikely until European car makers begin to match the Japanese in quality and efficiency. After all, Ford itself makes no effort to export its European models to Japan, preferring instead largely to sell Mazda's cars under the Ford badge.

'A fig leaf of moral respectability'

A similar rationale for trade restraints is the need to protect against unfairly subsidized imports which can, supposedly, drive domestic producers out of business. Free-trade purists would argue that under such circumstances it is the exporting country which actually suffers most by distorting its economy in a way which is unlikely, ultimately, to help the supported industry. The importing nation, on the other hand, gains from goods subsidized at foreign taxpayers' expense.

GATT does nonetheless recognize the right to protect against such unfair trade, and the usual method has been to impose countervailing duties to counterbalance the subsidy. However, once again it has been too easy for specious claims of unfair aid to foreign competitors to be used to excuse protection – while subsidies at home are conveniently forgotten.

At the same time as the United States imposed a surtax on Thai rice imports in 1986 on the grounds that the Thai government was providing tiny amounts of aid to its rice farmers (a mortgage programme provided a 0.02 per cent subsidy, for example), the US Department of Agriculture was providing nearly $1 billion to flood international markets with dumped rice. While the Thai rice programme spent less than $100 for each Thai rice farmer, the US programme spent the equivalent of more than $1 million for each full-time American rice grower between 1985 and 1990.[10]

Brazilian orange growers and Argentinean sheep farmers were similarly penalized for minuscule subsidies, while American citrus and sheep farmers were bankrolled by generous federal grants. In 1984 a Belgian steel company was even convicted of trading unfairly because, among other things, it received government aid for training its workers. Yet the US government systematically provides huge sums to allow American industry to do the same.

Low-cost credits for foreign exporters are loudly and regularly denounced as unfair by American politicians. But in the United States, even individual states have subsidized export loan guarantee programmes, supplementing the massive federal Export-Import Bank loans. According to Illinois Lieutenant Governor George H.Ryan: 'The key here is that we are not subsidizing our businesses – we are simply making low-risk, competitive-rate financing available to them when in practice it had not been available to them previously.' Quite. This is why the American trade expert, James Bovard, calls reciprocity 'a figleaf of moral respectability for American protectionists who claim they are shafting American consumers in order to teach foreigners a lesson.'[11]

The American system even allows countervailing duties to be maintained long after any supposed unfair subsidy has ended. In 1978 the US Commerce Department convicted Argentinean textile mills of receiving unfair subsidies. But in its annual reviews, the department found no subsidies from 1983 though to 1990. So the department finally announced its intention to revoke the duties – unless it heard an objection within thirty days from any interested party. The Amalgamated Clothing and Textile Workers' Union duly obliged and plans to cancel the duties were shelved. So much for level playing fields.

The whole argument that your own government should retaliate against the foolish decisions of foreign countries to subsidize or protect their industry is premised upon the assumption that the interests of producers are superior to those of consumers. This is a basic moral question. Should a government interfere in the free economic decisions of its citizens to make a contract to buy foreign goods? If the answer is yes, the interests of the consumer are being placed second to those of the producers. The resultant trade barrier in effect forcibly transfers income from the mass of citizens to the factory owner and a small number of workers. This is the moral basis of protectionism.

Of course, the protectionists go further, arguing that the trade barriers transcend the interests of the single factory or industry, benefiting the economy as a whole because the survival of a particular industry and its jobs is crucial. Almost invariably, however, trade barriers have served only to shield inefficiency and incompetence, or at best to preserve industries unsuited to the fundamental productive abilities of the economy in question. The result has been to put off necessary adjustment as well as to create high prices for consumers – which include other industries buying crucial supplies and components, with the consequent diversion of resources from efficient into inefficient industries and the disfiguring of the whole economy.

Protecting consumers

But perhaps the most alluring and persistent argument deployed by supporters of reciprocal and retaliatory trade measures is to appeal to the interest of consumers themselves. The argument is that the ultimate aim of unfair traders is to drive domestic producers out of the market, monopolize supply and so reap huge profits at consumers' expense. Trade barriers, they say, protect against that eventuality.

Perhaps consumers themselves should be left to make their own judgments as to which foreign goods represent a long-term threat to their economic well-being, rather than being nannied by politicians – especially when those politicians' own conclusions are clouded by a variety of considerations, not least among which is the extent to which their pockets have been lined by the companies soliciting protection.

The unfairest traders have anyway been among the most forlorn economies, such as India and Brazil – not wholly coincidentally. It seems highly unlikely that these nations, or their national champion corporations, are moving unerringly towards world domination. And if, say, the Japanese car manufacturers managed to drive the Big Three US car producers to the wall and then began pushing up prices, might not the Koreans see an opportunity to come in and undercut them?

Competition is the best guarantor against monopoly and high prices, and competition is not increased by government edicts designed to reduce the opportunities of its citizens to buy imported goods. In the words of the great American nineteenth-century free trader, William

Graham Sumner: 'The protective system puts us certainly in the hands of a home monopoly for fear of the impossible chance that we may fall into the hands of a foreign monopoly'.[12]

So even where exporting countries really do genuinely trade unfairly by protecting domestic markets or subsidizing exporters, the costs of retaliation are rarely worth it. The unilateral adoption of free trade, on the other hand, confers the benefits of low prices to the economy as a whole, benefits which almost invariably outweigh the disadvantages to home producers who, anyway, in an economy where the productive fundamentals are sound, will often respond by increasing efficiency, developing new products and so maintaining markets. Hong Kong, which has kept an open market and shunned retaliation against unfair traders, has also enjoyed the world's highest growth rate over the past three decades.

A dollar an hour

One justification for protection frequently deployed by trade unions is that competition from less developed nations is unfair because workers in poorer countries do not enjoy the same wages, working conditions and benefits as their counterparts in industrialized ones. This basis for protectionism has a distinguished history. As far back as 1916, American politicians were proposing banning imported goods made by fifteen-year-olds – even though millions of fifteen-year-olds were at that time working in the United States. By 1987, US congressmen were suggesting raising the age for unfair trade by embargoing goods from countries which refused to prohibit seventeen-year-olds from working at night – which would rule out the evening employees of many MacDonald's restaurants.[13]

American industry has recently eagerly seized on this line of argument to oppose the North America Free Trade Area pact with Mexico. The concept has, moreover, been institutionalized in the US 1988 Omnibus Trade Act which defines 'unfair trade' as, among other things, goods coming from countries without collective bargaining, statutory minimum wages, maximum hours of work, and health and safety rules.

One of the latest advocates of this particular brand of economic illiteracy was US presidential hopeful, Texas billionaire Ross Perot, who urged caution in accepting the proposed free-trade agreements with Mexico, saying: 'Just to suddenly throw the doors open will really, really, really, wipe out the jobs of millions of people in this country. A factory worker in Mexico makes a dollar an hour. I rest my case.'[14]

The popularity of this line is partly due to the fact that it cloaks its proponents in a misty-eyed veil of concern for Third World workers – always preferable to overt vested interest lobbying. But while there may well be grounds for restricting imports of goods which genuinely are made in ways which run counter to basic human rights, the main argument is completely specious. American workers are paid more than French ones. German workers enjoy better benefits than Italian ones. But does that justify the United States banning imports of goods from France; or Germany restricting Italian products? Is, moreover, a Bangladeshi clothing worker being 'exploited' if he is being paid only 50 cents an hour; or does this represent a relative advancement over alternative jobs – or lack of them?

The same debate has also taken place in Europe in the context of moves towards a free internal market within the European Community. Proponents of common social standards argue that trade can only be fair where such uniformity prevails. Yet how could Greece or Portugal hope to compete with Germany or the Netherlands if they had to bear the costs of German or Dutch levels of employee benefits, let alone wages?

Each country has labour conditions which are more or less appropriate to its level of development. Lower labour costs are an important source of competitive advantage for developing nations which can only afford higher wages and benefits as they become more productive. To argue that exports from such countries are unfair and should be restricted is to doom them to eternal economic backwardness. Moreover, the logical conclusion would be that only countries with exactly the same labour conditions, benefits and wages should trade with one another – which, of course, would mean the end of international trade.

Recently, this line of argument has also extended to vague talk of a 'social imbalance' between Japan and Europe, used particularly by French car manufacturers to justify anti-Japanese trade barriers. The idea is that Japanese workers meekly accept such bad working conditions and poor benefits that it constitutes an unfair advantage. This conveniently ignores the fact that the average Toyota worker earns around £24,000 a year, works a forty-hour week, enjoys an average four weeks' holiday and has a job for life. He also usually enjoys company-subsidized holidays and education for his children, lives in company-funded accommodation, probably eats in the same canteen as his boss and is almost certainly treated with more respect by his managers. It is true that

Japanese workers have different attitudes to their jobs, tending to work harder and more diligently. But that is hardly unfair.

'Unfair' advantages

Increasingly, basic, structural economic disparities have been cited as 'unfair' advantages and used to justify trade barriers. According to US Senator Hollings: 'Our rivals practice a bare-knuckles brand of controlled capitalism. ... They encourage savings. They do not give any interest deductions on consumer credits.'[15] So it is unfair that countries like Japan do not imitate the folly of some western countries by overtaxing savers and subsidizing consumption through tax breaks, so pushing up prices and interest rates as well as depriving industry of capital.

In both the 1988 US Omnibus Trade and Competitiveness Act and America's Structural Impediments Initiative (SII) talks with Japan, the notion of unfair trade practices has stretched further still into areas as diverse as domestic anti-monopoly policies, infrastructure spending, taxation and savings levels – in fact, the American menu in the SII talks runs to 240 items. But the idea that your competitors must change their domestic policies to suit your advantage if free trade is to be allowed is patently ridiculous.

It anyway seems perverse to delve deeper and deeper into the structure of Japan's economy in search of 'impediments' when the real problems are nearer home. For the harsh truth is that the real structural impediments to American exports are close at hand. Poor education and economic mismanagement are far more significant barriers to American industry than the Japanese distribution system. Or, as one observer cheekily pointed out: 'The strenuous effort required to close the door of many US cars is possibly the real 'non-tariff barrier' to the successful import of American cars to Japan.'[16]

American politicians have even concluded that any country which has a trade surplus with America must be an 'unfair' trader. In 1986 congressman Richard Gephardt proposed automatically to impose tariff surcharges on imports from nations with large surpluses. In 1987 he revised this to define an 'unwarranted trade surplus' as one which was 85 per cent larger than US exports. Senator Lloyd Bentsen preferred 65 per cent as a test of unfairness.[17] This pick-a-number definition of unfairness conveniently ignores the fact that during the 1950s the United States ran a huge trade surplus with Japan. Did that make the US an 'unfair' trader? In fact in those days the United States was somewhat less protectionist and Japan more so than is now the case.

Protecting the environment

Environmental considerations have also recently been invoked in support of trade restraints – such as the American ban on tuna caught with nets which were not 'dolphin-friendly'. There may well be genuine grounds for trade barriers in such instances. Certainly, in this case the United States gave the countries concerned good notice of the requirement to submit documentation proving that measures had been taken to protect marine mammals; and the embargo was lifted when this was complied with.

We should, however, beware protectionists in the guise of environmentalists. American industrial interests are particularly adept at this game. Successful campaigns have been waged by the soyabean lobby against the use of tropical oils on the grounds that they are often grown on deforested land, and by timber interests against imports of tropical hardwoods for similar reasons, campaigns which have found strong support among environmentalists and politicians alike.

Yet it seems strangely unjust for countries such as the United States – and indeed European nations too – which have chopped down most of their forests to object to developing nations doing the same. If the argument is that we need tropical forests as a global resource to preserve wildlife and absorb carbon dioxide – in part because we in the developed world have left so few trees standing – then instead of imposing trade sanctions on poorer nations for exporting timber, we should pay them for the carbon dioxide absorption service which they provide.

One important traditional principle of free international trade is that one country should not interfere in another's domestic sovereignty nor use other nations' rules as an excuse to deny access to their goods. For this would allow a country to restrict imports of a product solely because it originates in a country whose internal policies are different – a loophole which would allow any country unilaterally to impose its own standards and laws on others.

It is fair to say, however, that this breaks down when one country's environmental policies – or lack of them – directly impinges on another by causing, say, cross-border pollution, endangers a species or involves unacceptable cruelty. Hence the need for clear and enforceable rules and dispute-settlement procedures to ensure action is taken on a fair and multilateral basis, rather than by unilateral environmental vigilante action which merely clothes the naked protectionism beneath.

It is also worth reflecting that trade barriers are far more likely to harm the environment than free trade. The fiercely protectionist EC agricultural policy, for example, inflicts serious environmental damage by encouraging over-production and the unnecessary use of chemicals and fertilizers. Farm produce from countries like Argentina, Australia and Thailand, against which the EC barriers are aimed, use less than 10 per cent of the chemical fertilizer per acre used by European farmers. Trade barriers, moreover, that frustrate developing countries' ability to improve their living standards, and so gain access to modern technology and less environmentally damaging production methods, also hinder efforts to raise their standards of environmental protection.

A stronger GATT – or hostile blocs

The lesson surely is that the relationship between trade and environmental issues, labour conditions, subsidized exports or unfair structural advantages are now so complex that any trade-limiting action should always have to be sanctioned by GATT, not least to deter the temptation to use such concerns to cloak protectionism.

A greatly strengthened GATT is crucial to prevent the further build up of import quotas, anti-dumping actions, managed trade and bilateral deals in Europe and America. These do not just undermine and distort the world's economy, hindering the efficient allocation of production and resources, but are also steadily fragmenting the global trading system into three hostile trading blocs – Fortress Europe based on the European Community; an increasingly inward-looking North America, where the United States is concluding a series of trade agreements with Mexico and Canada; and the more outward-looking east Asian bloc centred on Japan.

Although each of these regional economic groupings is in the process of dismantling barriers against fellow bloc members, at the same time the American and European blocs are raising them against outsiders and so segmenting the global trading system. One of the North American Free Trade Area (Nafta) agreements, for example, specifies that Mexican garments must use North American yarn and cloth to qualify for duty-free entry into the US. And while Mexico has agreed to drop tariffs on most US products to zero, the fair trade promoters in Washington have pressed it to maintain tariffs on outside suppliers, so helping to make

Mexico captive to American suppliers who will enjoy a significant price advantage.[18]

Detroit has also levied its pound of flesh. For while existing US-Canadian free trade agreements specify that 50 per cent of a vehicle has to be manufactured in North America to escape import tariffs, the Big Three have persuaded their government to propose raising this to 65 per cent under the Nafta accord. Although the Mexicans and Canadians have resisted, the car companies have enough friends in the US Congress to cause Nafta problems unless their demands are acceded to. The result of such pandering to industrial vested interests is that open market arrangements within these groupings serve as stumbling blocks, rather than the building blocks of genuine global free trade.

Notes

1 Quoted in the *Financial Times*, 8 November 1991.

2 Patrick A.Messerlin and Yoshiyuki Noguchi, 'EC industrial policy: worse than before', in the *Financial Times*, 24 October 1991.

3 MITI survey of 3,331 Japanese companies with overseas affiliates.

4 *Car*, October 1991.

5 *Financial Times*, 23 September 1991.

6 Quoted in the *Financial Times*, 13 September 1991.

7 Isoshi Asahi, *The Secret of Japan's Trade Expansion*, Tokyo, 1934.

8 American International Automobile Dealers' Association estimate, quoted in James Bovard, *The Fair Trade Fraud*, St Martin's Press, New York, 1991.

9 *Financial Times*, 13 September 1991.

10 James Bovard, *The Fair Trade Fraud*, St Martin's Press, New York, 1991.

11 Ibid – many of the preceeding cases are quoted in Bovard.

12 William Graham Sumner, *Protectionism*, Henry Holt, New York, 1888.

13 Bovard, *The Fair Trade Fraud*.

14 Speech to the Association for Investment Management and Research national convention, 1992.

15 Congressional Record, 7 September 1988.

16 Mark Zimmerman, *Dealing with the Japanese*, George Allen & Unwin, London, 1985.

17 Bovard, *The Fair Trade Fraud*.

18 *Financial Times*, 9 June 1992.

16 Trade War

It is not true that people do not learn the lessons of history. They do: but then they forget.

Jan Tumlir, former chief economist at GATT

The crucial question is whether these trade tensions will go further, leading to political conflict and even war, as happened to some extent in the 1930s, and as recently predicted by some commentators.

Certainly, trade and politics have always been inextricably linked. Japan's imperial expansion in the 1930s was itself partly dictated by economic necessity. For Japan's rapidly growing population was at that time dependent on the United States together with British, Dutch and French colonies for oil, rubber and food. Mass emigration was not really an option in view of United States restrictions against immigrants from Japan, so imports were the only solution. But these had to be paid for by exports composed mainly of textiles and basic manufactured goods which, by the late 1920s, were meeting increasing tariffs and other barriers in the West and many of its colonies.

The loss of foreign markets and depression at home prompted internal repression and external aggression as Japan was impelled by a feeling that the western powers were hogging the world's resources and markets through their colonies. But Japan's subsequent push into China provoked the wrath of America, itself anxious not to be shut out of the potentially vast Chinese market. This resulted in American embargoes on exports of oil and other raw materials to Japan.

At that stage Japan had two options. First, it could back down and accede to all of the American demands – that is, relinquish its newly won Asian empire, cede control of its raw material supplies to the western powers with their Asian colonies, and accept the permanent status of a second-class power. Or it could fight – and with the oil situation becoming desperate, everything militated for the rapid, but ultimately disastrous strike on Pearl Harbor.

Trade tensions to political quarrels to military conflict?

Trade tensions were not alone responsible for the outbreak of war in the Pacific and elsewhere. But they contributed greatly to the rise of the militarists in Japan, who exploited widespread resentment at the way in which people perceived that they were being both shut out of western markets and denied access to the resources they urgently needed. So a war between Japan and America, considered virtually unthinkable just two decades earlier, became a reality.

Now, once again, the world is moving into a dangerous period of shifting economic power, provoking strains which uncomfortably echo those of the 1930s. Moreover, the beginnings of a backlash are evident in Japan, epitomized by a recent provocative book called *The Japan that Can Say 'No'* by 68-year-old Akio Morita, the cosmopolitan founder of Sony, and Shintaro Ishihara, a right-wing LDP Diet member with a reputation for being something of an *enfant terrible.*

The Morita-Ishihara book originally sold only a few copies and was not intended for publication abroad, but it was read by a Japanese-speaking American working for a Tokyo company. His office arranged for a private translation and before long copies found their way to the United States, first circulating in California's Silicon Valley and later on Capitol Hill.

The bluntness of much of the book's language shook American sensitivities to the core. Alarmed by increasing American dependence on Japanese technology, the Defense Department's Advanced Research Projects Agency, which channels state aid into high-tech industrial research, commissioned its own bootleg translation which it circulated widely to politicians and corporate leaders of companies most threatened by Japanese competition.

Congressmen and senators, rarely slow off the mark when it comes to Japan-bashing, were soon also making copies with the most intemperate passages underlined, passing them round and telling friends: 'I told you so', vying with each other in the strength of their denunciations. Needless to say, industrialists rapidly joined the fray, like Chrysler's Iacocca, who dubbed the book 'an insult to the American people'.

All of which was a shame because aside from a fair sprinkling of nonsense, a good proportion of the work, which is more a collection of essays than a book, makes some sense and there is plenty of frank admission of Japanese faults. Its main thesis, aside from the fact that America's problems are largely of its own making, is that Japan should be more forthright in its dealings with the West or it will continue to be trampled on.

The very fact that such a book was written indicates a change in Japanese attitudes, but the controversial anti-American strain contained within it – which closely parallels the style of the more hysterical school of American writing on Japan – is a more ominous indication of the complex of resentments that are currently bubbling beneath the surface in Japan.

It should, therefore, come as no surprise that a survey of Japanese junior high-school students named the United States as the nation Japan would most likely fight in a war, while more than half of those polled by a leading Japanese newspaper felt that the United States was unfairly indulging in Japan-bashing, a situation most feared would intensify.[1] At the same time, following French prime minister Edith Cresson's disparaging remarks about Japan, police had to mount guard over French interests in Tokyo to prevent attacks by infuriated right-wingers, while the Foreign Ministry summoned France's ambassador to deliver a stiff protest without precedent since 1945.

So it would be foolish to rule out the possibility of trade tensions leading first to political quarrels, and subsequently drifting to military conflict. For whatever hopes of a New World Order have been kindled by the failure of communism, nothing over the past 2,000 years has occurred to contradict Plato's maxim that 'only the dead have seen the end of war.'

Yet there are also important differences from the 1930s. Japan went to war with America in 1941 largely because the United States and the European colonial powers were denying it the oil and raw materials whose supply they dominated. Now, however, tensions are being provoked by Japanese exports and economic power rather than Japan's need for imports. Control over raw materials, moreover, is far more diverse than it was during the 1930s. An American embargo on oil, wheat and soya exports to Japan would be no more than a joke as Australia, New Zealand, Brazil, Argentina and any number of oil exporters gleefully rushed to fill the deficit.

In other areas, however, trade problems may provoke more dangerous developments. For although Japan is now the main victim of western trade barriers, the Third World, Turkey and the newly-emerging democracies of eastern Europe have also experienced trade problems with Europe and America.

Trade, not aid

Textiles is one of the few industries where less developed countries are able to compete with more advanced ones. This is because the opportunities for automation are relatively limited with the result that a high labour content is inevitable, giving lower-wage countries an important edge. Textiles is also the traditional springboard for industrial development. It is a huge industry, accounting for some 10 per cent of world trade in manufactures.

Yet imports of textiles and other basic goods from poorer nations are the very ones which the rich, industrialized Western countries restrict most, with serious consequences. For according to the World Bank, developing countries lose as much as a result of export restraints on such products as they currently receive in aid from those richer countries.[2] Chilean finance minister, Alejandro Foxley, goes further: 'If all the existing barriers that prevent developing countries from selling their goods could be removed at a stroke,' he says, 'this would do more good to the developing countries than doubling the flow of aid.'[3]

Damaging though they are to poorer countries, such trade restrictions can hardly be said to be crucial to the strategic industrial interests of the developed world. What possible justification can there be, for example, in imposing anti-dumping duties on exports of Chinese espadrilles, disposable lighters or paintbrushes to the EC? Europe's industrial future is not going to be assured by making cheap lighters, brushes or shoes. On the other hand they are among the few products that the Chinese can make and sell abroad successfully.

Would, moreover, the strategic interests of American industry really suffer were the US to allow Haiti to sell it more than the permitted quota of 8,030 tons of sugar? And isn't there something very mean and ignoble about a country as wealthy as the United States imposing anti-dumping duties on shop towels – cloths used for wiping machine parts – from Bangladesh, a country whose 108 million people have an average income of less than $200 a year, especially when imports amounted to a princely $2.46 million a year?

Why, furthermore, does a rich country like the United States need to be the keenest user of Multi-Fibre Arrangement (MFA) provisions, with no fewer than twenty-nine separate restraint agreements limiting textile and clothing imports from poorer countries such as Nepal, Mauritius, Trinidad and Tobago, Burma and El Salvador – the last of which the United States has been aiding militarily supposedly to support democracy and the free market system? (In fairness, the United States does not only restrict textile imports from poorer countries. It also imposes MFA quotas against Japan – the only country to do so – and slashed Japan's quota entitlement in 1990 by 25 per cent.)

On the one hand, Western governments help poorer countries with aid, but then prevent them from helping themselves by penalizing their industries with trade barriers. Sometimes the whole process is conveniently, if ludicrously, integrated. During the 1980s the United States slashed the amount of sugar that poorer Caribbean countries could sell to its citizens, but generously dumped almost $200 million of free food resulting from its own subsidized, protected farm programme, so making it even harder for Caribbean farmers to replace sugar with other crops.

Such policies only make it less likely that developing countries will be able to be weaned off of aid from richer ones. Trade, not aid, is what the poorer nations need. Of course, freer access to Western markets will not alone save the Third World. Developing countries themselves have been far too prone to protectionism and interventionist economic policies. A World Bank analysis of 60 developing countries in 1991 pointed out that those poorer nations which had the most market-oriented policies and which had invested in education had grown at a far faster rate than those with centrally-planned economies and less emphasis on education.[4]

Many Third World countries have now accepted this and a wave of liberalization and deregulation is sweeping through much of the developing world. Yet as they are undergoing the painful process of opening up their markets, the example they get from richer countries is not always very edifying. For only two industrialized nations are seriously dismantling trade barriers against poorer countries.

One is Sweden, which abandoned MFA restrictions in 1989. The other is Japan, which since 1989 has abolished or reduced tariffs on 154 separate categories of goods from tropical countries – 'the first such move on a large scale by any major industrialized nation', according to GATT.[5] But for the United States and other rich countries, it would seem that maintaining the job of a textile worker at several times the cost of putting that worker on a fully paid, permanent vacation is more important than letting countries like Haiti and Bangladesh develop badly needed export industries.

Stunting reform – Turkey and eastern Europe

Then there is the position of Turkey, precariously balanced between developing-nation status and industrialization, as well as between western liberal democracy and Islamic fundamentalism. Turkey occupies a pivotal position between Europe, the Middle East and Central Asia; it has been a linchpin of NATO, guarding Europe's southern flank against the Soviet threat since the war; it also allowed air bases on Turkish soil to be used during the Gulf War. Yet Turkey's reward for all of this, and for moving steadily towards genuine democracy, has been abrupt rebuffs for its attempts to join the European Community.

The stated reason is that Turkey's human rights record is not yet good enough. But the real underlying cause is the fear of Turkish textiles, agricultural goods and basic products like steel by powerful European industrial interests. To add insult to injury, over the past few years both the EC and the United States have imposed strict limits on exports of Turkish textiles under the MFA, virtually prohibited Turkish exports of fruit and vegetables, and severely restricted sales of Turkish steel products.

All of which makes Turkey more rather than less likely to turn its back on seventy years of steady westernization. And with the prospect of several unstable Islamic states emerging in central Asia from the rubble of the Soviet Union, the possibility of a snubbed Turkey turning increasingly eastward makes the politics of this crucial region all the more unpredictable.

To the north, the European Community made it clear to the newly emerging democracies of eastern Europe that rapid EC membership was out of the question, but offered Hungary, Czechoslovakia and Poland negotiations on an agreement of association with the EC. Even this limited ambition foundered on the rocks of Community protectionism when the most that the EC would offer was a ten-year transition to free trade. In the meantime, the Community agreed to make tariff cuts in all sectors except farm goods, glass, chemicals, coal, steel and textiles – the very commodities for which these countries most want access. More than half of Poland's exports to the EC, for example, comprise these products.

Eventually, the EC Commission did also offer to dismantle quotas on Polish steel over a five-year period – but only provided the Poles do not undercut EC prices. In textiles the Community wants to keep quotas for ten years, while on farm products even a very limited EC offer made in 1991 to provide access for a few hundred tons of Polish beef proved too much for the French, who blocked it late in 1991 at the behest of their farmers.

A visit by an EC Commissioner to Estonia in 1991 to show 'solidarity' with the Baltic state's claim for independence shortly after the failed Soviet coup was somewhat marred when an Estonian minister requested access to the EC market for his country's textiles, only to be told by the embarrassed Commissioner that EC solidarity did not extend quite that far and the Estonians would be better advised to find markets for such goods further east.

To add insult to injury, the European Bank for Reconstruction and Development (EBRD), established largely by the EC nations to finance development in eastern Europe, became entangled in trade tensions when the bank's vice-president, Ronald Freeman, complained that he had to tread warily in funding promising areas such as food, textile, steel and cars because these industries were sensitive 'hot buttons' in Brussels. A loan to a Hungarian car plant was, for example, delayed after French objections that tax concessions granted to the project encouraged unfair competition. French state subsidies to car maker Renault have totalled some £10 billion. The United States is little better, limiting a raft of imports form Eastern Europe. Poland, for example, is only allowed to sell it 350 tons of alloy tool steel a year. In the words of one frustrated OECD official: 'For the areas where the Poles, Hungarians and Czechs are most competitive, the industrialized countries are most protectionist.'[6]

Unfortunately such attitudes have proved contagious. Western European car manufacturers have made the establishment of plants in eastern Europe dependent on their rivals being excluded from those markets. Poland divided its import quota among just three western countries which were investing in the country, while appeals by General Motors, which has centred its east European investment in Hungary, resulted in Hungarian car-import quotas being tightened. Hungary went one better for Ford, issuing a government decree in the summer of 1992 which exempted from import tariffs vans meeting strict specifications. One foreign van qualified – the Ford Transit. Ford had just opened a £46 million component plant in western Hungary.

So the opportunity of creating a genuinely integrated European market, stretching from the Urals to the Atlantic, is receding. Instead of car manufacturers building plants of a genuinely economic scale and concentrating component production where the work can best be carried out, they are investing in a series of small-scale, localized ventures which are not competitive in a global sense and rely on protection for their viability. Instead of the eastern Europeans being allowed to evolve those industries most appropriate to their stage of development, freely exporting products to the West and buying more sophisticated goods in return, they are finding their progress restricted by the myopic, inward-looking mentality of the supposedly free-market nations to the west.

One of the advantages of free trade is that goods, services and capital move around – not people. At a time when western Europe is undergoing an anguished debate about the rising tide of migrants from the east, they should consider that one of the best ways of obviating the need for Poles, Hungarians, Czechs and Romanians to leave home is to help to ensure the opportunity for successful economic development in the east.

Yet as the former Eastern bloc nations struggle to escape from the disastrous centrally-planned economic system which has stunted their development since the war, they find that the vision of the economies of western Europe is restricted by the demands of inefficient industries. As a result, these so-called 'free market' economies are not prepared to extend the advantages of open markets to the very nations to which they have preached those advantages for so long. The obduracy of the Community is hampering a successful transition by eastern European countries to market economies and, by denying them access to western markets, is making future conflict more, rather than less, likely. Moreover, it is paradoxical that at the very time when the battle against communism has been won, in no small part due to the failure of socialist economic policies of interventionism, the West itself is slipping increasingly into a muddle of managed trade and state direction of key industries.

This is not to say that the road Europe and America are taking will lead to the type of economies the former communist countries are now seeking to reform. But any move towards more centrally controlled economic policies is likely further to damage western economic prospects, diverting attention from the real tasks of ensuring sound education and a stable monetary environment in which business can flourish.

The coming credit crunch

Europe and America should seriously ask whether it is worth risking so much for the sake of a few vested interests. For the result of the drift into protectionism may not merely be the relative impoverishment of the world economy. The dangers inherent in allowing the slide to continue are greater than that.

The choice is, on the one hand, between a steadily more pauperized and alienated developing world; the possibility of Turkey turning away from the West towards fundamentalism; an unstable, precariously democratic eastern Europe regressing into intolerant nationalism; and ever worsening tensions with an increasingly economically powerful east Asian economic zone: and, on the other hand, a more stable and prosperous world bonded in mutual dependence by trade.

This situation may be made more dangerous as a result of a coming credit crunch in the mid-1990s which will add to protectionist pressures. For whereas during the 1980s much of the funding for the global economy came from recycled German and Japanese surpluses and Arab oil money, the situation has drastically changed. Arab money is now tied up in the reconstruction of Kuwait and the strengthening of the Gulf area's defences, while the now huge German budget deficit brought about by the costs of reunification is also absorbing huge sums. Japanese finance, which has been significantly responsible for funding US budget deficits, is also becoming more cautious while problems in the Japanese stock market and financial system, together with a tighter monetary policy, have led to more of Japan's money staying at home.

While these three great engines of global finance are seemingly stuck in reverse, the extra demands for funds from the former eastern bloc nations and Middle East reconstruction will equal at least $80 billion a year between 1992 and 1996, according to an International Monetary Fund report,[7] requiring massive reductions in state budget deficits and huge increases in savings to provide the finance. But with the American budget deficit apparently institutionalized and savings actually falling in many Western countries, the pool of international capital seems dangerously low, a situation which may lead to severe economic problems and aggravated trade tensions as the 1990s wear on.

So although it may be difficult for politicians to hold out against the self-serving pleading of uncompetitive industrialists, it has now become critical to do so. The vehicle for this must be a reinvigorated GATT, to which the western industrialized nations must show a renewed commitment.

This commitment must involve more than just the rhetoric and self-serving manoeuvering which has characterized so much of the Uruguay Round. There has, for example, been more than just a suspicion that by insisting on putting agriculture before all else during the GATT talks, the United States was not so much wishing to lever open markets for an industry in which it has a significant competitive advantage; but rather that it was diverting attention and negotiating effort from other areas, such as industrial goods, where recent American trade actions have been retrogressive. In order for GATT to succeed, and indeed maybe even survive in an era when it has increasingly been bypassed, the organization has to be strengthened by giving it a genuine judicial role in trade disputes, taking decisions out of the hands of national politicians and so removing those decisions from the power of domestic vested interests.

Just as crucial are internal reforms in Europe and America, which must drop self-satisfied attitudes and be more prepared to learn from the Japanese, to improve education, to ensure more market-oriented economies and stable monetary conditions, so allowing the West to compete on more equal terms with Japan and the newly industrialized economies of east Asia. Above all, western industrialists will have to realize that they can only become competitive by accepting competition, rather than evading it.

Japan's responsibility

This is not to say that Japan itself does not have an important role and responsibility in the direction which the world economy takes in the run-up to the next century. The last few years has witnessed something of a debate as to how Japan can match her economic strength with an increasing role in world affairs. So far, this debate has centred on Japan providing more aid to developing countries and increasing its share of the burden of military spending.

American claims that Japan has greatly benefitted from the protective shield provided by American military might are, in the view of many, justified. But at this stage not much is to be gained by the Japanese imitating the Americans by significantly boosting military spending. Rather, Japan's new international role should involve being prepared to stand up for the genuine globalization of the world economy. This means Japan itself being prepared to make more concessions in difficult areas such as agriculture. It also means ending the traditional Japanese habit of meekly acquiescing to managed trade agreements and import quotas which may offer the easy option in the short term, but in the long run can only lead to the division and impoverishment of the world economy.

Settling trade disputes in smoke-filled rooms may have been Japan's only choice during the first decades after the war. But now Japan has the economic strength to go beyond such short-term palliatives and to play a major role in ensuring competition and open markets on a global scale.

The decision to break out of this vicious cycle of protectionism must also involve Japanese industry itself. Those companies which indirectly benefit in the short term from Western trade barriers – as a result of higher prices for their goods – should take a broader and more long-term view of what really is in their interests.

Japanese business and political leaders, moreover, must be prepared to lay aside their distaste for direct confrontation and to stand up to and counter the criticism that Japan is an unfair trader. Too often such condemnation is unjustified and merely a smokescreen for the erection of trade barriers in Europe and America.

But at a time of massive shifts in global political and economic power, the main obligation lies with the nations of the West to be big enough to admit that the responsibility for their problems lies at home. It would be a bitter irony if the United States, which played such a huge role in rescuing the world from tyranny in the 1940s and protecting it from communism in the post-war era, and the European Community which performed a crucial part in binding together the formerly warring nations of Europe, should themselves become the vehicles for the growing economic tensions which could fragment the world sometime in the next century.

Notes

1 Survey of 3,000 people in the *Mainichi Shimbun*, 18 June 1991.

2 *The Challenge of Development – World Development Report*, Oxford University Press, Oxford, 1991.

3 Quoted in the *Financial Times*, 28 October 1991.

4 *The Challenge of Development*, op. cit.

5 *GATT Review of Developments in the Trading System: September 1988 – February 1989*.

6 Quoted in the *Financial Times*, 11 May 1992.

7 International Monetary Fund, *World Economic Outlook*, second half of 1991.

Index

adaptation of foreign technology, 172–3
Advanced Battery Consortium, 198
aerospace industry, 84–5; *see also names of individual companies*
agriculture: farm policies, 125, 127–9, 233–4; tariffs, 3, 33, 217; trade barriers, 45
Airbus Industrie, 84, 100–1
alcohol trade, 49–51, 66–7
American Electronics Association, 178, 197–8
Anglo-Iranian Oil Company, 144
anti-dumping measures, ix, 5, 7, 8–9, 18, 19–22, 108, 118, 146, 187, 205, 206–7, 223, 228
anti-monopoly/-trust legislation, 98–9
Apple, 110, 198
Arab nations, 144, 233
Argentina, 28, 217, 227
Asia, East and South-east, 207–8
AT&T, 24, 99, 174, 178, 198
Australia, 130, 227

banana trade, 115–16
Bangladesh, 228–9
bankruptcies: Japan, 150, 163
Baunutzungs Verordnung (German retail law), 47
blood testing, trade barriers and, 116
BMC, 86–7, 97
BMW, 44–5, 113, 194
Boeing, 27, 84, 99, 100–1, 200
Brazil, viii, 21, 33, 92, 100, 124, 189, 217, 218, 227; computer industry, 95; 'informatica' law, 109
'breathing space' as purpose of protection, 114
Bretton Woods conference, 1–2
bribery and corruption, 117, 141

Britain, *see* United Kingdom
Bull (Groupe), 69, 74, 87, 199
Buy America Act, 60

Canada, 40, 41, 57, 60, 66–7, 124, 224
Canon, 11, 13, 15, 16, 17, 155–6, 157–8, 160, 170
capital, availability/cost of, 164, 166
Caribbean: banana trade, 115–16; sugar trade, 126, 229
Carlson, Chester, 14
cartels, 145–6
Caterpillar, 98, 111
Cessna Citation, 27
China, 28, 48, 144, 172, 173–4, 225, 228
Chrysler, 19, 56, 72–3, 77n., 81, 111, 113, 153, 198
citrus trade, 217
Cobden, Richard, 37, 71, 196–7
Coca Cola, 47, 190
coffee market: Renault and, 86
Colombia, 86
Columbia Pictures, 5, 35
Committee of European Copier Manufacturers, 10–11
commodity markets, 130
Common Agricultural Policy [EC], 127, 223
'comparative advantage', 212
competition, principle of, 97, 149
competitive advantage, national, 130–47
computer industry, 6, 31, 74, 85, 89, 150, 213; consortia, 198–200; disk drive industry, 19–20; microchip industry, 23–6, 178; notebook computers, 150–1, 156, 157; personal computers, 23; *see also names of individual companies*
Concorde, 84–5, 199

236

Index

condoms, 88; trade barriers and, 116
consortia, government-backed, 198–200
construction contracting industry, 177
consumption, excessive, 42, 45
'copying' of ideas, 172–3, 176, 179
copyrights, 175
credit restrictions, 143
Cresson, Edith, 1, 43, 146–7, 227
Czechoslovakia, 230–2

D-Rams, 110, 213
Daihatsu, 81, 153
Daimler Benz, 153–4, 211; *see also* Mercedes Benz
debt finance, 162–4
decentralization of responsibility: Japanese industry, 137
defence and military spending: Japan, 142, 234; United States, 89
Defense Advanced Projects Agency (Darpa), 89, 198
deficits (balance of payments), 2
Demming, W. Edwards, 171–2
Democratic Party [US], 32, 69
developing countries, 3, 8, 220, 227–9
DIN (Deutsche Industrie-Norm), 51
division of labour, international, 208
domestic consumption, 143–4, 164
dumping, 7–8, 126–8, 151–2; *see also* anti-dumping duties
Dunlop, 190, 192

Eastern Europe, 8, 28, 105, 227–8, 230–3
education, vocational, 195–6; lack of, 221
electronics industry, 6, 70, 72, 83, 85, 151, 155, 156, 175, 202, 213; *see also names of individual companies*; computer industry
employment, viii, 117–19, 142, 171, 206
environment, the, 43, 112, 147, 222–3
equity finance, 163, 181
Estonia, 231
European Bank for Reconstruction and Development, 231
European Commission, 11–13, 62, 64, 206
European Community, 235; and Eastern Europe, 230–2; and Turkey, 230; anti-dumping measures, 7–9, 11–13, 18; Common Agricultural Policy, 127, 223; import restrictions, 61–2, 216; over-subsidy of steel industry, 100; relative wage levels, 220; research and development programmes, 201–2
exports, 151, 189–90, 215; credits, 87, 100
Export Risk Guarantee programme [Switzerland], 87–8

Fairchild Semiconductor 35, 165
Fiat, 113, 159–60, 165
Finland: and EC import quotas, 62
flotation, 163
food industries, 121–8; *see also individual commodities*; agriculture
Food Motor Company, 43, 45, 48–9, 55–6, 74, 111, 113, 152–3, 165, 183, 189, 198, 209, 216, 231
France: prime minister's remarks and relations with Japan, 227
Fujitsu, 25, 74, 96, 161, 165

GATT (General Agreement on Tariffs and Trade), 1–4, 7, 18, 27–8, 34, 50, 51, 58, 60, 126–7, 212, 216, 223, 229, 233–4; Geneva round, 3; Tokyo round, 3; Uruguay round, 1, 4, 60–1, 104, 123, 127, 233
GEC, 165, 199
General Electric, 24, 89–90, 105, 155
General Motors, 73–4, 88, 99, 113, 153, 160, 165, 166, 188, 193, 194, 198, 209
Germany: and US import quotas, 56; competition with Japan, 177, 189; education, 148; import restrictions, 62, 114, 214; military vehicles, 115; reunification, costs of, 233; road haulage toll, 63; subsidies to industry, 87
Gestetner, 17, 43
group ethos, 131, 169, 193
growth, economic: priority in Japan, 143–4, 145, 181
Grundig, 151–2

Haiti, 228–9
Haloid Company, 14
Harley-Davidson, 155, 187–8
HDTV (high-definition television), 198–9, 201
Hewlett Packard, 25, 198
Hills, Carla, 32–3
Hitachi, 20, 157–8, 178, 202

237

Index

Honda, 44–5, 81, 149, 152–3, 155, 157–8, 166, 193–4, 202, 207
Hong Kong, 6, 9, 189, 219
hovertrain technology, 177, 201
Hungary, 230–2

IBM, 14, 15, 17, 24, 31, 43, 85, 99, 110, 171–2, 190, 198, 209
ICL, 74, 85, 95–6
import restrictions, 8–9, 36, 54–7, 113, 188; quotas, 6, 54–6, 61–2, 126, 233, 228–31; *see also* anti-dumping measures; import restrictions: quotas
India, viii, 33, 92, 95, 100, 189, 218
Industrial Reorganization Corporation [UK], 86, 97
industrial sophistication, comparative levels of, ix, 213–14, 228–31
industrial unrest, 131–2, 169
inflation, control of, 164
information technology industry, 25; *see also* computer industry
Intel, 24, 25, 198
interdependence, principle of, 211–12
interest rates, 164
International Monetary Fund (IMF), 2, 108, 208, 233
International Standards Organization, 51
International Trade Organization, 2
Italy, 87, 164, 165

Jaguar, 44, 97, 194
Japan: ageing of population, 179: creditor status, 6; cultural biases, 40, 45, 47, 50; domestic market, 150; education and training, 131–40, 147, 148, 161, 168, 191, 195–6; GDP/GNP, 40–1; group ethos, 131, 169; history, 38, 48, 79, 131, 144, 173–4, 190–1, 215, 225; infant mortality, 143; labour relations, 168–70; land shortage, 180; life expectancy, 142–3, 147, 179; social elite emerging, 180
Japan that can say 'no', The (A. Morita & S. Ishihara), 226–7
Japanese Consumer Product Safety Association, 51
JAPEX, 81
jobs *see* employment
joint manufacture, US-Japanese; motor industry, 73–4

juku schools, 133, 135, 139–40
just-in-time parts delivery system, 171

Kawasaki, 79, 156, 203
keiretsu system, 158–60
Kodak, 15, 17, 174
Korea, North, 212
Korea, South, 6, 28, 32, 101, 102, 104, 113, 126, 174, 178–9, 208, 213, 218; and Western import quotas, 21, 57, 61–2
kyohokai suppliers, 158

labour unions, 31–2, 132, 217; in-house enterprise unions (Japan), 169–70; *see also* industrial unrest
Land Rover, 88, 114, 153–4, 165
Leyland, 86–7, 97, 165
Liberal Democratic Party [Japan], 122, 141, 181
licences, overseas, 175–6, 178
lifetime employment system (Japanese industry), 171
loan finance, 163
local content requirements, 206
lower-cost goods, trade bariers and, ix, 112, 116, 228–31

McDonald's, 47, 190, 219
Malaysia, 208
managed trade, ix, 27–8, 223, 232
market forces: government intervention compatible with, 101–2
market share, 151; long-term, 162
marketing: costs ignored in anti-dumping regulations, 9
Massachusetts Institute of Technology, 58, 183
Matsushita, 23, 138, 157–8, 166, 174, 178, 184, 208
Mazda, 45, 48–9, 74, 81, 100, 153, 166, 169–70, 194, 216; indicted for 'dumping', 19
MCC consortium, 200
Mega Project, 198
Meiji, *Emperor*, 79, 135, 174
memory chips, 110, 178, 213
Mercedes Benz, 44–5, 183, 194; *see also* Daimler Benz
Mexico, 209, 219, 223–4
microcars, 112
microrobots, 177

238

Index

MITI (Minstry of International Trade and Industry) [Japan], viii, 73, 78–83, 91–2, 97–8, 100–5, 150, 178, 180
Mitsubishi group, 5, 34, 73, 77n., 79, 81, 98, 157, 166, 178, 213
Morita, Akio, 149, 168, 175, 192, 226–7
motivation in industry, 168–70, 203
motor industry, 55–6, 61, 64, 76, 81, 86, 112–13, 118, 152–5, 166, 175–6, 182–4, 194, 210–11, 216, 224, 231; *see also names of individual companies*
motorcycle industry, 113, 155, 187–8, 193–4, 202–3; *see also names of individual companies*
Motorola, 89, 178, 198
Multi-Fibre Arrangement (MFA), 1974, 3, 103–5, 108, 114, 228–9, 230

NAFTA (North American Free Trade Area), 223–4
NASA, 89–90
NASP project, 88–90
National Consumer Council, 18, 108
national poverty, Japanese perception of, 48
NEC, 20, 23, 58, 138, 155–6, 177, 178
new technology, 175, 178, 183–4
New York Telephone Company, 137
New Zealand, 205, 227
Nigeria, 95
Nissan, 44, 81, 100, 137, 160, 166, 169, 170, 175, 194
Nixon, Richard, 54, 59, 123, 182
Norway: and EC import quotas, 62
nuclear power industry, 105; *see also names of individual companies*

Oce, 13, 17
OECD (Organization for Economic Cooperation and Development), ix, 40, 87, 105, 205
oil industry, 81–2, 144; crisis, 192, 225–6, 227; *see also names of individual companies*
Olivetti, 13, 17, 43, 74
Omnibus Trade Act, 1988 [US], 219, 221
Organization for Trade Cooperation (proposed), 2

patent, 175–6
Pentagon, the, 25, 89, 94, 165

Peugeot, 43, 113, 210
Philippines, 127, 208
Philips, 24, 43, 75, 151–2, 165–6, 178, 198–9
photocopier industry, 10–17, 30–1, 74, 113–14
Plan Calcul, 86
Poland, 230–2
population density: Japan, 147
Porsche, 175, 194
pricing, 151; price-fixing, 146
process industries, 213
product design and innovation, 155, 160–2
'production assistance' [EC governments], 87
production capacity, 151–2

quality control: Japan 51, 170

Reagan, Ronald, 55, 88, 126
reciprocal retaliatory action, 215–16
Reciprocity Fair Trader Association [UK], 36
regional development policies, 96
Renault, 44, 86, 112, 113, 210, 231
research and development, 176; National Research and Development Council, 201; state funding, 90, 91, 200–2
retailing and distribution, 46–7
rice trade, 121–3, 216–17
Ricoh, 157–8, 161
Rolls-Royce, 27–8

Saab-Scania, 85, 194
Samsung conglomerate, 178–9
savings, 143–4, 164, 191, 204
scarcity of indigenous natural resources: possible advantages, 131, 135
'segment retreat', 194
Seiko, 156, 157, 184
Self Help (S. Smiles), 135
self-sufficiency, impracticality of, 212
semiconductor industry, 6, 18, 22, 23, 26, 70, 85, 178, 190, 198–9, 213; Semiconductor Accord, 1986, 26; Semiconductor Industry Association [US], 23, 26; trade barriers and, 109, 114, 119; *see also names of individual companies*
seniority system [Japanese industry], 170

239

Index

services, financial: tariffs, 3
SGS-Thomson group, 85–6
share finance, 162–3, 181
'shared fate' attitude [Japanese industry], 168
Sharp, 13, 157–8, 201
sheep farming, 217
Shinto, 136, 174
shogun regime [Japan], 174
Shunto (Japanese wage round), 170
Siemens-Nixdorf, 69, 86, 155, 198–9, 202
Silicon Valley, 23, 99, 196, 226
Singapore, 6
SKF, 20
ski equipment, 51, 190
small car market, 112, 153, 194
Smoot-Hawley Act, 1930 [US], 37, 186
sogoshosha trading houses, 157
Sony, 19–20, 24, 35, 82, 100, 149, 152, 157–8, 168, 169, 175, 184, 192
statistical analysis: in quality control, 171
steel industry, vii, 21, 55–6, 62, 81, 82, 95, 96, 100, 109, 156, 187; *see also names of individual companies*
stock prices, 181
'strategic' considerations, 54, 70
strikes, 131–2, 169
Structural Impediments, Initiative [US], 221
Subaru, 81, 153
sugar trade, 117, 118, 126–7, 228–9
Sumitomo group, 81, 157, 177, 192
Super 301 clause, 26, 32
superconductors, 177, 198
Suzuki, 81, 153, 157–8
Sweden, 20, 85, 88, 130, 165, 229
Switzerland, 32, 56, 87–8, 127, 156, 164

Taiwan, 6, 28, 32, 101, 174, 179, 208; and Western import quotas, 56, 61–2
takeover, 163–6
Takeshita, Noboru, 141, 181
tariffs, 3, 4, 33, 71, 109–10, 215, 223–4; *see also* GATT
taxation, 64, 164, 204; Japan, 141–2, 143, 180
teamwork, principle of, 193
telecommunications industry, 85
Texas Instruments, 23, 198
textiles industry, 3, 103–5, 114, 118, 217, 228–9; *see also names of individual companies*; Multi-Fibre Arrangement, 1974
Thailand, 208: Western import restrictions, 62, 216
third markets, 76
Thomson, 72, 75, 85–6, 198
tobacco, 123
Tokyo Motor Show, 1991, 182
Toshiba, 75, 150, 157, 178
Toyota, 44, 73, 75, 76, 81, 100, 113, 152–5, 157–8, 166, 169, 171, 182–3, 193, 194, 220; indicted for 'dumping', 19
Trade Act, 1988 [US], 26
trade barriers, viii, ix, 26, 36, 45, 67, 108–19, 187, 205–24 *passim*, 225–32, 235; covert (non-tariff), 4, 46, 52, 58–9, 61; *Report on foreign trade barriers* [US], 32–3; unintended advantages to competitors, 76; *see also* import restrictions: quotas
trade crisis, world, 186, 206
trademarks, 175
trading blocs, ix, 4, 207, 223
Trading with the Enemy Act [US], 59
transplant production, 205
Triumph, 193, 203
tropical forests, 222
truck exports, European: US tariff, 215
Tumlir, Jan, 7, 225
Turkey, 205, 227–8, 230

unemployment, viii
unfair trade, allegations of, vii, ix, 187, 216–17, 219, 221–2, 231
Unilever, 190; Nippon Lever, 46–7
United Auto Workers' union [US], 55–6, 193
United Kingdom: and 'fairness', 68; economic decline, 196–7; import restrictions, 36–7; opposition to haulage restrictions, 63; ownership of US companies, 35
United Kingdom Patent Office, 202
United Nations, 2
United States: economic history, 37, 196–7; education, 196; foreign policy, 1945, 197
United States Department of Defense Manufacturing Technology Program, 92
United States Export-Import Bank, 87, 99

United States International Trade Commission, 55
United States Merchant Marine, 117; Merchant Marine Act, 58
United States National Academy of Engineering, 176
university graduates: in government, 80
upgrading of technological levels, 101

Very High Speed Integrated Circuit project, 89
Volkswagen, 44, 75, 87, 113, 115, 183, 215
volume markets, 195; volume/margin strategy, 193–4
voluntary restraint agreements (VRAs), 4, 7, 18, 22, 55–6, 64

wage levels, relative, 220
war: as result of trade conflicts, ix–x, 226; Gulf War, 1991, 70; Vietnam War, 144
warrant bonds, 181
watchmaking industry, 156; *see also* Seiko
Westinghouse, 24, 99, 105
World Bank, 228, 229

Xerox Corporation, 11, 13–17, 43, 98–9, 118, 152, 207; Fuji Xerox, 12, 16–17; Rank Xerox, 12, 17, 74

yen: appreciation, 182

zaibatsu industrial groups, 157